RIDING

Angela Rippon
RIDING

Sidgwick & Jackson
London

To Kate and Susan. Together, they'll
make a rider out of me yet!

Page one: Kate's ears pricked and eager –
we both have a lot of fun in training
Frontispiece: Kate, fat and contented,
during her summer holidays

First published in Great Britain in 1980
by Sidgwick and Jackson Limited

Copyright © 1980 Angela Rippon

Designed by Paul Watkins
Picture research by Marion Eason

ISBN 0 283 98659 X

Typeset in Monophoto Plantin by
Type Planning Services Limited,
Anlaby, Hull, England.

Printed in Great Britain by
A. Wheaton & Co. Ltd., Exeter
for Sidgwick and Jackson Limited
1 Tavistock Chambers, Bloomsbury Way
London WC1A 2SG

Acknowledgements
During the course of writing this
book I've lost track of the number of
people whose brains I've picked,
whose help and advice I've sought,
and who deserve my thanks: people
like Alan Ball and Bill Thompson,
who both spent hours explaining the
mysteries and skills of course-
building; Peter Cannon and his team
at the British Horse Society
Headquarters in Kenilworth; Mike
Howard, MFH retired, who helped
on the hunting chapter; Sue
Armstrong, who patiently and
willingly read and checked my
original text; Wendy Jackson who
deciphered my writing and typed the
manuscript; Shirley Bosley who gives
care and attention to Kate; and lastly
the scores of others who never said
no when I rang for information, or
shouted for help.

To them all – those named and those
anonymous – my thanks. Without
you, there never would have been a
book!

Contents

Introduction

An ambition fulfilled. . . . On my way to the winner's enclosure at Goodwood, 17 May 1977

I stood leaning on the rails at the starting line at Goodwood and thought, 'My God, a mile is a hell of a long way.' The mile in question was the Old Mile at Goodwood race-track in West Sussex. As I stood there with trainer Mick Masson, and my husband Chris, the place was all but deserted.

The white rails at the start of the track curved away to the right in a long gentle arc in front of the empty grandstand, and on past the red and white disc that marked the finishing line. In an hour and a half or so, those rails and terraces would be lined with hundreds of cheering punters, and the odds were that a lot of them would be betting on *me*, because I was about to realize one of my wildest ambitions, and ride a racehorse in a race, on the flat.

For someone who had been riding for barely seven years, and mostly just week-end hacking at that, it was a pretty crazy ambition. And the fact that it happened at all, was the result of someone else's misfortune, and pure chance.

On Monday, 2 May 1977, I arrived in London to begin a week of work that would include reading B.B.C. news bulletins, attending a rehearsal with the Royal Philharmonic Orchestra, writing a two-thousand-word article for a motoring magazine, preparing an interview with the head of the Home Civil Service, attending press conferences, dress fittings, and photo calls, and was to culminate in the presentation on the Saturday night of the Eurovision Song Contest from the Wembley Conference Centre. Not exactly one of my quieter weeks.

On Tuesday afternoon the phone rang: the caller was the public relations consultant for a famous cosmetics company.

In January, he explained, the company had decided to sponsor a series of ladies' match races: a simple knock-out competition in which two riders competed against each other, and the winner went on to meet the winner of another match in a quarter-final, then a semi, then the final. Eight lady jockeys had agreed to take part. Unfortunately, that week-end, one of the riders had fallen badly, injured her spine, and was now flat on her back in a cast in Frenchay Hospital, Bristol – would I like to take her place in the match?

Then, as an afterthought, 'The race is in fifteen days time on May 17th.'

My immediate reaction was 'No way'. But my opportunist subconscious was saying 'Why not? What a marvellous opportunity!'

I said I'd think about it. I did, and said yes.

After that the timetable was positively lunatic. The organisers had found a trainer who'd be prepared to let me have a horse. But what I needed more was a jockey's licence. The Stewards of the Jockey Club required at least seven days notice before the race, to issue the permit, and then only after I had been recommended as fit to ride by a registered trainer. On paper, we had fifteen days; in practice, there were only nine.

The earliest that I could get to Mick Masson's stable at Lewes in East Sussex for a trial run was Sunday, 8 May, the morning after the song contest. Eurovision was not one of the easiest jobs I've ever done, to put it mildly. And the only thing I really wanted to do the morning after the night before, was to sleep. As it was, by ten o'clock, I was in a helicopter rising over the top of Battersea Power Station on my way to Lewes for what was supposed to be a 'secret' training session.

I had agreed to ride out providing there was no publicity. I had reached saturation point with the song contest, seeing journalists from all over Europe as well as the British press, and I wanted to do something without the camera and notebook to record every second. After all, this wasn't a publicity stunt. The whole point was for Mick Masson to assure himself that I could ride, and I needed to prove something to myself.

We went to the site of the old Lewes racecourse, a redundant track that provides an ideal training ground for all the racing stables in the area. I had been told I would be riding a horse called Briars Vanter but the owner got cold feet (understandably) so instead there was Maxes Taxi, a dark bay with enormous presence and a kind eye. 'You'll like him,' said Mick's wife Sally, 'he is a real gent.'

Mick gave me a leg-up into the saddle, and I got my first wave of mild nausea – the feeling which in me passes for fright. The stable jockey, Harry Ballantyne, was mounted on a lightly built chestnut and looked perfectly at home in his crash-helmet and old jodhpurs with his knees drawn up around his elbows. I felt decidedly out of place in my velvet riding cap, neatly pressed riding trousers and long boots, and extremely uncomfortable as my stirrups were yanked up so that instead of sitting as I was used to, with my legs wrapped around the horse's stomach, they were perched somewhere up near its neck. My muscles began to ache, my seat felt very precarious, and we hadn't even moved off yet. The fact that I could ride at all wasn't in question. But riding a racehorse is quite unlike any other riding and Mick Masson took one look at my 'back up, heels down' position as taught at the riding school and said, with some amusement, 'I think you'll find it easier if you forget that. Don't balance on the balls of your feet, let the stirrup slip through to the arch. Point your toes down. Get up on your knees and stay there. Keep your body low and let your hands move with the horse's mouth. Apart from that, enjoy yourself.'

As I moved off with Harry towards the starting line I got the first impression of the enormous strength of the horse and an uncanny bouncy feeling that came from the fine, springy hocks. We were to trot quietly to the bottom of the gallops, turn, and then let them go. The gallops were clearly defined as the only mown area on that part of the Downs, and the width of the straight was marked with small conifer branches. All I had to do was keep a straight line and stay on. It was odd, but now the only thing that worried me was staying on at the start. I've watched the way racehorses snatch away in a sudden explosion of power at the starting line and I had visions of being ignominiously thrown back over his rump, so ending my racing career before I'd even begun.

We were just a few paces from the starting line. 'Ready?' said Harry. I nodded. We turned slowly but the old horse had gone through this routine too often to be fooled by a new jockey. I could feel the anticipation thrill through his body. His ears pricked, the muscles tightened ready for the spring, his head was turned towards the straight, and we shot off. I had been ready for the break, and had gone forward with him. It wasn't half as bad as I'd expected and once I had got over the initial shock, I managed to balance myself on my knees, get my body positioned over his neck and then ride for the sheer hell of it.

Max had a long, strong stride which gave me confidence. To me he felt as solid and safe as the Rock of Gibraltar, and as fast as a Lightning jet. The wind was whistling past my ears, there was the unexpectedly loud drumming noise as hooves glanced off turf in rapid succession.

I suddenly found myself laughing out loud. I wasn't frightened any more – just caught up in the thrill and sheer excitement of speed. Harry pulled up alongside. 'You O.K.?' he mouthed. 'Yes,' I said, and meant it.

As we neared the finishing line he pulled ahead. I began working my legs like pistons, and put in a challenge. Max changed up into another gear and flashed into the lead. The old horse didn't take too much stopping – like I said, he'd done all this before. He was the perfect schoolmaster, truly a real gent. Harry had obviously let me win, but I didn't care. Mick looked decidedly happier than he had before we'd set off, and I was ready for another gallop, I'd enjoyed it so much. We did one more circuit, then back to the stables.

There was a gang of press photographers there, but by then I didn't mind too much. At least they had let me ride in peace, and Mick was happy to recommend me for a licence.

'What's the name of the horse you'll be riding?' I was asked. 'Maxes Taxi,' I said. 'No,' said Mick, 'Star Performance,' and the fine chestnut that Harry had ridden came into the yard.

That morning we'd ridden two short bursts of half a mile each. Max was a seven-furlong horse. He had a fast, strong burst of energy for seven furlongs, but would fade over the last furlong in a mile race. I'd ridden him because he was such a good schoolmaster. My next ride on a racehorse, a week later, would be my first, and only, practice on the horse I would ride at Goodwood – Star Performance.

The next week I was back at work. My amateur jockey's permit came through, number 135, together with a set of rules of racing from the Jockey Club. I took to walking up and down the six flights of stairs in Television Centre to the news studio to try to strengthen my legs and improve my 'puff'. They were hardly ideal conditions to train for a race, but I had no alternative.

I got home to Devon on 12 May and had an hour's riding lesson each day, which included fast work, with stirrups up, over a small set of cross-country fences. When I went back to Lewes the following Sunday, I was fitter than I had been the week-end before, and much less apprehensive.

Star Performance was an entirely different horse to Max. He was of a lighter build and seemed to take shorter, bouncier strides – and was much faster. After the first three-quarter-mile gallop I could see why Mick hadn't let me ride him first. I did a second run over the three-quarter-mile gallop and that was it. On Monday I was interviewing the Archbishop of Canterbury. On Tuesday I raced.

When the day arrived I felt very unprepared. I had no doubts about my ability to ride – only in my ability to last the course. I was nowhere near as fit as I would have liked to have been; I'd only sat on the horse I was going to ride twice, and I'd never ever ridden for a mile, flat out. My opponent, on the other hand,

In the stableyard at Lewes with Maxes Taxi – I had to prove to Mick Masson that I could ride at Goodwood

Debbie Johnsey, was an Olympic show-jumper who spent her life in the saddle – and the betting was in her favour. Which is why, as I leant on the railings at the start of the course, I got that old feeling of nausea and thought, 'My God, a mile is a hell of a long way.'

I'd been drawn to run on the outside. This was a distinct disadvantage as it meant taking a slightly wider sweep to try to get in on the rails to take the shortest line to the winning-post. Before the race, Mick Masson walked around the course with me and told me how to ride it.

The tactics, he explained, would be to burst away as fast as possible, and go all out over the first furlong to get ahead of Bird Cherry, Debbie Johnsey's mount, and then hug the rails. 'Keep going flat out for three furlongs by which time you'll reach the sharpest part of the bend on the course. You can ease off a bit here, let the horse run on and save your own strength until you get to the seven-furlong marker. By then, you'll be going past the grandstand, facing up hill towards the line. Pick the horse up and ride like the devil, but don't stop short of the line, ride for a

line beyond the finish, that way you'll finish strongly.' By the time we had walked to the finishing-post I was exhausted, and the crowds had started to arrive. There was no going back now.

We got back to the weighing-in room where the changing-rooms were. At that time, there were still very few ladies racing. Our changing-room was the doctor's surgery. It was slightly off-putting being surrounded by the paraphernalia for strapping broken collar-bones, and mending broken heads. But there wasn't time to brood over the possible consequences of falling off, for I was taken in hand by a large man in a long apron, Mr Tim Nelligan, the valet. He was responsible for kitting me out.

Along with his assistant, he would turn up early in the day at the race meetings, bringing with him washed breeches and polished boots for all the jockeys on the circuit. He'd brought with him a selection of spare breeches and boots, and crash-helmets. We found a set that fitted, and then I was handed my 'colours'. Mick Masson had taken out of retirement the colours worn by his father's jockey when he raced some thirty years before. The shirt was black, with gold crosses front and back, hoops on the sleeves, and black and gold quarters on the cap. It was a gesture of confidence – and one I greatly appreciated.

I went away to get changed. The boots felt most extraordinary. I'd been used to long, stiff, riding wellingtons, these boots were more like fine kid gloves, and the soles were so fine I could feel my toes on the ground. Mr Nelligan gave me the once over to make sure I was properly dressed and allowed a nod of approval. Chris, my husband, threw his head back, roared with laughter and said, 'I've never seen you look so scruffy.' Mr Nelligan looked disapproving, Chris was ushered away, and I went off to be weighed with the saddle.

The tack was taken away, the horse saddled up, and at 1.15 Debbie Johnsey and I walked down the steps to the saddling enclosure to be met by a sea of photographers. We made our way through them to our horses and while we checked girths, tightened the straps on our helmets, and prepared to mount, the cameras moved in. It is amazing that no one was kicked. I was in a state of high tension, and I'm sure the horse was too. We made our way out of the saddling enclosure on to the track. To reach the starting line we had to canter down the length of the course, which meant going past the stands. They say a horse always reacts to the tensions of the rider. Well, I was strung up like a high-wire act, and Star Performance reacted accordingly. He bounced into a strong canter, and took off. 'Oh no,' I thought, 'he's going to run away with me – in front of the stands.' I gathered all my strength and balance, and tried to look nonchalant as we whizzed over the turf. I didn't doubt that the horse had enough energy to ride a mile there and back, but I knew my own strength would only last for as long as the race and I didn't want to arrive at the starting line worn out.

The long bend in the course was coming up on my left.

However, I kept the horse going on straight. This confused him, and gave me a chance to check his stride. There was a small slipway back to the left that would take me to the start. A St John Ambulance man said, 'This isn't the way, dear.' 'I know,' I replied, and managed to get the horse back to a springy, quieter jog.

I reached the start line feeling that I'd already run half the race and asking myself, 'What am I doing here?' There wasn't time to wait for an answer. The starter was counting the seconds up to 1.30. We got in position. He didn't have a flag, just a white handkerchief, which hung on the air for a second. His arm dropped, we shot forward and in less than ten strides I'd gained ground on Bird Cherry.

When I knew I was well clear and wouldn't crowd her on to the rails, I pulled over and headed for the bend. On our walk, Mick had said this was the place to ease off. When it came to it I really had no choice. I was exhausted with the effort of the first dash. I tried to shift my position slightly to give my aching knees and back some respite, but this only unbalanced the horse. So I stayed where I was, crouched over my knees, my bottom in the air, my mouth open, gasping for breath.

As we rounded the bend and started to go past the stands, I heard another roar over the sound of the hooves – the crowds in the stands were shouting and cheering us both on. My calves were rubbing against the side of the saddle and started to really pinch. Star Performance was pulling like an express train and I suddenly thought, 'I'm going to fall off.' But ego is a wonderful preservative, and the thought of making a fool of myself in front of all those people kept me firmly in the saddle and determined to reach the line. Suddenly Star's ears went back. He, like me, had heard another set of hooves accompanying his own. Bird Cherry was staging a challenge. The roar from the crowds got louder. I dug my heels in and threw myself into the action of the horse. He rolled into overdrive and just kept going.

The run into the finish at Goodwood is all uphill, and believe me, as we rode past the final furlong marker, I felt as though there was still a whole mile to go. That is the longest furlong in the world – the finishing line, the most enticing. We crossed over with Star a full seven lengths out in front, and living up to his name, feeling as though he could run the whole race again.

I was exhausted, excited, giggly, and somewhat over-whelmed. When I got off the horse, I almost fell over as I'd dredged up every last ounce of stamina and there was nothing left. I looked a mess, but I didn't care. I used to be a happy week-end hacker who'd just pootled around the moors, dreaming of the far-fetched idea of riding a really fit fast racehorse over the turf. As I rode Star Performance into the winners' enclosure, there were noise and people and cameras and a delighted Mick Masson. Before I dismounted into the turmoil of bodies, I sat, just for a second, and thought, 'Well, Ange, you've done it. And what's more – you've won.'

1 Starting Off

I am not an expert rider. Every time I see one of the national newspapers describe me as 'experienced horsewoman' or 'well known rider', I cringe with embarrassment.

I'm nothing more than a week-end hacker who has had the opportunity of riding a number of interesting horses in exciting situations, and the sense to realize that if I'm going to ride at all, then I'm going to do it properly. Because of the nature of my job, my private life and hobbies get as much press attention as my public work and so most people know I ride for pleasure and associate me with horses. As a result, it's amazing how many people seem to think that I came from a 'privileged' background with wealthy parents and a pony on the front lawn, and that I've been riding since jodhpurs would fit over my nappies.

Nothing like it. I was born in one of the poorer parts of Plymouth, to hard-working parents who certainly never had money to spare for luxuries like riding. In fact, I didn't have any contact with horses at all until I was seventeen. A girlfriend at school, who rode horses round the family farm, suggested a gang of us should go for a Sunday morning ride at a stable on the edge of Dartmoor.

It seemed like a good idea at the time. We were all steeped in work for mock A levels, and needed something to take our minds off exams. I had a Saturday job in a Plymouth shop where I earned nineteen shillings and sixpence for the day. So ten shillings for an hour's ride was well within my scope.

The bus journey from Plymouth to the moor took the best part of an hour. Then we walked half a mile to the stables, and were put on a set of tired old nags who viewed the prospect of another hour's ride, over the same bit of moorland, with about as much enthusiasm as a wooden fairground horse on the 'golden gallopers' roundabout. At least the painted horses have spring in their step and fire in their nostrils. The real things had sadness in their eyes, and a resigned 'plod' in their gait. The only time they showed any sign of life was when we turned for home. That was when I fell off, hit my ankle on a granite boulder, and determined never to go near another horse again – which I didn't for at least eight years.

Buying a house on Dartmoor changed all that. I've always loved the countryside and finding myself living slap in the middle of some of the wildest, most beautiful open moorland in Britain, I came to the conclusion that, as much as I enjoy walking, the only way to see the moor properly, to appreciate fully its size and scope – was on horseback.

I enrolled at a local riding school, and turned up for the first of eight lessons in jeans, wellingtons and a conspicuously new black velvet cap. The first hour was a painful experience. While the teacher shouted instructions and encouragement, I presented a living, working definition of the word 'uncoordinated'. While the horse maintained one rhythm, I achieved another. The only time my bottom came down on the seat was when the saddle was coming up, and when the instructor said she was going to put a pound note between my knees and the saddle to improve my grip, I knew I was about to lose a fortune.

Monday morning was sheer purgatory. There were no lifts in the studio I was working at, and walking up four flights of stairs to my office that morning, was an experience I shall never forget. I didn't just ache, I hurt in every conceivable muscle and joint from the waist down. Suffice to say, I understood completely why Will Hay always walked as though an express train could pass between his knees.

It did get better. In the weeks that followed, I had a crash course in walking, trotting, cantering, jumping over tiny obstacles no more than a foot high, and a particularly fiendish torture known as lunging. The whole point of this exercise is to improve balance and 'seat', in other words, your position when you sit in the saddle. To achieve this you're left without either reins or stirrups, perched in the saddle clinging on to the front for grim death while the instructor guides the horse around in a circle on the end of a long lead or lunge rein, in a walk, trot and canter. 'It is good for you,' I was told. And it was. My impersonation of Will Hay was much improved on Monday morning.

Eventually I was considered fit to be let loose on the moors and enjoyed several years of just pottering about on Sunday mornings for an hour or so, with occasional all-day treks in the summer. The craggy granite tors, wooded river valleys, rolling commons and high-hedged lanes became familiar week-end landscape. Even after all these years, I still can't quite get over the thrill of sitting on top of a tor, looking across a wide expanse of green rolling moorland to another outcrop of granite some three miles away, knowing that in less than ten or fifteen minutes I can be cantering up the side of the hill and looking back to my vantage point across the valley. I'd never walk it in that time, if at all. Such is the freedom offered by the strength and speed of a horse.

I suppose I would have gone on just hacking across the moors for ever, if I hadn't got ambitions about jumping. I'm still not quite sure why I got the idea that I'd like to fly through the air on the top of a ton of thundering horseflesh, but the fact that I did brought me into contact with a trainer called Sue Armstrong. 'Can you ride?' she asked. 'Yes, I can,' I said with all the confidence of five years in the saddle, albeit on Sunday mornings. She asked me to walk, trot and canter around the schooling area, then pop over a small jump of white poles about two feet high. 'H'mm,' she grunted, 'I don't know who jumped higher, you or the horse.' She was obviously not impressed. It took her just ten minutes to realize that in five years, left to my own devices, I'd picked up all sorts of bad habits and poor riding technique. So she started from scratch to teach me to ride. That was nearly five years ago, and I'm still learning.

I tell you all this to put this book, and my reason for writing it, into perspective. What I've learned in the past nine years is that the riding world has two distinctive groups: an inner and an outer circle. The inner circle is made up of people who've either ridden or had associations with horses for most of their lives. The language of the horse world is their everyday vocabulary, and while their *riding* technique may have been taught, their *attitude* comes from instinct.

The rest of us are in the outer circle. People who just love or have an interest in horses, and all things horsy, who enjoy county shows or cross-country events for the spectacle, the show-jumping for the tension, and who work in an office, factory or shop from Monday to Friday and ride at week-ends on hired horses for the sheer enjoyment of it. For us, much of what goes on in the real horse world is a closed book, and will remain so. I've heard people talking about surcingles, and pelhams, checking for soundness and wind-galls as though everyone in the world knew what they were talking about. Of course, you can always ask, and a good instructor or yard owner will always explain. But not all do, and you can be made to look an idiot for not knowing.

I was once asked to help bandage a horse's legs to protect them while it travelled in a horse-box. A young girl had already started on the front legs. Faced with the rear end I asked 'How do you do this?' 'Don't you know?' she gasped incredulously. Now I might well have been interviewing the Prime Minister the day before, or presenting a live television programme in front of 12 million people, but the fact that I didn't know how to tie travelling bandages on a horse's legs made me less than insignificant in the eye of that precocious madam, who knew it all!

From my own experience, I know that most people get involved with riding in a haphazard way. Someone says, 'Why don't we go riding this week-end?' and before you know where you are, you are in a saddle and out in open country.

Providing you survive the first round, and have enough determination to stay on, whatever speed the horse does, you will actually start to enjoy the experience. But there is so much more to riding than that.

Whenever I see a horse galloping away with someone totally out of control, or a rider bringing his horse to a standstill by yanking and sawing on the bit, with his feet stuck out in front for greater leverage, I think, poor horse, and poor rider, because neither is really having much fun.

Riding is one of the fastest growing leisure activities in the country. Every year new stables are opening up, as more and more people turn to the horse for pleasure and relaxation. If you read this book, you won't ever become an Olympic contender, but it might answer some of the questions you've never known how to ask, and help to make the world of horses and riding more enjoyable and interesting than you ever thought – for you and the horse.

2 Where to Learn

Checking tack and grooming in a riding school

Once you have made up your mind that you want to ride, you are faced with two clear alternatives. Do you tag along at the end of a line with friends and pick up what you can, as you can, or do you take lessons? Obviously anyone who works with horses will advise that a set of basic lessons is the best foundation. If you know how to walk, trot, canter, start the horse, stop it, and keep it under control, then you're more likely to look upon a week-end ride as a thing to be enjoyed, rather than an hour-long battle of strength and nerve with the horse anxious to get a move on, and you determined not to fall off.

Finding a teacher is fairly simple. Choosing the right one for *you* may take time, trial and error. If you are already riding, ask at the stable if they give lessons, or if they can recommend someone who will. Or ask in the local saddle shop. If they are specialists in saddlery and equipment, they will know everyone who is anyone in the horse world by reputation, as well as ability! Look in the yellow pages of the telephone directory under 'Riding establishments,' phone them and ask them what facilities they have. A sanded manège (or schooling area) suggests a school that is reasonably well equipped. An indoor school might be more appealing, especially if you are taking up riding in the winter.

Some schools offer 'teaching rides', where you are not confined to the limits of a schooling ring but are taught the basic principles while you hack gently over open countryside or along bridleways.

Ask them how much they charge. Prices do vary enormously so don't take the first one because it sounds cheap, or because you are afraid to say no, if it is expensive. Also check on the qualifications of the person who is going to do the teaching. The minimum requirement for a recognized instructor is the British Horse Society (B.H.S.) Assistant Instructors Certificate, commonly known as the A.I. Qualifications after that are graded as follows: the Intermediate Instructors Certificate, the British Horse Society Instructors Certificate (the B.H.S.I.), and finally the British Horse Society Fellowship. According to the B.H.S., 'This is the ultimate B.H.S. examination for instructors, and suffice to say that to pass it requires a very high degree of competence in every aspect of equitation and stable management.'

Do not be tempted to make a block booking of, say, six lessons. Just book one, and see how you get on. You may dislike the teacher on sight, mistrust the horses, or feel that you are not really learning a thing. Don't feel bad about changing instructors. You are there to enjoy yourself, not to be bullied, or suffer purgatory, so test the water before you plunge in.

A lot of people will decide that as all they want to do is get out on a horse on a Sunday morning for a bit of fresh air, lessons aren't necessary. For them it is a case of 'follow my leader' and learn the hard way. Eventually they will master the rhythm of the sitting trot, stop feeling panicky every time the horse breaks into a canter and get the horse to stop more or less where and when they want it to.

But there is really much more to riding than that. So if you feel perhaps you could give the horse an easier, or more comfortable ride, and get more fun out of it yourself, then read on.

Stables

In my time, I've seen just about every type of stable that is going. From the incredibly elegant paved walks and architect-designed stalls of a wealthy racehorse trainer, to a ramshackle collection of corrugated tin huts set in the middle of what looked like a slurry heap.

Riding stables come in all shapes, sizes and conditions. As a rank beginner, how do you know whether the one you have been taken to is good, bad or indifferent? You don't need to be an expert on stable management or horseflesh, just aware of one or two obvious things to look for.

To begin with, location. That's fairly simple. If the stable is bang in the middle of urban development and doesn't have a

schooling ring, or land of its own, then your ride is almost certainly going to be limited to trotting around the lanes and houses and will not be very exciting. If it has a few fields or better still an indoor school, or manège, a schooling ring, then what you are in for is an hour's instruction at the walk and trot, eventually progressing to a canter, gallop, and schooling exercises over small jumps.

If, however, what you want is the freedom to canter over rolling green acres, then you will have to head for the nearest bit of countryside. But make sure that there is some common land available somewhere, or you'll be back to trotting on tarmac, around the lanes. That can be quite pleasant and absorbing, if you've an interest in wild birds and hedgerow plants, but week after week, around the same lanes, could become very boring. And if you get the idea that *that* is all riding has to offer, you may give up before the real thrill of the sport has had a chance to make an impression. It will depend very much on where you live, of course, but try to find a stable that offers a variety of scenery and rides, otherwise you'll never know what you are missing.

Licensing

Any riding stable or school offering horses for hire *must* be licensed by the local authority, and to get that licence it has to make certain provisions to protect the welfare and safety of horse and rider.

So if you want to make sure that the stable you are going to is bona fide, and not just some fly-by-night profiteer, ring the local council and ask. If the stable is not licensed, don't go. *It* will be breaking the law, and *you* will be unprotected by it. If it is licensed, then at least you'll have the confidence of knowing that you are protected by the safeguards written into the Riding Establishments Acts 1964 and 1970. This all sounds very formal, but, believe me, it is very necessary. Very few people would dream of driving a car without a licence and insurance, and horses are far more unpredictable than cars!

I don't know how comforting this will be to you before you've even sat on a horse, but if you do have an accident as a result of negligence by the stable owner (and that includes falling off because the horse was not suitable for a beginner, or because the saddle fell to pieces), then at least you can claim damages or compensation. One of the provisions for granting a licence is that the stable should be adequately insured to cover accidents or damage. A public health officer will check over the yard to see that effluent from the stables can be piped away, and that the 'muck heap' of manure and soiled straw from the beds is far enough away from the stable yard not to be a health hazard. (The wise stable owner will make sure that the location offers easy access to keen gardeners who will be only too pleased to remove the problem altogether.)

The council's veterinary officer will want to be sure that the

21

horses offered for hire are fit for work, and he'll make a note of those *not* to be used. These include mares heavy in foal, or with a foal of less than three months, and horses under three years of age. This is because horses aren't broken until they are three rising four. Before then, they simply are not strong enough to carry weight on their backs. Anyone trying to rush the process could do irreparable damage.

The vet will check that the stables are sufficiently large, light and airy. They needn't be palatial, but boxes that are too small to allow the horse to lie down, or are dank and airless, simply would not be acceptable. Where horses are to be kept out at grass there should be at least one acre per horse available for grazing. He will examine the condition of the tack, general competence of the person running the yard, and the fire precautions. There should also be enough staff to send one qualified rider with every ride. Novices and beginners should never be sent out un- escorted, and your escort must be sixteen or over.

When the inspectors have been satisfied, and any necessary planning permission has been granted, then the licence will be issued. So, before you even step over the threshold you will know that the *licensed* yard has at least met with the *minimum* requirements under law.

But they say first impressions count most and, as a rule, you can get a pretty good idea of the sort of ride you'll have from a quick glance round the yard.

There are just over 2,500 licensed riding stables in Great Britain. They can be inspected at any time, without prior notice, by the council's representative, and if they don't come up to scratch then, at least, certain horses can be taken out of work, at most, the licence taken away. But while some councils are scrupulous in carrying out the terms of the Act to the last letter, making many surprise visits to establishments and maintaining high standards, others simply don't have the manpower, time or, one might unkindly suggest, the inclination to keep as close an eye as they might. So regardless of the legal status, always make a few 'eyeball checks' yourself.

How to assess stables and horses
No yard will be absolutely spick and span, without a trace of mud, muck or straw somewhere. You cannot combine horses and the British climate and keep everything in pristine showroom condition. But a yard that is ankle-deep in mud and slurry, has junk littered about in untidy dirty heaps, and looks badly maintained and run down, probably is, and the horses won't be much better.

Even the oldest, most humble yard can be kept clean with a broom, droppings can be picked up, and buckets washed and stacked neatly. Having rubbish lying around is dangerous. It can harbour germs, and get in the way of excitable horses. If you can see that someone has taken the trouble to keep a yard tidy, then it is more than likely that they will have taken trouble over the horses too.

If you have never ridden before, or are still a beginner, it is unlikely that you will be given the liveliest horse in the stable. Something with a quiet, docile temperament, and a kind eye is what you will want, but it should be healthy and fit for work. You don't have to rank as a main-ring show judge to know whether a horse is fit for its purpose. Working horses should not be skinny. You shouldn't be able to play a tune on their ribs, count the vertebrae in the back, or see the hip-bones standing up like coat-hangers, and the neck should be firm, not hollow and scraggy. They should be 'well covered' with flesh, muscle and a layer of fat. Don't be fooled by a thick coat. Just run your hand gently over the neck, across the ribs and then down over the back. Your fingers will tell you whether or not the skin is firm without being tightly stretched over the bones, and whether or not there is any cushion of flesh under the coat.

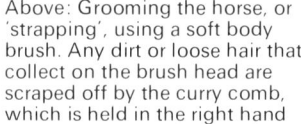

Below left: Checking the back of
the legs for injury or swelling

Below right: Picking out the
hooves, using a hoof pick. Use a
downward movement, never up

Above: Grooming the horse, or
'strapping', using a soft body
brush. Any dirt or loose hair that
collect on the brush head are
scraped off by the curry comb,
which is held in the right hand

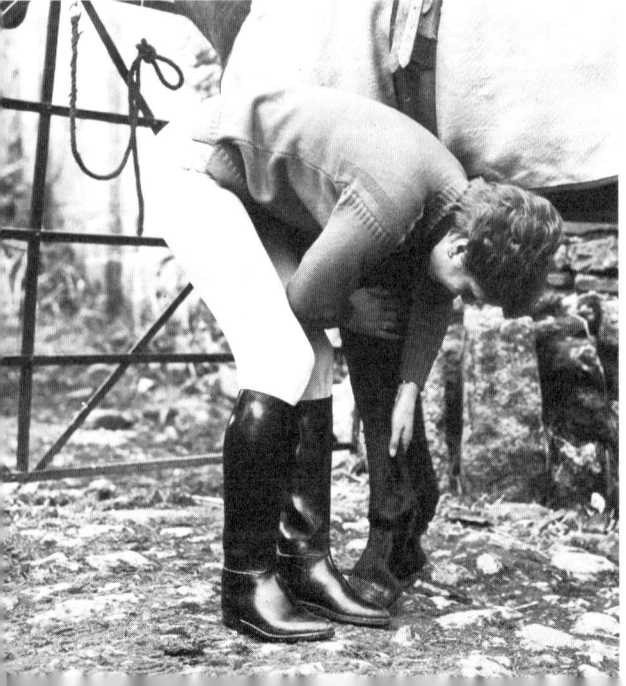

Horses that are kept out, rather than stabled, will almost certainly keep their thick woolly coats, and because horses love to roll, in the winter particularly, they will be brought into the yard covered in mud. Sometimes, if the mud is still wet, it is best left until it can be taken off with a stiff dry brush. But some attempt should have been made at grooming and you should never be asked to ride a horse that hasn't had almost, if not all, of the mud removed.

The legs should be smooth. Anything with lumps and bumps is suspect, and the hooves should be neatly trimmed. Any turning up at the bottom suggests that they haven't been trimmed properly, or that the blacksmith is overdue.

The shoes should fit evenly around the base of the hoof and you should be able to see a good depth of iron. If all you can see is a faint sliver, then you will know that the horses are not shod regularly. This should be done every four to six weeks. Like humans, some horses are heavier on their shoes than others.

Look at the general appearance and health of the skin on the horse. If there are scabs or sores ask the owner to identify them. Some horses are allergic to flies and in the summer suffer from a particularly unpleasant complaint called sweet itch. The poor animal becomes so badly bitten that it breaks out in sores, usually around the mane and tail, spreading up over the hindquarters. The more the sores itch, the more the horse will scratch and rub, and so the sores spread, not healing properly until the winter when the flies have gone and the vet's medication takes effect. If it is sweet itch, it may look horrible, but won't affect the horse's performance, or you. But if the scabs are ringworm, easily identified by the ring formation of the scar, then these can be passed on to humans, and should be avoided at all cost.

There are other sores to look for, perhaps less obvious. You will only find them around the bridle on the head, around and under the saddle. They are caused quite simply by badly fitting tack which has rubbed away the flesh. On the head, the places to look are just behind the ears, down the side of the cheeks, and where the noseband fits across the front of the face. On the saddle, the places to look are around the pressure points where the saddle comes into contact with the horse's back and sides, and also the girth, the band that goes under the horse's stomach to hold the saddle in place. If this is too tight, or badly fitting, the combination of pressure and perspiration will produce girth galls. If the sores are really bad then the horse should not be ridden.

Horses are not particularly tolerant of pain, and a niggling painful spot can change their temperament dramatically. Imagine how you would feel walking five miles in new shoes that had already rubbed huge blisters on your heels, and you will get some idea of what you are asking the horse to go through.

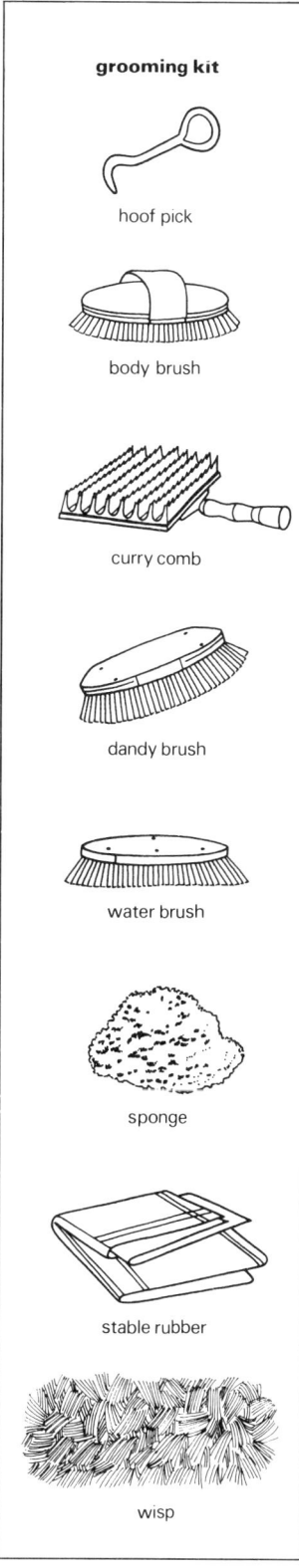

grooming kit

hoof pick

body brush

curry comb

dandy brush

water brush

sponge

stable rubber

wisp

Checking the tack

If you have satisfied yourself that the horse is sound, now look at the tack. It is important that it should be well maintained and supple, that way it will be safe and comfortable. When it is cleaned regularly with saddle soap, leather will stay soft and pliable, and take on a dark, slightly 'greasy' look. On the bridle you should be able to undo and reset the buckles and straps without any difficulty, and the stitching around the buckles on both the bridle and the reins should be sound with no sign of wear. This is something you can check quickly and simply by just running your fingers over the leather. If it feels dry and hard, shows signs of cracking, and is irremovably locked into rusted buckles, then it hasn't been maintained, and you should look very carefully at the stitching. On old, badly maintained tack, the stitching becomes dry and brittle, and if put under strain is likely to snap.

By the way, if you are a beginner or novice, you should not be asked to ride a horse with more than one set of reins. Double reins come with what are known as 'double bridles'. They control two bits and should only be used by experienced hands. If the stable tells you the only way to control the horse is with a double, then you should not be riding it anyway.

The saddle should be supple. It is safer, and more comfortable for you and the horse. First of all, there should be plenty of padding, rather like a cushion, at the part of the saddle known as the lining where it rests on the horse's back. In a good, well fitting saddle, the cushion or lining will hold the saddle off the spine, leaving a clear channel from pommel at the front to cantle at the back. If the padding has worn down with use, then a careful owner should have the saddle restuffed so that it doesn't pinch or put pressure on the spine.

The simple act of walking, rising at the trot, and cantering, makes the rider use muscles he never knew he had, and the effect on untrained limbs can be traumatic. Couple that with a saddle that is as hard and flat as a schoolroom bench and the painful after-effects are awful to contemplate.

At the side of the saddle, under the flap, you will find the hook on which the stirrup leathers are held in place. They should not be rusty. If they are, the stirrup leathers will jam in place. The whole idea of the hook is that if you do fall off and get your foot jammed in the stirrup, the leather should slide off the bar so that you are not dragged on your back for miles. The girth buckles should be well stitched and sound, and the girth itself not so thin that it will bite and pinch into the horse's stomach.

Finally, stirrup irons come in all sizes. Yours should be not so large that they allow your foot to flop around, nor so small that they jam your boot in place.

I bet you are thinking, by the time I've done that lot, I will have used up half of the hour I've booked for a ride. Not at all. It takes just a few minutes and they are the sort of checks that even the most experienced of riders would make before getting on a strange horse.

If all this sounds as though I am painting a gloomy picture of a country littered with rundown, seedy stables, with fly-bitten scraggy old horses, I'm not. But if you know the worst to expect, then anything better than that is a bonus.

The British Horse Society
Where riding businesses are concerned local authorities are only licensing bodies, not horse or stable *experts*. The experts are the British Horse Society (B.H.S.) and their yardstick for testing and approving a riding school, trekking centre, livery yard or training centre will be far more stringent than anything the council can apply and is therefore a better guide.

The British Horse Society, the ruling body of the sport in this country, has an approved and recognized register of its own. To date, some 520 of the country's licensed establishments are on the society's list. Their officers can visit at any time, without prior notice, to ensure that the highest standards are maintained, and the yard can display the B.H.S. badge of approval, the society's symbol depicting a horse's head surrounded by a horseshoe. If at any time, the establishment fails to live up to B.H.S. requirements, then the badge, and recognition, are removed.

The remaining 2,000 or so yards can be checked at any time by the representatives of the local authority responsible for issuing the licence, or the Riding Establishments Act Committee, which includes representatives from the B.H.S.

Their last report makes interesting reading. Of the 2,596 establishments they visited, 240 were below acceptable standards, and so were operating without any licence at all. They found bad stabling and management, dangerous saddlery, poor shoeing, use of animals under age, and animals in such poor condition that thirty-three were taken out of service.

Now the stable you choose, whether it is B.H.S. registered or not, is no doubt properly licensed and run by people who know what they are doing, who care about the condition of their horses and saddlery, and offer the best service they know how. But there are some who don't. They measure the success of their business by how much money they can make on a good Sunday in the summer, and the fact that no one has caught them out, so far. If you get stuck with a place like that, then at least you should be armed with enough knowledge not to get taken for a sucker.

3 What to Wear

Headgear

If you have a vision of copying the television ads where people gallop through the surf, barefooted and with the wind blowing through their hair, forget it. To begin with, no school worth its salt will let you even sit on a horse without a hard riding hat. Any yard that hires out horses should be well prepared with a collection of sound, spare hats in various sizes. Most owners recognize that anyone who is just 'coming along to see if I like it' isn't going to spend anything from £10 for a riding hat, in case, after the first hour, they can't stand the sight of a horse and never want to go near a stable again. A hard hat is essential, with the emphasis on the hard. Modern riding caps are made from layers of fibreglass and padding so that they are light and comfortable to wear, but strong enough to withstand quite a considerable impact.

I once went to a yard where the tack room had an impressive pile of hats to offer customers. It all looked very efficient, until you came to try them on. Some of the newer ones were fine, but the older hats, that had faded from their original black or navy velvet to a sort of dirty khaki after years of exposure to the elements, were so soft and pliable, they were more like cloth caps than hard hats, and totally useless. If you had a fall on your head in one of those, it might muffle the sound of your skull cracking, but it wouldn't stop it happening.

You should wear the hat so that it fits squarely on the head; not tilted back at a rakish angle or so far forward that the peak flops over your eyes. And it should *fit*. If it is too tight across the forehead and temple you'll just get a bad headache; if it is too loose, then it will flop around while you are trotting or cantering, and if you do come off then the chances are that the hat will go flying first, leaving your skull totally unprotected.

No doubt there will be friends in your group who think it is smart to wear just a headscarf or a flat cap. It isn't smart, it is stupid, and tempting providence. Some years ago, my father and I were riding two fairly quiet beasts at a slow amble up a steep hill, flanked on either side by high thick Devon hedges. Dad is an easy-going sort of chap, and if his horse wanted to wander over and nibble at the grass on the banks, he didn't mind too much. But the horse decided that the grass half-way up the bank was much sweeter than that on the ground, so she suddenly launched her front legs on to the bank and stood at a forty-five-degree angle. The sudden and violent jerk completely unseated my father who fell backwards, over her rump. As he landed on his back, his head hit the road with a loud crack. He lay quite motionless and I really thought he was dead. He wasn't but he had been knocked unconscious. The back of his hat was squashed, and had bits of stone embedded in it, but his skull was in one piece. Without the hat, we'd have been picking his brains out of the tarmac for weeks.

The day I landed on my skull, the horse had been *standing* in

My hacking gear: rubber riding boots, jodphurs, riding gloves and hard hat the yard. It happened just as I was getting on. As I was in mid-air, with one foot in the left-hand stirrup, the other flying over her back, she took fright, shied, and bolted across the yard. I was catapulted over her head, and shot like a ramrod, head first, into a granite post. The impact tilted my hat forward slightly, and as the horse went over the top of me, one of her hooves sliced into the back of my head and took out a V-shaped chunk. I saw multicoloured stars and stripes for nearly half an hour, needed two stitches in the cut, and had a violent pain from what felt like a screwdriver being pushed through my skull for the next three weeks. But without that hat, I'd have been reduced to a cabbage. Granite pillars aren't known for their give. So, like I said, it isn't silly to wear a hat, it's essential.

Footwear

The other piece of important riding equipment is at the other end so to speak; what you wear on your feet. If you are going to buy the proper gear, then you'll need either jodhpur boots, or long boots. The jodhpur boots are a little like men's slip-on shoes to look at, except that they come up well above the ankles, with elasticated sides, to give a firm grip on the foot. The soles are flat and the heels small. Riding boots are traditionally made of leather, but when they cost upwards of £100 these days, you are more likely to find them on the legs of professionals or dedicated amateurs. The rubber boot, or riding wellington, is much more popular, and cheaper, starting at about £11. Whereas the leg in an ordinary 'gardening' wellington will go straight up and down, on riding boots you'll see that the leg slopes forward slightly towards the toe. This is because when you're sitting correctly in the saddle your toe will point up, your heel down, and your leg will then naturally tilt forward slightly, so the boot is made to accommodate this.

There is usually extra padding on the inside part of the leg to give just a little extra protection to the calves when they are working on the side of the horse. The sole is flat, the heel small, and the whole boot will be cut on 'slim' lines to grip the ankle and fit snugly around the calf. And you will usually find that they are lined with fine nylon stockinet to help them slip on and off more easily. A word of warning. Don't ever ride with bare feet inside the boots: as the perspiration builds up, your skin will stick to the lining and then getting the boot off, which isn't easy at the best of times, is worse than getting a cork out of a wine bottle. If you can wear a sock of some kind, even in the summer, it will make life much easier.

The painless way to take a boot off is to jam your heel into a boot jack and heave. Most stables have a jack as basic equipment, if not, you'll need something pretty solid, like a doorstep to loosen your heel. If that fails, then you will just have to sit on the floor and let someone else heave at your foot. Not very elegant, but practical.

If you don't want to splash out on boots, then don't be tempted to think that ordinary wellingtons will do instead. The sort that flop around your calves, and have half an inch of G.T. tread on them, are useless. When you are in the saddle, you need to balance evenly on the ball of your foot. If there is a tread of any kind, it is likely to jam the stirrup in the grooves (fatal if you come off) or make your balance uneven. So if your boots are not suitable, much better to wear strong shoes; not slip-ons, or sandals, or high heels, or 'fashion' shoes, but something that conforms to the plain sole and small heel of the riding boot, with laces, so that they hug your heels and stay on firmly. If you are riding with your weight on the balls of your feet, you don't want your heel slipping out of the shoe, or, worse still, the whole foot slipping out. It is uncomfortable at best, dangerous at worst.

riding hat

Trousers

As for the rest of your gear, eventually you may want to buy your own riding trousers, breeches, or jodhpurs. They are made of stretchable fabric that will give in all the right places and have extra padding on the inside leg around the knee joint at the top of the calf. You will find, when you are riding, that it is this part of your leg that takes the most wear, and if it is not properly protected you will get chafe or even bruise marks from constant rubbing against the saddle, and horse. But jodhpurs are not essential. As long as your trousers are not too tight (that would be most uncomfortable), or too thin (that would not give any protection against rubbing at all), almost anything will do and jeans are ideal.

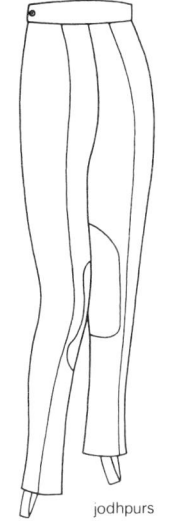
jodhpurs

In fact, a lot of regular, or professional, riders – people who spend a large part of the day in the saddle, exercising and hacking – often wear jeans in preference to jodhpurs. But they cover them with chaps, which are leggins made from a soft leather which keeps them warm, dry, and gives total protection to the whole of the inside leg in a way that jodhpurs and boots never could.

Apart from that, wear whatever is comfortable and suits the climate for the time of year. But keep it simple. Clothes that flap around, or need to be adjusted every five minutes will be uncomfortable for you and unsettling for the horse.

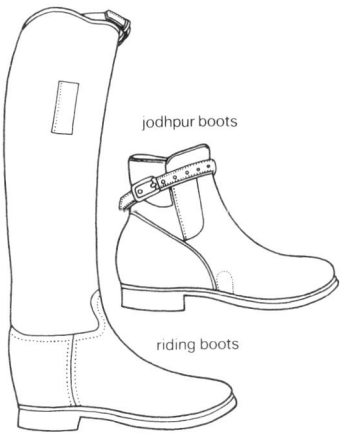
jodhpur boots

riding boots

In the summer, stay cool and cover yourself and your hat with fly repellent (why do flies always make for the head?), and in the winter invest in a really thick pair of socks, and a pair of gloves. There is nothing more miserable than being stuck out on a ride with numb toes and frozen fingers knowing that it is half an hour or more before you can warm up in the stable. A steady trot, or stiff canter will get the circulation going, and keep most of your body warm, but you can't keep that pace up for an hour, and it is the fingers and toes that will succumb to the cold first.

4 Getting Under Way

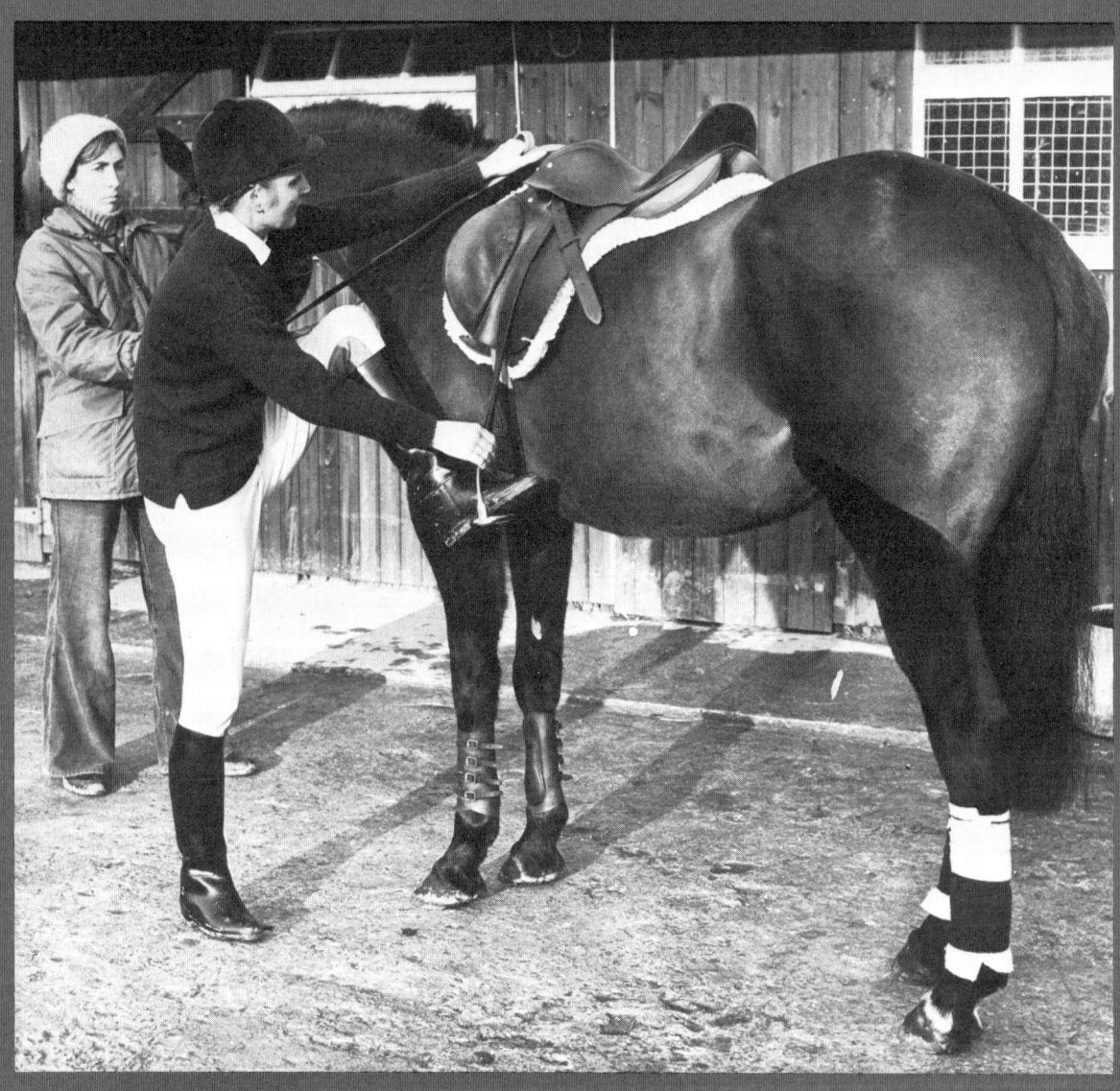

Faced with getting into the saddle for the first time, the stirrup can look an awful long way off the ground, and the horse enormous. I've watched so many people who obviously regard mounting as a sort of lurch and scramble, when really it needn't be too much of an effort at all.

How to mount

You always mount from the left side, and if you are in a yard where the ground is uneven, or slopes, then make sure that you place the horse so that you stand on the higher ground. Mounting against the gradient makes it a long haul to the top.

First, check the girth. To do this, pull up the flap of the saddle, and pull the girth straps through the buckles until you are satisfied that the girth is firm around the horse's stomach. Then make sure that someone from the stable is standing at the horse's head to hold it steady while you mount. Horses can get fidgety and there is nothing more unsettling for a beginner than to find that everything starts moving under him while he is still in mid-air.

The helper can also put his weight on to the right-hand stirrup to ensure that the saddle doesn't slip, and to help distribute weight across the horse's back.

Make sure that the reins are over the horse's head, then prepare to mount. Stand with *your* left shoulder level with the horse's shoulder, facing the rear end. Take the reins in your left hand to control the horse, and hold on lightly, just for balance, to the horse's neck in front of the saddle. With your right hand, hold the stirrup iron and place your left foot firmly in, up to the arch.

Take a firm grip on the back of the saddle (the cantle), point your toe downwards, so you don't dig the horse in the ribs. Push your body up towards the saddle, swing your right leg over the horse's back without kicking it in the rump – then sit lightly down into the saddle. Try not to 'flop' down, the effect of twelve stone or so landing in the middle of the back, dropped from a great height, is uncomfortable, and unsettling.

Sit well in the middle of the saddle and check the length of your stirrups. If they are too long, you will lose both your balance and the stirrups, and spend the whole ride groping for them. If they are too short, this will tip you too far forward, and probably give your unaccustomed muscles a painful bout of cramp. A good guide is to let your legs dangle free of the stirrups, and then adjust the length using the buckle under the skirt until they reach a point level with the bottom of your ankle-bone.

Slip your feet back into the stirrups, with your weight resting on the balls of your feet, toes pointing forwards. If you push your foot 'home' to the arch there won't be any elasticity in your foot, and it will be difficult to balance well once the horse starts moving. Think of it this way. If you stand holding the back of a

Getting on: left foot in the stirrup, left hand holding the reins and lightly balanced on the withers

chair, feet slightly apart, and crouch up and down bending your knees, it is easier to control your movement if you do it balancing on the balls of your feet. If you stand flat-footed it is likely that you will not be able to bend at all. Exactly the same thing applies when you are riding a horse. Let the stirrup leathers lie flat before you place your feet in the irons, otherwise there is a chance that you will put your foot in the back of the iron and twist the leathers. Then they will chafe against your shins.

Now you're in the saddle, this is as good a time as any to tell you how to get off. And rightaway you can forget anything you've ever seen in Western movies. It's all very well for John Wayne to leave one foot in the stirrup and nonchalantly swing the other over the horse's quarters as if he is getting off a bicycle – but not you.

If the horse were to shy suddenly or move off while you were in mid-flight, you'd be overbalanced and would land with a nasty crunch. You might even get your foot caught in the stirrup and get dragged along the ground. (I am sure all these protestations of doom seem far-fetched to a lot of you – but they

Getting off: putting the reins in the left hand; taking both feet out of the stirrups; leaning forward; swinging the right leg over the horse's hindquarters; taking the weight on the arms and dropping lightly to the floor

really DO happen.)

The safe way to get off a horse is also the simplest. Put the reins in one hand. Take both feet out of the stirrups. Place your hands in front of you, either on the saddle or the horse's neck to take your weight and give you balance. Lean forward, bringing your right leg over the horse's quarter, and 'spring' off on to the ground.

As soon as you get off the horse, loop the reins over your arms then run the stirrups up on their leathers. Hold the front loop of the leathers in your left hand, then slide the stirrup iron up the back run of the loop until it reaches the buckle end. Then tuck the long loop of the leather into the stirrup, and pull down straight so that the iron is secured up out of the way. Horses don't like things hitting them in the ribs, so never lead a horse with the stirrups swinging. Also, if you have to lead a horse into the stable, a swinging stirrup could get caught in the door, and make a clanking noise to startle the horse. So it is safer always to run them up.

But let's suppose that finding yourself *in* the saddle, you're happy to stay there for the ride.

How to hold the reins

Now pick up the reins. Hold them so that they lie across the palm of your hand with the end nearest the horse's neck passing between your ring (third) finger and little finger. The slack, at the other end, should pass over the index finger and be held in place by the thumb. Let the loop of the reins fall to the left-hand side. Adjust your hold on the reins until you can feel a light contact with the bit in the horse's mouth through your ring finger. But it should only be light. My first instructor told me always to think of the bit as a piece of cotton. Properly used it would wear well, too much pressure and it would snap.

If you ride with your reins so loose that you have no contact at all, then the horse will slop along with its head down going where it likes and doing what it pleases. Admittedly, if you go out in a riding-school line the horses will tend to follow each other and the amount of steering you will need to do will be minimal. But if the horse should shy suddenly or stumble, you will be thrown off balance. Conversely, if you pull the reins too tight, and hold them with stiff immovable hands, you'll cause unnecessary pain to the horse's mouth and neck. It will keep fighting against you and you will both have a miserable ride.

Walking

You are now ready to move off. Sit upright in the saddle, but not bolt upright and stiff. If you are like a ramrod balancing on top of something that is moving, every bone in your body will be buffeted and jarred. Try to relax, and move with the horse. To use a disco equivalent, let your backbone flip. If you keep your seat in the saddle, the force of movement from the horse's hindquarters, as it moves forward at the walk, will flex your back and push your hips backwards and forwards with the motion of the horse. At the front end, the horse's head will be moving in and out automatically and in order to keep contact with the bit your hands and arms must go with that movement, backwards and forwards like gentle pistons. That way you will not be perched precariously on top of the saddle – you will be riding as one with the horse.

At one time, riding instructors would always tell you 'to grip with your knees'. Nowadays, less emphasis is put on the knees, and more on the whole leg. Think of yourself as sitting on a greasy pole and 'wrap' your legs around the horse's body giving light contact from the thigh, through the knee to the calf. If you keep your toes pointing forward and your heels down, it shouldn't be too difficult to achieve.

I remember feeling pigeon-toed, knock-kneed and bandy, the first time I sat like that. My instructor said that's how it should feel, so if that is your feeling, take heart, you are getting there.

Walking, of course, is the easy bit. So, funnily enough, is cantering (more of that later on). It is the rising trot that is the real killer for most beginners.

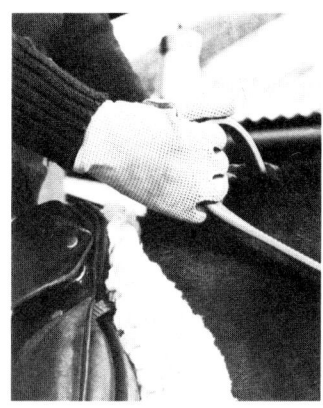

Correct position for the hands, the reins passing between the ring and little fingers and held in place by the thumb

Opposite: In the saddle and ready for the off

Kate at the walk. She's carrying her head too high and resisting the bit. For once, my position is almost correct with shoulder, hip and ankle in line

Trotting

Look at any group of new riders and sooner or later you will see someone valiantly pushing himself up and down, red in the face with the effort, usually managing no more than an uncomfortable-looking double bounce with the seat crashing down to hit the saddle – ouch. The secret when you are just beginning to learn, is to let the horse do the work for you. To prepare to trot, first gather up the reins. The faster a horse moves, the more it draws in its head, so you will need to take a shorter and firmer hold. On a well schooled animal you should only need to squeeze with your legs to push him forwards. But many hacking-yard horses need a little more persuasion. So if it doesn't respond to a squeeze, 'niggle' at it with your heels. At the same time give firm forward pressure from your seat, as you would if you were pushing off on a bicycle. A sharp vicious thump in the ribs is the thug's idea of an accelerator. It is rarely necessary, yet you see the uninformed doing it every day.

What you are asking the horse to do is to produce more energy and power from its hindquarters because that is where the engine is. When you use the correct aids of long leg and seat, it is like dabbing the accelerator. You are telling the horse that you want it to alter its gait and increase power and speed. It is the resulting driving force from the hindquarters that will help push you forwards to achieve a rising trot.

The thing to remember is that the action is not so much up and down, as slightly forward and back. Keep your weight evenly distributed on the balls of both feet and slightly increase the pressure with your legs. Try to keep the leg, from your knee to your foot, fairly still and use your knees as a point of balance and bend, like a fulcrum. The action is similar to lowering your seat on a dining-room chair. As you stand up, your feet stay flat on the floor, your lower leg is straight, and your hips swivel forward over the knees. If you were to sit down immediately, neither your feet nor your legs would move and your hips would lower on to the seat from your knee joint. On a horse, though, you don't have to force yourself backwards and forwards. The power from the hindquarters will do that for you. If you try to push yourself out of the saddle, the action will probably take longer than the natural swing of the horse. So, as you are coming back to rest on the saddle, the horse will be a beat ahead of you, and coming up for another 'rise'. That is when your rear end starts to get buffeted, and your balance goes to pot. Keep the action simple, gentle and relaxed. As the horse throws you forward, take your balance on your knees and gently lower yourself down again. Lean your shoulders slightly forward. If you strain back, you will overbalance. Listen to the noise the hooves are making as they strike the ground. You will hear a definite one-two, one-two rhythm being struck out. Repeat the

Kate trotting and beginning to 'track up' – that is, bringing her hind feet up to the mark left by her front feet rhythm to yourself and move your hips in time with your counting. Eventually you will get the feel of the steady rhythmic stride and your own body will coordinate quite easily with the horse.

Cantering

Your first transition to canter will probably be the easiest thing you have ever done, simply because *you* won't have done anything about it at all. Most riding-school horses are great 'follow my leaders' and creatures of habit. There will undoubtedly be parts of the ride where you can canter safely, and the horses will always associate that bit of ground with a change of pace, regardless of what *you* might want to do.

On an escorted ride the leader will usually warn, 'This is where we canter, all right?' If it isn't all right, then say so. A responsible leader will make sure that the rest of the ride moves at your pace and that you are not left behind. Horses are sociable creatures and are used to staying together on a ride. They will not want to be left on their own. It is the herd instinct. If you try to keep them back from 'the herd', they will pull and fight to catch up and if you are at all nervous of going fast, then you will be in real trouble.

Suppose that you do suddenly find yourself going at a faster pace. First rule, don't panic. I know it is easier said than done,

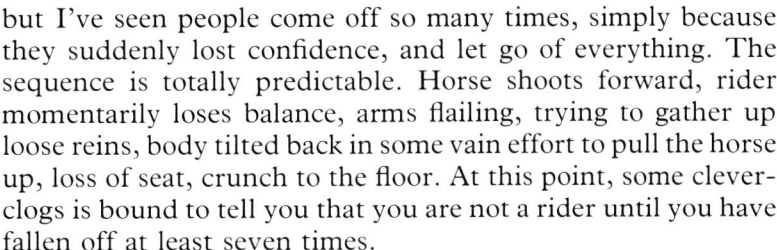

The pace Kate enjoys most, an active canter uphill. Note the shift in body weight over the knees, and the shorter rein

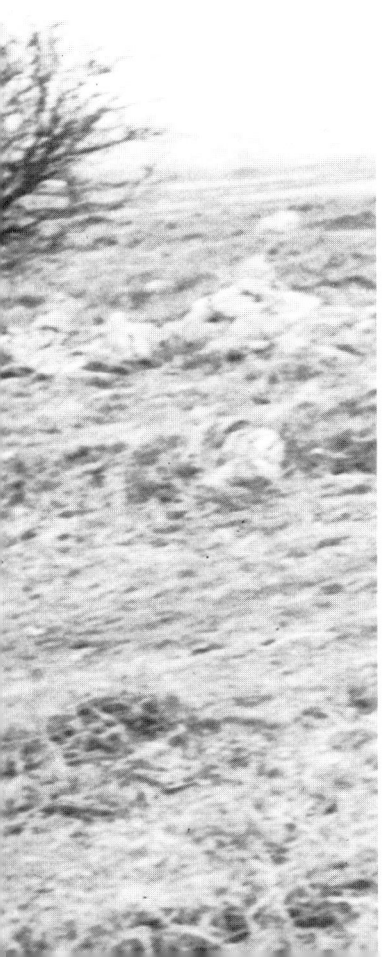

but I've seen people come off so many times, simply because they suddenly lost confidence, and let go of everything. The sequence is totally predictable. Horse shoots forward, rider momentarily loses balance, arms flailing, trying to gather up loose reins, body tilted back in some vain effort to pull the horse up, loss of seat, crunch to the floor. At this point, some clever-clogs is bound to tell you that you are not a rider until you have fallen off at least seven times.

Admittedly, you will come off a few times, especially as you go on putting your own ability to the test by trying more difficult and demanding things. It happens even to the most experienced of riders, as you will have seen on television, but you learn to ride horses by sitting on their backs, not rolling on the ground. And the general idea is not to come off, but to stay on and enjoy your ride.

As soon as someone on the ride indicates that you are going to go faster, gather up your reins and have a stronger contact. The faster a horse goes, the further up the reins you need to position your hands. Just look at the difference between the position of the hands on a rider performing the slow measured precision of a dressage test, and a jockey riding a race over the finishing line. On the first, the back will be upright, the hands about an inch away from the pommel on the saddle. On the second, the rider will be hunched over the horse's neck, his hands barely twelve inches from the bit.

Having positioned your hands, shift your weight further forward by taking your bottom off the saddle, and balancing on the balls of your feet and your knees, gripping with your thighs. Don't hang on to the mouth, but feel it through your fingers and let your arms move with the action of the horse's head. Don't be tempted to sit up, or lean back. As a beginner, that is the quickest way of losing your balance. If you keep your weight forward over the horse's shoulder, you will have a smoother ride, and more control.

At this stage, don't try a fancy 'sit' to the canter. To do that well you need a really supple back, good balance and, ultimately, the ability to use the aids of leg, hands and back in coordination. In the beginning, it is more important that you should build up confidence in your own ability to stay on, and start to enjoy the exhilaration of speed, albeit rather gentle. By the time you are ready to gallop, the next speed on from the canter, and the fastest of the horse's four paces, you need only follow the same principles of shorter reins and forward body, only more so.

Eventually, you won't want to follow the gang, and canter only when everyone else does, but when you choose. And it isn't just a case of kicking furiously at the horse's ribs and whacking it over the rear with a crop. I know people do employ those 'aids' and the horse will break into a canter. But it is a crude language to the horse, who will respond just as well, and more generously, with more subtle messages.

Shorten the reins, sit to the trot and push into the saddle with your back as if you are revving up an accelerator, only using your seat rather than your foot. At the same time, give a strong leg aid with either the left or right leg pressed firmly against the horse's flank, just behind the girth. Make it a forward pressure from the calf so that the horse is getting two messages, from your seat and from the leg, asking it to bring its hindquarters underneath, producing stronger impulsion.

You may find that all the horse does is trot more quickly, without ever breaking into a canter. This could be either because he is too darn lazy, in which case vocal encouragement and a firm touch on the rear with a crop will send the message home, or it could be that your hands are not going forward with the horse. It is no good pushing forward from the back, if you are pulling up at the front. You will be giving the horse two entirely conflicting sets of instructions. The back saying 'go forward', the front saying 'hold on'. The poor thing will not know what to do and hitting it will only confuse it even more.

So keep your hands relaxed so that you can pick up the movement of the horse, without losing contact. When you have been riding for a while you will find that your back will have sufficient strength and flexion to take a sitting canter. You stay firmly in the saddle with your backbone 'giving' to the action of the horse, and your arms following the flow of the head. Once you have mastered it, it is a most comfortable stride. But it is tiring, so if you don't want to end each ride as an exhausted heap, you will find it more practical to alternate between sitting, and balancing over your knees.

Stopping

So now you can walk, trot and canter. But as my husband asked the first, and only, time he ever sat on a horse, 'Where are the brakes on this damn thing?' or words to that effect. What you *don't* do to stop or slow a horse is stick your feet forward, lean back and yank on the bit. And *never never* 'saw' on the bit by raking your hands from side to side. A horse's mouth is incredibly tender. 'Sawing' on the delicate 'bars' of the mouth is a vicious and painful exercise and anyone who needs to resort to that tactic is riding out of his class.

The 'brakes', like the accelerator, are in your hands, your seat and your back.

There is a very funny Bob Newhart L.P. called The Driving Instructor. In it the hapless lady driver (who you never hear in the one-sided conversation) explains that in the previous driving lesson she learned 'the other way of stopping'. 'What's that?' asks the instructor. 'Throwing it into reverse!' Well it may be catastrophic on a car, but that is how it works on a horse.

Think again about the principle of the toboggan. If you want to stop, you dig your heels into the ground. *Don't* dig your *heels* forward on the horse but employ the same bracing action with your back and your seat so that your body resists the forward movement of the horse.

To change from the canter to the trot, sit in the saddle, and stop giving any forward aids. Flex firmly back with your hands in time with the horse's head movement. This whole 'reverse' action will slow the horse back to a trot. From a trot to a walk, the 'reverse aids' are the same. The faster the horse has been going forward, the stronger the aids must be to slow it down. But the rule is strong and firm, not rough and ready.

Finally, to come back to a halt, use a firm back, strong seat, gentle flexion on the bit, and a very firm 'sqeezing' action with the legs so that you almost feel as though you are drawing yourself up in the saddle.

No horse will stop, or change its pace immediately. Even in the highest level of *haute école* dressage, there will be a few paces of preparation. You won't see them (or you shouldn't), but they will be there. So do not expect the animal to stop immediately. It *will* slow down in a few paces. It will stop after a few strides. And you will have achieved the transition in the smoothest, most comfortable way for both you and the horse.

I know that most riding-school 'plugs' have set routines and routes and will tend to stop and start when it suits them, or the rest of the ride (if you will let them). But every horse should have been schooled to respond to the most elementary of the aids, when it was first broken. They may have had some of their willingness to oblige knocked out of them after years of rough hands and sharp heels. But they never forget.

Riding

You will have gathered by now that riding a horse is not just a simple matter of sitting in the saddle and letting it happen. Done properly, it requires a tremendous amount of muscular energy. So a word of warning. However keen you may be, don't push your unaccustomed flabby muscles too far too soon. Only ride within the limits of your strength or you will wear yourself out and riding won't be fun so much as an endurance test. As your muscles harden, your riding will become stronger, and easier.

If you are content to stop, start or go fast in line with the rest of the ride, you need only learn to cope with the different paces, and leave the horse to do the rest. But if you do want the independence of riding to suit yourself, so that you are not just being *taken* for a ride, but *going* for a ride, then you will need to apply the aids with patience, and firm resolve, and then even the most abused horse will respond.

If your stable is one where horses are used to being ridden properly, then you will begin to experience what it is that keeps so many people in the saddle. Not the thrill of control over another living creature, but a partnership with a horse that enjoys its ride as much as you, and suddenly riding will take on quite a different complexion.

5 Study Your Horse

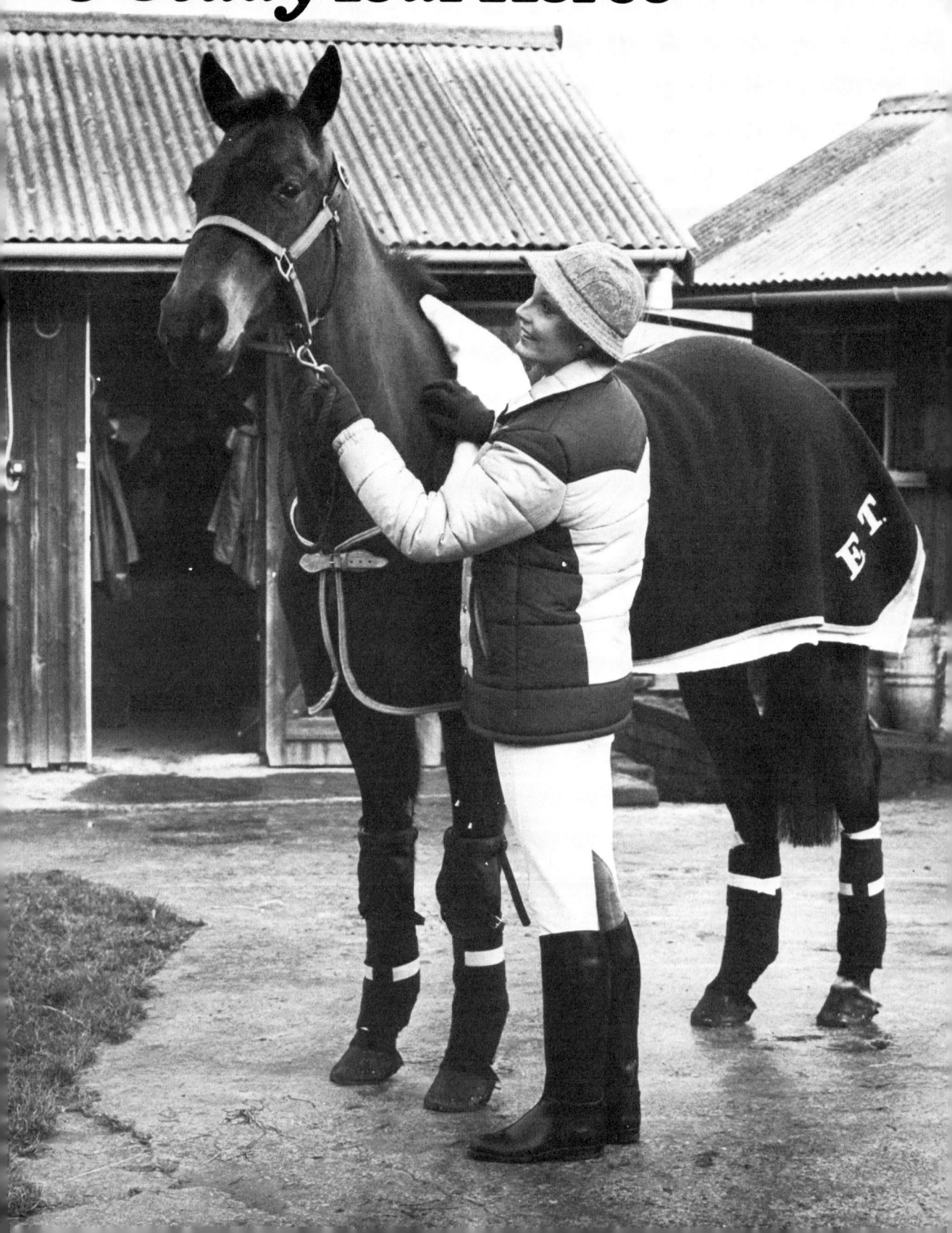

After a hectic few days away in London, Birmingham or wherever, I find there is nothing more relaxing than to get out on the horse to the middle of the moor. Somewhere so quiet that all you can hear is the scolding of the skylark and the steady chomp of Dartmoor ponies eating grass. With most people their reason for riding has more to do with being out in the fresh air than aiming for the dizzy heights of the competitive sport.

For me, it is the ultimate 'switch off'. But don't be fooled. Even as you sit there drinking in the fresh air, and enjoying the scenery, at least part of your mind and body should stay fully alert. Horses are not inanimate lumps. They are complex living creatures – clever, delicate, strong, willing, cantankerous, reliable, or thoroughly unpredictable. These are just some of the characteristics you will find all rolled up in the same animal. So it should help you to enjoy your association with the horse much more if you begin to understand those things that make its life more comfortable physically and also what makes it tick – what goes on inside its head. Though according to at least one renowned horseman of my acquaintance, 'Horses are like women, you can never understand them!'

Before they were domesticated, horses lived as wild herds roaming the grassy plains of Europe and Asia. Horses are non-aggressive. There is nothing about their physical shape that would make them good fighters. They can kick with powerful hooves, and bite with sharp teeth, but they are not killers. Though they were preyed upon by carnivores. So they needed sharp hearing and an acute sense of smell to detect the approach of an enemy, and a powerful explosion of sudden speed to run away. That is why horses stand up when they are dozing. There are not many lions on the loose these days in Devon, Yorkshire, or the Home Counties, but the instinct is inbred.

If you have ever watched a horse getting up when it has been lying down, you will see what a complicated, time-consuming business it is of flailing, spindly legs, heaving up a half-ton body. So you can be sure that when you do see a horse sprawled out and lying in the sun, or sleeping in its stable, that it feels very secure and safe from danger.

Horses are not necessarily intelligent, but they do have very good memories and learn by repetition. When working on a dressage test for a competition, which involves performing a series of exercises at the walk, trot and canter in a set sequence, you have to do bits of it at a time, interspersed with other, non-connected exercises. If you keep on doing the complete test over and over again, the horse will soon get too clever, and anticipate each movement, rather than wait for the aids.

Similarly, a horse from a riding school will soon get to know all the regular routes. If you let him, he will take you out and decide where you trot, walk and canter. And as soon as you head for home, even the most sluggish horse will suddenly become bright-eyed and bushy-tailed.

Horses have a limited vocabulary. They whinny or whicker to each other when they need the confidence of companionship. A horse taken to a show, or hunt, finding itself surrounded by strangers will call out in the hope that another horse will recognize it and reply. On a ride, if you get separated, your horse will call out to locate the rest of the ride. If it is used to working in a crowd, it will need to know that it hasn't suddenly been deserted. They will 'scream' with terror, 'squeal' with delight, and sometimes give an odd blowing sound through their teeth and nose as a form of greeting or recognition. But like most animals, their widest vocabulary is in their 'body language'.

As well as being the instruments of an acute and highly developed sense of hearing, the ears themselves are sensitive. They are *also* a good indicator of the horse's state of mind. Watch any good horse at work, whether it is jumping fences in a show-ring, galloping over a cross-country course, or schooling in an arena. When it is alert and interested in what it is doing, the ears will be 'pricked' forward in keen anticipation. On a gentle hack, you will find that the ears are constantly revolving like radar antennae, picking up information about horses, traffic, people, anything and everything that is going on around. When the ears are laid back, flat against the head, that is a sign of bad temper. So is curling the upper lip back and exposing the teeth. It may look as if they are laughing. In fact, they are doing the opposite.

If a horse lays its ears back as you are about to mount, get someone to stand at the head. If they are really bad tempered about something, they could be quite unpredictable, so don't take chances. If you are out on a ride, the horse may flatten its ears as a sign to another horse that it doesn't want it to come near. As the rider, don't force the issue. You could end up in the middle of a kicking match. It can be an indication that they are being bitten to pieces by flies, in which case, you will have to search around to find the offender. Or maybe you, the rider, are doing something to cause pain or discomfort. Whatever it is, eliminate the cause. You and the horse will be happier for it.

The eye will indicate fear. Usually, all you will see is a large dark shiny pool of brown (very, very rarely blue), fringed by soft folds of skin and long coarse lashes. When a horse is frightened, the eye socket is dilated, and you can see, literally 'the whites of their eyes'.

The sense of smell, as in all animals, is highly developed. On a ride, you will often see horses sniffing at the droppings of others. It may look disgusting, but it is their way of identifying who passed that way before them. You will hear many people say that horses can always tell when you are frightened of them, and it is true, they can. The sensitive ears will pick up any hint of tremor in your voice. Their ultra-sensitive skin will trace even the slightest tremble in your hands, back or legs, and their noses will pick up the scent of fear. It doesn't matter how much you may disguise the pure 'human' smell with soaps, deodorants and perfumes, the human body gives off a distinctive odour that is sharpened from certain glands when we are frightened, or even just a *little* bit scared. It may only be faint, but to a horse, it is a message as loud and clear as a shout to human ears. Whether the horse will exploit or pander to your fear is very much up to the horse!

The horse's tail is a useful tool. It is fairly efficient at flicking off flies. It is also a barometer of its temperament. If the tail is swishing in an agitated way, you can be sure the rest of the horse is pretty agitated too.

If you have ever looked through the 'Horses for sale' columns of your local newspapers, you will have often seen animals described as 'bomb-proof'. Obviously, it doesn't mean that they will withstand the impact of a four-pound grenade. It is an indication that the horse will not shy or bolt when faced with a tractor, a slamming car door, or any of the other terrors awaiting you on a ride in town or country.

At a commercial riding school or stable, most horses for hire will fall into this category. Horses can be expensive, but clients are more so!

Even so, *don't* relax your concentration entirely. My own horse, Kate, is a pretty even-tempered creature. But she is well bred and highly strung, which makes her, from time to time, totally unpredictable. While on one day she may allow an articulated lorry or galloping horse to pass without so much as a glance, the following day the world will be full of danger. The robin popping out a hedge will be a marauding vulture. A sheep lying peacefully in the shade of a gorse bush will be a wolf in sheep's clothing, and a piece of corrugated metal clanking on a gate will hold untold terrors if we pass too close.

Now it could be because she is in season, and is feeling a bit temperamental anyway. Or because she has decided to challenge my authority as master. If you are to have a successful partnership with a horse, one of you must be the senior partner. You must work in harmony, with each appreciating the skill, courage and enjoyment of the other. But, let's face it, a horse is a bigger, fitter, stronger animal than any human. If that power and strength were not controlled they could at worst acciden-tally kill or maim you, at least make your ride unpleasant and uncomfortable. So the human must be able to control, without squashing, the horse's spirit. Most horses are happy to accept the situation, but from time to time, they will 'challenge' you. If that happens, you must make it quite clear, firmly, but not unkindly, that you are the boss. There is *no* call for laying into a horse with a crop. If you are a novice rider on a riding-school horse you will not have the knowledge to determine why the horse misbehaved. In which case, you certainly do not have the right to assume the role of taskmaster.

So, coping with the naughty horse will just be a question of asserting authority. If you ask at the stable before you go out about possible 'vices' or dislikes, you will at least be prepared. Much more serious are the things that really do frighten the genuinely nervous horse. Remember that if you are nervous, you will be sending out loud signals to the horse. And a nervous horse with a nervous rider will lose all confidence.

If you are on a road, and you know the horse is frightened by traffic, or lorries, tuck yourself in beside a 'bomb-proof' animal. Stay calm yourself, talk quietly to the animal, even stroke its neck. The soothing assurance from you and the confidence of the calmer animal beside it will work wonders.

Be like the horse, listen, and anticipate danger, so you are not taken unawares. And if you see a vehicle looming up, give a clear slowing-down signal to the driver. Most country people meet this kind of problem every day on country roads and lanes, and will automatically switch off the engine and stop so that you can pass by. But you will come up against drivers who are just plain ignorant, or genuinely don't understand the problems. (More of them later in another chapter.) In that case, being prepared is your best defence.

All sorts of things that are innocuous to you or me, can startle a horse. Be aware of things like farm gates. A dog may suddenly run out or a cow unexpectedly appear in the gap. Paper may be hurled around in the wind. A tin may clank noisily on tarmac near a car. Anticipate that people or children in a bus shelter may suddenly pop up from nowhere and remember that a horse doesn't have particularly clear eyesight. What we see as a clearly defined object, may just be a grey hazy blur to a horse.

I have often gone past a field where men have been working behind the hedge. *I* have seen them quite clearly, but Kate has

been disturbed by a shapeless, noisy mass that *she* can't identify. I usually find that by asking people to move into the open so that the horse can see them clearly is enough to settle her down. The people do not mind and the horse is assured. It may all seem very silly and unnecessary to us, but horses are not human. They don't think or react like us and it is wrong to try to superimpose human reactions on an equine. Instead, think horsey, it is safer.

A horse that suddenly shies can be very unsettling. By anticipating possible trouble-spots, you are already coping with half the problem. The rest lies in your seat. No matter how relaxed you are in the saddle, keep contact with your legs, and light contact with your hands. That way your reflexes will react much more quickly. You might be unbalanced, but you won't be unseated.

And it is so easily done. A few years ago a friend and I were taking our horses slowly through a wooded section of Dartmoor. Earlier, a third rider had peeled off and left us to take a short cut back to the stable. We were chatting aimlessly about what we had done the previous week. Everything was very peaceful, not a trauma for miles, or so we thought. Suddenly three sheep ran out on to the narrow path in front of us. My companion's horse shied violently and turned 180 degrees. We hadn't been concentrating, and were caught completely unawares. She had a crashing fall, but somehow hung onto the reins. But the horse had been frightened, and headed off to find the stable companion that had left us earlier. We caught the horse, and continued the ride. But my friend had a cracked rib, and lost her nerve. She has never ridden since, which is a pity.

We both learned a lesson – the hard way.

Typical Dartmoor riding country, plenty of room for us and the native ponies

6 Riding Hints

Picking our way carefully
through granite clitter on the
edge of a Dartmoor tor

Riding out for pleasure should be just that – an hour or so spent in the saddle which you find relaxing and enjoyable. Not a regimented, super-disciplined hour with the instructor shouting out 'Don't do that,' every few minutes without any explanation of why.

There are several do's and don'ts that you should be aware of and a few hints about horse lore that should stop you doing serious damage to the horse or you. These are just a few of the ones I have picked up over the years.

Fit your pace to the surface

Try not to canter on hard road surfaces like tarmac or concrete. If you become a keen hunt follower, you may well see riders caught up in the speed of the chase cantering along lanes, but it is not generally acceptable. Firstly, because it can be dangerous. A horse travelling at speed on a smooth surface with metal shoes stands a good chance of losing balance and going down, causing severe damage to itself, and you. They are more difficult to stop. Like applying the brakes on a car on a slippery surface, horses can skid. It is also bad for the horse's legs. Their limbs don't have built-in shock absorbers as the Almighty didn't intend that they should ever ride on anything but springy turf. So every time the legs come into contact with a hard road surface at speed, it sends a shock wave up through the bone. Imagine the feeling you would get if you put your foot to the ground thinking there was a step below you, and there wasn't. That jarring on your foot is the sort of thing that happens to the horse's legs. It *can* lame them and cause 'splints', a bony growth between the cannon-bone and one of the splint-bones. In other words, the leg is 'concussed'.

If you are riding across rough, uneven ground, with loose stones and shale around, walk, don't trot or canter. Or better still, avoid it all together. If you can't, then allow your horse to pick its own way through, avoiding the largest and sharpest of the stones. At speed it wouldn't be so accurate, and could do real damage to itself and you by losing its footing and falling over. However, even at a walk, this kind of ground can still be tricky. The horse could bruise the sole of its foot by getting a stone jammed in the soft tissue around the shoe. It could go lame, and it isn't unknown for a horse to twist a foot so sharply that it breaks a leg. So go easy.

Horses should be strong enough, and sufficiently well balanced, to go up and down hills without much difficulty. But if a hill on a road is particularly steep, and you are going down, it is often better to get off the horse and walk, rather than risk riding. On grass there is no problem (unless you are trying to tackle a one-in-four slope) as the horse can get purchase and grip without sliding and if there is plenty of room you can zigzag down the side of a hill to take the steepness out of it. But on a road, it is a different matter.

The surface may be slippery and greasy with an accumulation of oil from cars, aggravated by rain showers. Or it may be so well worn that it is like glass under the steel shoes. If a horse starts slipping, with your weight on top of it, it could get panicky. Hop off and walk beside the horse. It will be much easier for him, and if he does start to slip uncontrollably, then you can at least give him some help by just putting your shoulder into the shoulder of the horse and act as a live brake. It will be just enough to steady the horse, and give it confidence. Of course, in an ideal world, a well balanced horse that is well shod will not have too many problems with hills. But remember that riding-school horses do hours of work. Their shoes can wear down quickly and if you are riding the day before the blacksmith is due, there will only be the minimum amount of tread and grip left on the shoe.

If you ride throughout the year, then sooner or later in your 'winter' season you are going to come up against snow and ice. It can be quite pleasant riding in the snow, especially on days when the sky is that brilliant clear blue that only comes with frosty days, the air crisp, and the snow white and crunchy. Your main problem will be snow 'balling' in the horse's hooves. As

they move over the ground snow will collect, and build up in the hollow parts of the feet.

Usually these lumps knock out on their own, but it's uncomfortable for the horse, and it can be dangerous if you get a build-up of ice on all four hooves. It's like putting the horse up on icy stilts. You'll lose all grip with the ground, and the horse is likely to slip all over the place. To prevent it, you can fill the hoof with thick grease, or even ride the horse (providing it is to be a fairly leisurely ride), in leather or sacking bootees. But riding schools are hardly likely to keep a whole stock of these for just one or two snowy week-ends in the year. So be prepared for a slow and careful ride – or none at all.

Ice is quite a different kettle of fish. If you meet ice on the road – get off and walk the horse. Try to make for the gutter where the gravel or tarmac should be rougher, and where winter debris may have built up to give the horse some purchase.

On open ground, ice can be just as treacherous. If the ground is frozen rock hard don't *ever* try to canter. Apart from the fact that you'd probably slide all over the place, the effect on the horse's legs would be that of riding on concrete. And when the surface begins to thaw don't be misled into thinking that it will be safe. Ground that has been deep-frozen during the winter takes weeks to thaw out properly. The first few days of sun may thaw the surface – but underneath it will still be solid, and that combination of a greasy surface and frozen subsoil is deadly.

Loose and shed shoes

If your horse develops a loose shoe, take it easy. When walking on a hard surface it is easy to hear when a shoe is wearing loose. The hoof will make a hollow ringing sound as it hits the floor. A bit like a tap shoe doing a double shuffle. If you are on grass, then it is slightly more difficult to hear because the sound is absorbed by the soft ground. You are more likely to hear a soft clanking sound as the shoe flops up and down on the hoof. A loose shoe is about as uncomfortable on a horse as it is on a human. So keep to a walk, trot – *slowly* – if you must, but don't canter. That is the quickest way of losing the shoe altogether. While you are riding, keep an eye on the shoe, then if it does come off, you stand a chance of picking it up, and taking it back to the stable with you. If it is not too badly worn down, it could be re-nailed to the hoof. And with farriers charging anything from £7 to £15 for a full set of new shoes for riding-school horses, the stable owner will be only too grateful to you for saving them yet another bill.

If the shoe *does* come off, you can do one of two things. Ride slowly home on the grass, or get off and walk.

A horse that is regularly shod should not be ridden without shoes. The soft, unprotected, inside sole of the foot will become sore and ragged. When you get back to the stable, make sure the owner knows that the shoe is either loose, or has come off. They may be able to secure the loose shoe temporarily, but if it has been lost, then the horse should be returned to the stable, or field and *not* asked to work again until it has been re-shod.

Broken tack

It doesn't happen often, but it is possible that while you are riding, some part of the horse's tack may snap. If, like the proverbial boy scout you are always prepared with a bit of string, or a rubber band tucked in your pocket, then it is usually possible to do a running repair. And, of course, you can manage to ride without certain things, in an emergency. You *can* ride without a noseband. It *is* possible to ride without a bit. A knot in the reins is as good as a buckle. And provided you are happy to sit and relax in the saddle at a gentle walk, you *could* ride home without stirrups. However, if the girth breaks, then you are in real trouble and that means a long walk home. But the best insurance against any accident with the tack is, as I said at the beginning, to check its condition before you set out. If you are not happy with it, point it out to the owner, and get it changed.

It is unlikely that well maintained tack will let you down, but not impossible. When Captain Mark Phillips was just three fences into the cross-country section of a major three-day event at Badminton, the reins fell away from his horse's bridle and the animal careered off the course, temporarily out of control and he was eliminated. So it can happen to the best of riders.

The horse's needs

If your horse wants to pass water, then you MUST stand up in the stirrups and take your weight off the saddle. A horse's kidneys are situated just under the spot where the lining, the deep cushions on the back of the saddle, bear down on the hindquarters. It is important that the kidneys are not restricted, to avoid any discomfort to the horse.

People are often concerned to see horses slavering at the mouth as if they have been at a tube of toothpaste, and frothing on the neck like an advert for soap powder. Both are quite natural. When a horse is really working 'on the bit', this means that it is giving plenty of impulsion from behind, and flexing its jaw in front to give that beautifully arched outline, typical of a well schooled horse. As the horse flexes its jaw, it champs on the bit. The more it champs, the more saliva it produces. In some horses, this shows as just a small amount of frothy saliva around the edge of the bit on the bars, or outer corners of the horse's mouth. On others, it is a mass of creamy white foam. Either way, it is not a sign of cruelty, but that the horse is working well.

As for the froth on the neck or between the hindquarters, that occurs naturally when a horse starts to sweat. Again, not a sign of cruelty – 'working the horse into a lather' – but of a hot horse.

It is not a good idea to let horses eat while they are on a ride. To begin with, they cannot chew grass properly with a mouth

full of steel or vulcanite bit. So what ends up in their stomachs is likely to be half chewed and lumpy. And despite their size and strength, horses are incredibly delicate internally, and susceptible to all sorts of stomach upsets if their food and water are not administered properly. If you were just going to amble about for an hour at a slow walk, it would not be too serious. But most people want to 'ride' and that means trotting and cantering. No horse can work on a full stomach. So a good stable routine will allow at least an hour between feeding, and doing work of any kind. If you allow the horse to chomp away at the hedgerows in between bouts of strenuous or fast work, then you are asking for trouble. It could produce an uncomfortable form of equine indigestion, or you could create a blockage of lumpy partially digested food.

There is only one exception. If you are walking your horse slowly back to the stable, and you know that he will not be asked to go out on the next ride, but will have an hour or so's rest, then it is O.K. to let the horse take a few nibbles at the grass. But it should be looked on as a titbit, a reward for a good ride, not a whacking great meal. That way, the digestive system will be able to cope.

Keeping horses away from poisonous plants

If you are going to let the horse graze, either on the way home, or if you have stopped for a quick half at the village pub, then you should be aware of the plants that are poisonous to horses. On the whole, horses are fairly fussy about what they eat and naturally avoid the 'nasties'. But they might just idly nibble at an overhanging branch, or take a mouthful of passing hedgerow out of boredom or devilment. So if you can recognize the poisonous plants, that is the time to hang on to the reins, and make sure that the horse doesn't grab a quick snack.

Some of them are fairly obvious because they are poisonous to just about everything, but it is worth listing the major ones just the same.

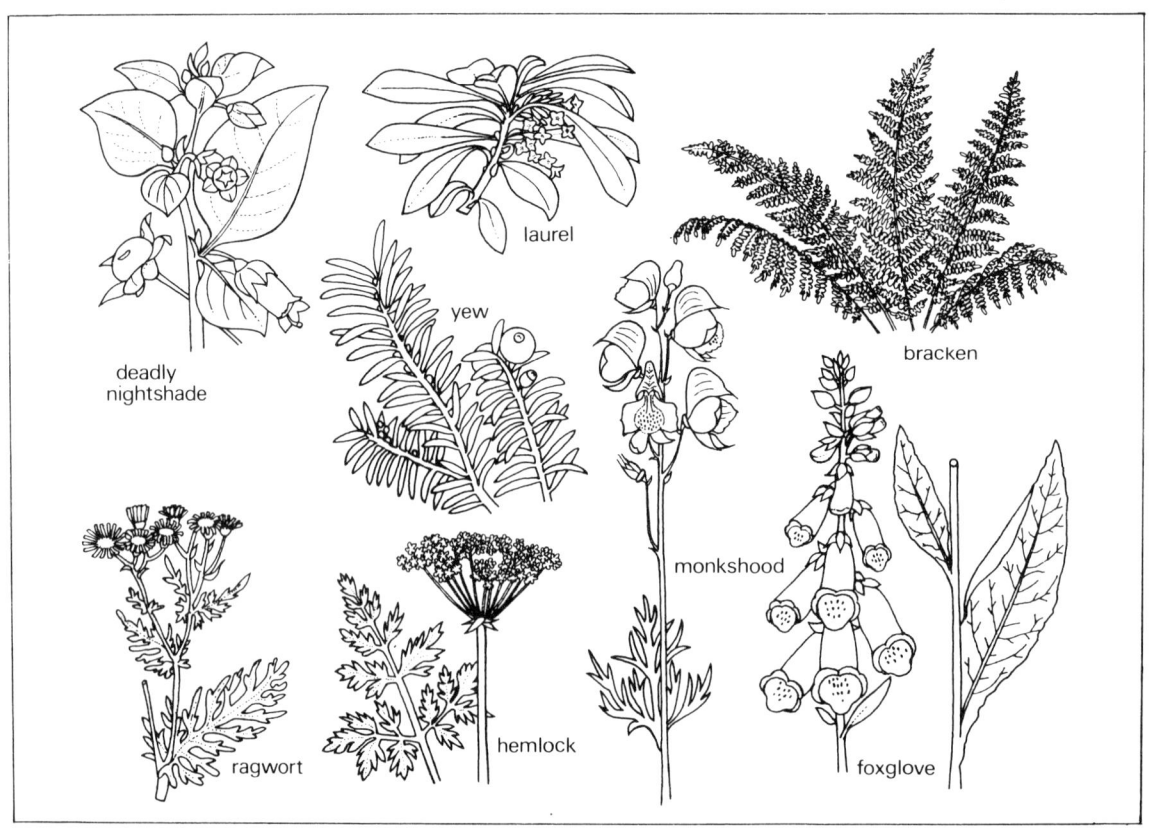

Deadly nightshade (or any of the nightshade family). Small, barrel-like purple flowers, with white stamens. In the autumn the flower matures to a blackish blue berry.

Yew. Dark green needles of leaves – looks like a ragged Christmas tree.

Laurel. Distinctive large broad-leafed tree.

Bracken. On Dartmoor you will notice that even when the grazing is poor, the wild ponies will not touch the plentiful fronds of bracken.

Ragwort. A bright-yellow hedgerow plant. Looks a bit like small dandelions clustered together, about a dozen or so to one stem.

Hemlock. Clusters of small white flowers, not unlike ground elder.

Monkshood. Large purple flower that looks just like the hood on a monk's habit. Not unlike the garden flower, aquilegia.

Foxgloves. Few horses are likely to take in a mouthful of foxglove from the hedgerow because, unlike some of the other deadly flowers, they are large and quite distinctive. But the poison digitalis does come from the plant, so it is worth being wary of it.

Water for the horse

If you come to a stream, it is fairly natural to let your horse have a drink. But choose your time, and don't let it drink too much.

If you have just done a lot of very fast work, a stiff canter or gallop, and the horse is very hot, don't let it drink at all. Ice-cold water going into a hot horse, will bring on an attack of colic – severe stomach pains. And don't let it drink just *before* you intend to set off at a brisk trot or canter. The effect of all that water sloshing around inside its stomach would be like a lead weight. So let the horse drink in the middle of a stage when you are walking – and then only enough to quench its thirst. Too much water, particularly on a hot day, even when you are just walking, is likely to induce colic, which even in a mild form, is unpleasant and better avoided.

Non-violent instructions

Don't 'yank' your horse's head around if you want it to turn or move across to the left or right. When you want a horse to turn you need to use a combination of leg and hand working together. To turn left, move the left hand out to bring the head around, at the same time gently squeezing and asking for a forward motion with both legs but bringing the right leg back slightly to just behind the girth. Effectively, you are bending the horse around your left leg. If you want to go right, reverse the process! right hand leading, left leg pushing. In fact, make it a rule never to yank, pull, snag, or be rough on the horse's mouth. Do everything firmly, but gently – you will get a much more responsive horse.

Don't keep thumping the horse in the ribs to make it 'go', or as a punishment. There are times when you need to 'kick on' with two or three firm leg movements – just before a jump, or if the horse is sluggish going into a canter. But a constant booting in the ribs is unnecessary, unkind, and will eventually make the animal's side 'dead to the leg'. In other words, the area around the girth will be so hardened to constant thumping, that when someone tries to ride the horse properly, giving correct aids through the leg, the horse simply won't respond. Instead of constant thumping, much better to give one firm slap with a crop to wake the horse up, or to let know it has done something wrong. Only ever use the crop on the flanks, just behind the girth, or, lightly, on the shoulder. Don't *ever* hit a horse about the head, and don't wait until the animal gets back to the yard, and then set about it in the stable. You may think these warnings quite unnecessary, but, believe me, some R.S.P.C.A. or B.H.S. reports on the treatment of horses make chilling reading.

Lameness

You will often hear people talk of horses being out of work because they are lame. An experienced rider will be able to tell at once watching the paces of another animal, or feeling the stride of his own, as soon as the horse is lame. For a novice, it may be more difficult, or at least less noticeable.

Normally a horse will trot at a steady rhythm of one-two, one-two. If it goes lame, the rhythm may change slightly as the horse comes down heavily on one leg to relieve the pain on another. You may also feel a change through your seat as the horse, quite literally 'limps' on one leg. Once you know what you are looking for, you will see, hear, or feel it quite clearly, though it is possible in some cases, for the lameness to be so slight in the early stages that you will not hear or feel a thing. Then you must rely on the eye of another person to notice that the horse is walking or trotting unevenly or 'being careful' with one of its legs. The lameness may be caused by many things, from a fairly simple soreness of the back, to a more serious injury. Either way, you must get off at once and walk the horse back to its stable.

Rolling

Horses love to roll. Left to themselves in a field, or stable, it is their way of giving the back a good scratch. Unfortunately, you may come across a horse that thinks it can still roll, even when there is someone on its back. Some may try it if they have been standing around for a long time in a group while you are busily talking. Others may even attempt a sort of 'aqua roll' if you get near water. Your warning sign will be that the horse will try to lean over on one side, and start to drop its front shoulder. It once happened to me (on dry land), so quickly that I suddenly found myself standing on the ground with my feet still in the stirrups. I was able to coax the horse back up from a standing position.

That was sheer luck. Usually, you have only two alternatives: either to catch the movement before the horse goes down, and keep it upright; or, if it has gone too far, to get off and out of the way quickly. Half a ton of horse steamrollering over your legs is not a happy experience. Fortunately, few horses will roll over a saddle. If one did, it could damage its spine (not to mention the saddle).

Bucking

Bucking is not necessarily the sign of a difficult or dangerous horse. Many horses will buck out of sheer joy of living. It's exuberance, or excitement, not a vicious attempt to unseat you. A small, playful buck is fairly easy to cope with. If you stay relaxed in the saddle you will just ride it out. Often a horse will buck with pleasure as you kick into a canter. When that happens you will usually absorb the impact with the increased speed and will hardly notice it. So don't be too ready to chastise a horse that bucks. Like you, it may just be out to enjoy itself.

In fact, the easiest way to stop a horse from bucking more than once, is to kick it on. It cannot keep going up and down if it is being made to put all its energy into going forward.

A horse that gives off a series of savage, bad-tempered bucks is quite a different matter. Take heart. Any horse with that sort of disposition will rarely find its way into a riding school. If it does, it won't last long. But if you are on a horse that bucks violently, either because someone has just stubbed their cigarette out on its rump (it has happened), or because it wants you off, there are ways of riding it out, depending on the severity of the buck, and your own riding skill and nerve.

In order to get good leverage into the buck, the horse will get its head right down almost between the front legs. So the first thing is to try and get the head up. Pull in all the rein you can manage and when you have got the head up, keep it there. Sit deep in the saddle and let your back flex with the horse and if you can manage to remember, push the horse forward to dispel some of the upward energy. If you are strong, keep your nerve and don't panic, it is likely that you will survive the experience.

Rearing

Rearing is, I feel, much more unpleasant and dangerous than bucking. Once a horse is up on its hind legs, flailing about in mid-air, it could so easily overbalance, crashing down on its back, and you. It is a serious fault in a horse, and again, those guilty of it, rarely end up in public stables. The only thing you can do is throw your weight forward as far as possible as though you were trying to put your arms around the horse's neck. Throw the reins forward and try to get the head down.

Bolting

A bolting horse can be terrifying. I once sat on a small grey horse that treated every piece of long straight grass as a potential race-track, and would take off like a bullet out of a gun at the sight of a straight. The first time I rode him I didn't realize this, and was simply run away with on a long stretch of open moor. I got the reins short, gripped like fury with my knees, and actually prayed, 'Please, God, don't let me fall off – not at this speed.'

I didn't have a clue how to stop him, so I just hung on for grim death – hoping that when we got to the bank of gorse bushes at the end of the run, he would stop by himself. As we got nearer, I suddenly panicked and thought, 'What do I do if he decides to jump them?' Fortunately, he didn't and stopped. I was like jelly. Years later I got someone to explain what I should have done and I've never been frightened by the phenomenal speed of a horse since.

The first rule is – don't panic. If you sit up, drop the reins and lose control, you will be off in a nasty heap on the floor. Take a firm hold on the reins, but *don't* stick your feet out front and just pull with all your strength on the bit. Horses are cowards and always run away from pain. The pain you cause to its mouth by a straight pulling action will make it gallop away from you even faster to try and escape.

Keep your seat, and with your reins fairly short, put your left fist into the horse's neck just above the pommel of the saddle. With the right hand, give and take on the bit so that you bring the horse's head around, and begin to slow him down. If you are in a field or open space, turn the horse to make a large circle. Your aim should be not necessarily to stop immediately, but to slow him down to a controllable speed. Then bring him back to a trot and walk. Of course you may not have the room to bring the horse back by degrees. With a ditch, or wall, or railway line looming up, the action will have to be strong, even severe, as you won't have the luxury of time and space. If drastic action is needed (but only then), make a sawing action on the bit, and keep trying to bring the horse's head around. In a straight fight of sheer strength, the horse will always win. What you have to do is try to shift the balance and direction of the horse so that you are back in control.

Falling off
Until now, we have assumed that regardless of what the horse may throw at you, you have stayed in the saddle. If that happens, you are lucky. Unfortunately as a novice, with soft muscles, the chances are that given any one of the previous examples, you and the horse will part company.

The experts will tell you that there is a 'proper' way to fall. If you can keep fairly relaxed, and take the impact out of landing by 'rolling' into a fall, then the chances are that you will end up just winded. Watch National Hunt jockeys when they hit the floor. They roll into a tight ball, and even though there may be horses and bodies flying all around them, more often than not they get up, and walk back to the dressing-room. It is too easy to say that they are good at falling because they get so much practice, because sometimes they *are* injured quite badly. (Dick Francis, the Queen Mother's former National Hunt jockey – now a successful thriller writer – tells some horrendous stories of jockeys riding with broken collar-bones and fractured wrists.) So perhaps what they are *really* expert at is pretending they are *not* hurt.

As a novice rider you may find yourself dumped on the floor because the horse bolted, reared, bucked or shied, or because you simply lost your nerve. This means you may go flying over its neck at speed, drop inelegantly over the back end or just throw yourself out of the saddle in panic. If you have time to think about anything while you are in mid-air, then try to think about landing without legs and arms flailing. That is when they tend to break. In practice, I have found that each fall is different. You just have to take it as it comes, and hope for the best. If you are winded, don't get up too quickly. Give yourself time to catch your breath, and to make sure that nothing is broken.

I once took a crashing fall at a steeplechase fence in a hunter trial competition. I bounced on my spine, then landed in a heap on my face. I was so winded I felt physically sick, so I just lay there, sprawled out on my face till the nausea passed, while my breath filtered back, and wiggled all my toes and fingers to make sure nothing was broken. What is the point of getting up, I thought, when all I am going to do is fall down again. As soon as I had decided that everything was still where it should be, and I had got my breath back – I got back on the horse and finished the course.

You should do the same. If you come off, and you are not injured, get back on the horse again as soon as you can. Otherwise you may just lose your nerve, and that would be a pity.

If someone is genuinely injured on a ride, don't try to move him. If you are in a crowd, let two riders go off to find the nearest telephone and ring for an ambulance. Two, because riding-school horses don't like leaving the herd, and so two together will be more willing to separate from the main group. Also, it saves any problems in the unlikely event of one lone rider either getting lost, or having an accident himself. If there are only two of you out for a ride, then you will have to leave the injured person. Make them comfortable and warm, and leave something like a jacket or scarf on the nearest tree as a marker. You may feel you know exactly where you left a person lying on the road, but on an open moor or in a thick wood, it is easy to lose your bearings.

If you have a badly injured horse on your hands, follow the same procedure. Don't move the animal. Keep it calm. Phone the owner of the stable and, if you are on a road, the police.

Most riders have fallen off at some time in their lives – it is a risk that goes with the hobby – like jamming your fingers in the car door. But don't be unduly worried, or anxious about it. The more you ride, the more experienced you will become and so the better you will be equipped to avoid the obvious pitfalls.

Rubstic's jockey going into a roll as horse and rider fall during the 1980 Grand National

So you have fallen off. You are not injured. And you are ready and willing to get back in the saddle. First, catch your horse. If you are lucky, the animal will not be injured. If you are unlucky, it will have set off at high speed, and will either be heading for home, or tantalizingly nibbling grass just a few feet away, making a dash for freedom every time you get close.

The first rule is that a runaway horse should not be chased by another rider. The sound of galloping hooves will only make the horse run away even faster, whether because it is frightened, or because it starts to race with the pursuer. With main roads or cattle grids around it is dangerous to panic the horse into even greater speed. Left to itself, it will slow down eventually. If you are going to catch a horse on horseback, follow slowly, then get off your own horse, and walk up to the runaway with a handful of grass, or some other titbit. Talk quietly and soothingly, coaxing it close enough to catch hold of the reins.

If you are pursuing on foot, do the same. Often a horse will play up and let you get close, then suddenly dash away. No matter how much you are tempted, don't run after it. And whatever you may be *thinking*, keep calm, and persevere with the slow, coaxing approach. Ninety-nine times out of a hundred it works. If you have got the horse that is the one in a hundred, then be prepared to meet up with it back at the stable.

Working horses reasonably

Don't return a horse to the stable in a hot, sweaty, exhausted condition. Once you are within about half a mile of the stable, let the horse walk on a long rein. This will give it a chance to stretch its neck, relax, and cool off slowly and naturally. You can also loosen the girth by a hole or two. Just enough to let the horse 'blow out', not enough to let the saddle slip. If you have ever been to a race-track, you will see that after a race, horses are dressed in a sweat rug, a thing like a string vest, and walked around in circles. This allows their bodies to cool down gradually, brings the heartbeat back to normal, and stops the muscles seizing up. Human athletes do the same. You will never see a runner burst through the tape and stop dead. They nearly always jog on a few yards more, at a slower pace. Horses are the same – they need to ease off gently.

Don't lead the horse like a dog on the end of a leash. Once you have jumped off, slip the reins over the horse's head, and stand on the left side of the horse (the near side). Hold the buckle end of the reins in your left hand. Your right hand should hold the reins about 6 in (150 mm) under the horse's chin, with your index finger between the reins. This way you are still controlling the bit, albeit lightly. Don't wander off from the horse. Walk with your shoulder level with the horse's shoulder. That way you will be in complete control of the horse, stand less risk of being kicked, and your heels and feet will be well clear of the front hooves.

In most good riding stables a horse has his work 'paced out' during the day so that he isn't flogged to death. But some people treat horses like hire cars, on the principle of more use producing more money, and they spend all day plodding in and out on a conveyor belt.

So take note if the horse handed to you is one that has just come in off a ride. If the skin is damp, and the sides are heaving in and out, then it has had a hard ride, and you must not ask too much of it too early. When you get back to the yard, notice whether or not your horse is then handed on to yet another rider. If so, then it might be a kindness to point out the sort of work it has already been asked to do. If all you have done is plod round for an hour at a gentle walk with only the occasional burst of trotting, then a fit well-fed horse will cope with that sort of work most of the day. But a lot of riders look on horses as galloping machines, and a couple of hours of hard, fast work will tire out even the fittest animal.

Leading a horse into its box

If you are asked to put a horse into its box, make sure the stirrups are up, walk it in a straight line to the entrance – not on a sharp curve round a corner – and as you get to the stable door, walk slightly ahead of the horse, looking back at it to make sure that it doesn't hit its hindquarters on the door jambs. (You should do the same taking a horse out of its box.) Walk straight into the stable heading for the back wall, and make sure that all the animal's body is inside the box before you start to turn the head round towards the door. Keep the reins in one hand (if you let them trail on the floor *at any time* you risk the horse getting its foot caught in the loop), pull the lower half of the stable door to, and secure it.

Leading Kate out of her stable, and looking back to make sure that she comes out straight without hitting her flanks on the door

The easiest way to carry the tack, with the bridle over my shoulder and the saddle resting on my arm

Tacking up

At most stables, you will find that your horse is already tacked up when you arrive, and that it will be taken away from you and dealt with when you get back. So there is never any need to learn about fitting, or removing the saddle and bridle. But many people like to do this as part of getting to know the horse. Whether you carry the bridle in your hand, or slung over your arm doesn't matter but it must be carried by the top loop of the headband, with the reins also looped over your arm – not trailing their full length on the floor. Carry the saddle so that it is sitting on your arm with the pommel end nearest your elbow, and the cantle at the wrist end. Don't lay a saddle flat on the floor as this will stretch the side panels. If it must go on the floor, then stand it on its pommel end, leaning up against something with the underneath part of the saddle facing outwards, taking care not to scratch or damage the leather. It is much better if you can rest the saddle over the stable door or on top of a convenient gate or fence. The girth strap will be resting over the seat of the saddle – either detached at both sides, or attached with just one set of buckles.

As a beginner, you don't want the horse roaming all over the

Tightening the girth before mounting, but don't forget to check it after you have ridden a few hundred yards, to adjust any slack after the horses stomach muscles have tightened up

stable while you are trying to put the tack on. So either get your instructor, or someone from the stable to tie the horse up with a head-collar, or just hold it steady.

Approach the horse from the left side, at all times, when putting on or taking off its tack. Place the saddle high on the shoulders, and gently slide it back into position so that all the hairs on the back are lying flat, not sticking up and likely to cause irritation. Walk around to the right side and pull the girth towards you. If the girth is already attached on this side make sure that the buckle guard, a small flap of leather, is pulled over the bbuckles. If it is not attached, then hitch the buckles to the first two girth straps on the saddle. The third is there as a safety back-up, if either of the others ever snap. Pull down the buckle guard, and replace the saddle flap. Walk around to the left again, and secure the other end of the girth to the straps in exactly the same way. Don't ever just throw the girth over the saddle from the left-hand side. The buckles could hit and damage the horse. Don't do the girth up too tight at this stage. You must pull up the buckles. If it is not attached, then hitch the buckles to the you have ridden a few hundred yards by which time the horse's stomach will have tightened up.

Putting on the bridle, not as difficult as it looks, and even easier when you have a cooperative horse

The bridle is slightly more complex. The novice rider will probably use the most simple of bridles and bits – a snaffle with a cavesson noseband. Hold the bridle by the headpiece in your left hand, with the buckle end of the reins in your right. Slip the reins over the horse's head. Slip your right arm under the horse's jaw and grasp the entire bridle in your right hand, just below the brow-band. The horse's head is now cradled in your arm, and you can keep the face still by lightly resting your right hand on the nose. Hold the bit on the flat palm of your left hand. Using your left thumb to ease the horse's mouth open, slip the bit into the mouth without knocking the front teeth. Slip the headpiece over the ears, and do this gently as ears are very sensitive.

Attach the throat-latch, and check the fitting by placing your hand, sideways on, between the leather and the horse's cheek. Ideally there should be enough room to take the full width of a normal hand. Secure the noseband, and again, there should be enough room to allow either two fingers, or a thumb to pass between the band and the nose. Once you have finished, always get someone to check the horse over. Badly, or incorrectly fitting tack could lead to an accident, or severe discomfort for the horse.

When removing the tack, loop the reins over your arm, and again, work from the left side. Make sure the stirrups have been run up, then begin with the girth. Undo the buckles from the left, and pass the buckle ends under the horse's stomach. Don't

throw them or just let them swing. Walk around to the right, and lay the girth over the top of the saddle seat. Return to the left side, and slide the saddle off. Place it either on the floor, as described on page 00, or over a suitable bar. Now undo both the noseband and throat-latch buckles. Take the headpiece in both hands, and draw the whole bridle gently down off the horse's face. The animal will automatically open its mouth and let the bit fall free.

If you are going to put the tack away in the tack room, rinse the bit clean, hang the bridle up by the headpiece, and place the saddle on either a saddle horse, or a saddle mount, which will protrude from the wall. Always place the saddle with the pommel end nearest the wall, and the cantel facing outwards.

Titbits

Giving titbits at the end of a ride is the way most people want to show their gratitude to, or affection for, a horse, especially one that they ride regularly.

Apples, sugar lumps, carrots, and peppermints are all recognized horsy delicacies. (Though I know of several animals, racehorses particularly, whose taste runs to stout, chocolate bars and marshmallows.)

If you are going to give the horse a reward, take an apple or carrot. Don't let the horse eat with the bit in its mouth. It really is very difficult for a horse to champ on something solid when its

Checking the fitting on the throat lash – there should be enough slack to take the width of your hand

mouth is already full with one, and sometimes two bits. If your horse is going back into a box or being turned out, give the apple or carrot once all the tack has been removed. If it is going straight out on another ride, a sugar lump or mint is ideal.

When you are offering food to a horse, put it in the centre of the palm of your hand. Hold your hand quite flat and offer it to the horse's mouth. The animal will take the food quite cleanly and make no attempt to bite you. Don't snatch your hand away quickly. This will startle the horse. And don't curl your fingers up. If you do, then you must expect the horse to assume that they are a tasty morsel too!

Inspecting a horse's feet

If you have to pick up a horse's feet for any reason, don't make a grab for the hoof and expect the animal to oblige. Speak to the horse, stand with your shoulder close to the leg, and run your hand nearest the animal's side down the whole length of the leg starting from the withers (at the front) or the hindquarters (at the rear) – follow the back contour of the leg to just above the hoof. Slip your hand around the back of the leg so that you can take a hold at the front at the base of the fetlock, and lift. This ensures that the horse isn't frightened by any sudden movement. Horses associate the action with a request to lift their feet.

If you ever need to do any work around a horse's legs, or under its stomach, don't be tempted to kneel on the ground beside the horse. Crouch instead. That way you keep your weight and balance on your feet, so that if the horse steps towards you, you can get out of its way quickly. If you're down on your knees, by the time you've moved, you will probably have been trampled on!

Wet horses

Don't ever put a rain-soaked horse back in its stable, and just leave it. That is the quickest way for a horse to catch a chill. Once you have untacked, rub the animal down all over with a handful of clean straw to absorb the worst of the moisture. And make sure that the legs are as dry and free from mud as you can manage. A good way of drying out a really wet horse is to lay a layer of straw across its back, and then cover this with a stable rug, sacking side in. This combination will keep the animal warm, and allow the air to circulate as it drys out. You may also find in some stables that horses will have straw bandages put on their legs if they have got very wet and muddy. Similarly, this consists of a layer of straw held loosely in place by stable bandages. It dries them out and helps the circulation. At the other extreme, where facilities are more limited, you may have to settle for just a few sacks thrown over the hindquarters and withers, and a quick massage on the legs to get the blood going. Not every stable expects its customers to 'muck in' and help with the stable management of the horse. But I have found that

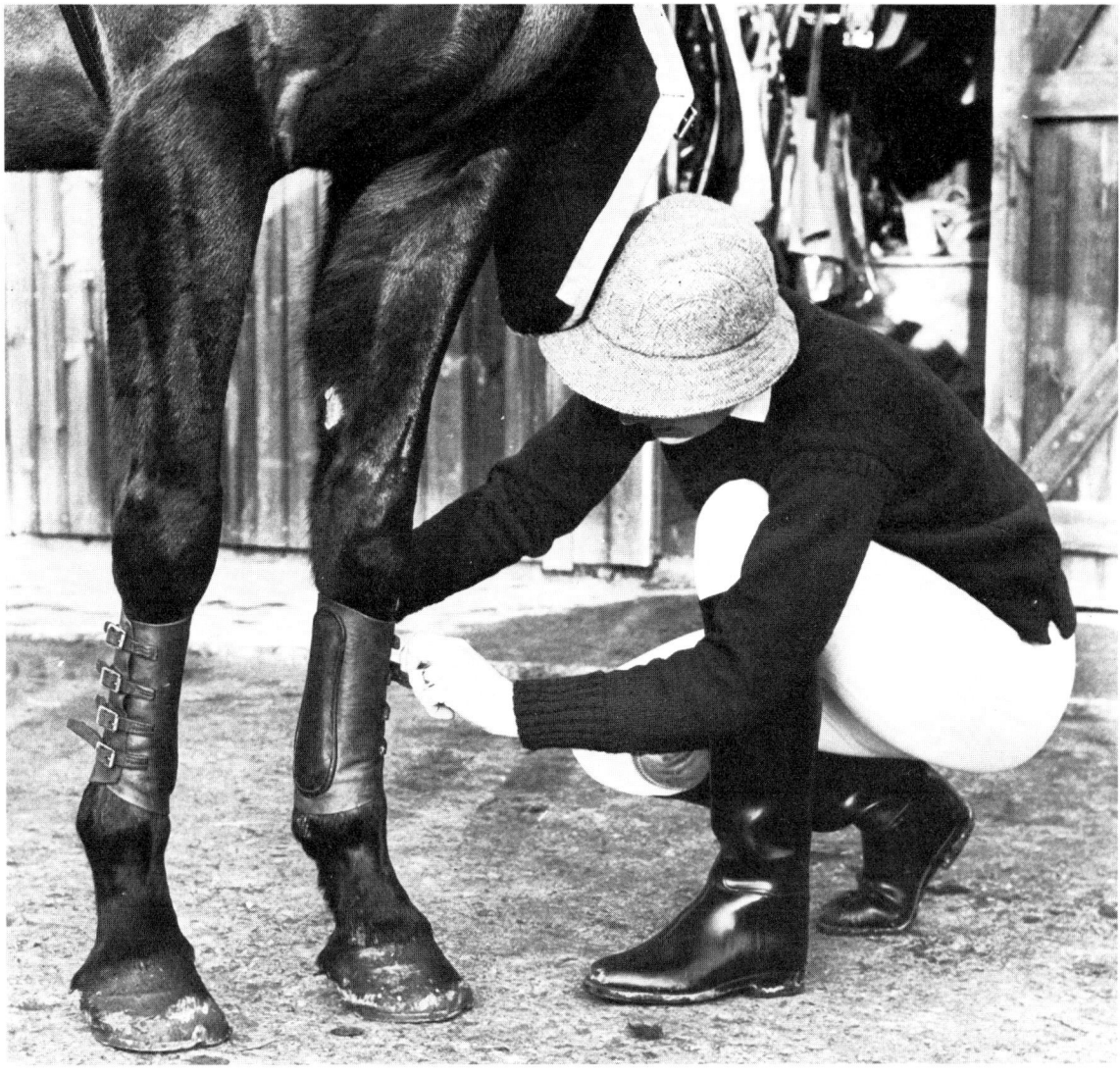

most people like to be involved. And besides, the exercise involving rubbing down, and rugging up a wet or muddy horse not only gets the circulation going in your own wet and frozen toes and fingers, it helps to ensure that there will still be a horse, willing and able to be ridden, next week-end.

Do put an anti-sweat rug over the horse if you get it back to the stable and find that the skin is still damp with perspiration. A sweat rug is a giant string vest. It keeps the horse warm, and allows the skin to breathe, and dry out slowly.

Generally

Do make a rule, that all your movements in handling the horse will be firm, but calm. Don't shout, make sudden and violent movements, or handle the animal roughty. Not, of course, unless you want a neurotic horse on your hands.

These brushing boots will protect Kate's legs while we're riding and give her tendons support. Note, always crouch when working around a horse's legs, never kneel, in case you need to get out of the way quickly

7 Riding on Roads

Once you've leapt off the ground and into the saddle, it's a mistake to believe that what you have under you is now a four-footed pedestrian, and that you can ride where and how you like. Not so. Wherever you ride, there are restrictions, and hazards.

Riding on a road, whether it's a country lane, or main trunk route, is potentially the most dangerous aspect of the sport. Firstly because too many riders don't obey the simple rules of road safety, and secondly, because some drivers refuse to exercise either care or consideration when approaching horses.

On main roads, horses don't simply have a right to be on the road – it is where they *ought* to be, because, by law, horses should not be ridden on pavements. A horse and its rider are just as much 'traffic' as is a juggernaut lorry, and they go on highways not in competition with cars, but as legitimate road users.

If you're going to ride on a busy road, with other traffic, you must be quite confident that you can handle the horse and be prepared to show as much road sense as if you were riding a bicycle, or driving a car.

Keep to the left. Let the horse walk or trot, but never canter. Ride with both hands on the reins – except when signalling. If turning left or right, or negotiating a roundabout – use clear, positive hand signals and get yourself in the correct position on the road – again, exactly the same as driving a car.

If you have to cross a road, position yourself so that the horse isn't buffeted or frightened by the speed of passing vehicles, but still close enough to the edge for drivers to realize that you are waiting to cross. When the road is safely clear, walk across purposefully, but don't let the animal rush at it and risk slipping. Also, *never* make a dash between what looks like a safe gap. You could totally misjudge the speed of what is coming towards you.

If drivers stop for you, or show you consideration in any way – always acknowledge it. If you have to ride along a main road, and the animal is just too frightened to cope – get off and walk beside the horse, placing yourself between it and the traffic.

If you are in a group, never ride more than two abreast. Don't trail about and get left behind. If the other horses suddenly disappear around a corner, your own could get panicky and make a sudden dash after them.

Try to keep the horse's hindquarters square so that they don't suddenly swing out in the path of another vehicle.

A busy road that is expected to be used a lot by horses as well, is supposed to be provided with a grass verge for the use of riders. Unfortunately, few local authorities bother.

In the countryside, you do have access to bridleways, green roads, and whole chunks of the country's main long-distance footpaths.

If a right of way is described as a 'footpath' you have a right to ride along that – unless the local district council has decided that

Motorists in our Devon village are used to meeting horses and riders on the roads

Turning right at a junction, just like any other 'vehicle'

horses will churn the path up too much for the comfort of walkers. In which case, you will be barred, and there will be notices to warn you accordingly. The royal parks, like Hyde Park in central London, Richmond and Windsor Great Park, all have restrictions on access and use by riders, and these are clearly written up at the entrance to the parks.

The fact that an area is designated as common land does not mean it is common to everyone including horses. It means that 'commoners' have rights to the land, and don't necessarily want riders (or even pedestrians) crawling all over it. What you may have are bridleways crossing the common. These should be clearly marked, and you must stick to them. The common land on my doorstep is the vast Dartmoor National Park. Fortunately, few restrictions are applied to riders on Dartmoor, which provides those of us who live in this part of the world with thousands of open rolling acres – for me, the finest riding country in the land.

If you are in any doubt about access, get hold of a 1:50,000 Ordnance Survey map. Footpaths will be marked with a red dotted line, and bridleways by a red dash. If you are still in doubt, apply to the county council in the area for the region's Definitive Map. That will give a complete, up-to-date record of all paths and bridleways in the area.

Country lanes may have less traffic than main roads, but are no less hazardous. If you have high, dense hedges on either side,

use your ears as much as your eyes to warn of approaching traffic. If you hear a car coming, don't get into a position where you both meet on a bend. If necessary, stop and wait on a straight section of road – it will give the driver a better chance of seeing you.

If the lane is wide enough for passing traffic, keep your horse straight, and well into the left side, and allow the vehicle to pass. Where there is a single track, find a passing spot and then wave the car on. Don't allow any car – no matter how impatient the driver may seem – to panic you into action. Stay calm, and be safe.

You would think, being a nation of horse lovers, that at least some of them would drive cars! As it is, while a few people show great patience and understanding when they meet a rider, many car drivers see horses as a nuisance, a hold-up, and unnecessary competition for road space.

The rules for drivers are quite simple, and are spelled out succinctly on the B.H.S. road-safety car-stickers. Pass slow and wide.

Follow that, and you won't go far wrong, but one or two other considerations would help as well.

Be aware when you're in the country, that you are likely to meet up with a rider sooner or later. So don't hammer along country lanes or round bends. Meeting another car is bad enough, but cars mend – horses don't.

Waiting to cross a main road, having placed myself at the junction, where I have a clear view of the traffic, and they have a clear view of me

If you come up behind a horse, slow down, and pass, giving plenty of room, don't try to squeeze past. Even the most placid horse may suddenly be startled by something in the hedge. If it suddenly shies to one side, you want plenty of room for manoeuvre. If you meet a horse coming towards you, the rider may well stop and signal you on. But if *you* decide to wait then make sure that the horse is well clear of your rear bumper before you drive off. A sudden burst from the exhaust can be startling.

Don't let children wave things out of the window at horses, and if you are on holiday, with polythene flapping about on the roof rack, or have anything outside the car likely to startle a horse, give an extra wide berth, and ease off on the accelerator.

If you see a rider waiting at the side of the road and you are in a long line of traffic, the rider will be very grateful if you slow down, and let the horse across, especially if the horse is fidgeting – believe me, it's a bit like sitting on a keg of dynamite with a short fuse!

If you have to wait for a suitable passing place, drive slowly behind the horse leaving plenty of room. Don't nudge impatiently up behind the horse. When you do finally pass, do so slowly, not in a sudden burst of noisy acceleration.

I've often sat at the edge of the main road across Dartmoor waiting for a gap in the traffic, with families driving past saying 'Oh look at the nice horse,' but not bothering to stop. It only takes between five and ten seconds to cross a road. If you stopped, the children would have a much better look at the horse – and you wouldn't be delayed *that* much on your journey.

Don't toot your horn at riders – especially if you're coming up behind them. Lorry drivers would help if they kept off those

loud, hissing air brakes. I once saw a young woman in a group of four riders become hysterical when a large lorry came up behind them in a narrow village street. The horse was put off by the hissing brakes and began turning and rearing in the middle of the road. The driver sat in his cab letting the brakes on and off, with a huge grin on his face – thoroughly enjoying the spectacle.

Eventually someone came out of a cottage and led the horse into his drive. It calmed the horse, and spoilt the driver's fun. When you are passing a horse, take extra care if the road is wet, or has new chippings laid. Horses don't like their legs being sprayed with water, or small sharp stones, any more than you would.

On the main road, remember that the horse has a right to be there and should be treated like any other slow-moving vehicle. Watch the rider's hand signals – and if they indicate that they want you to slow down – then do. It may be safer for you both in the long run.

Accidents do happen. If you are involved as the driver, you must stop, and if there is injury to horse, or rider, or both, you must call the police as well as either an ambulance or vet. When you contact the police, tell them that a horse is involved – it may be easier for them to ring for a vet than you. If the rider is injured, follow the basic first-aid rules for the type of injury sustained. Keep him warm, dry and comfortable – and if you are in any doubt, don't move him. If the horse is injured but on its feet, keep it calm and make sure someone can stay with it by flagging down another motorist if necessary. If the horse is down, then don't make any attempt to yank it up. If it is just winded and not badly injured, then let it get up in its own way. But if the horse is obviously badly injured, and not likely to get up – first, don't move it, then get someone to sit by its head, on the neck, if necessary. This will keep it calm and prevent any violent struggling.

If you are able, remove the horse's saddle – gently and calmly. Keep the horse as quiet as you can. Not an easy thing to accomplish if it is terrified and in pain, but try. Make sure someone stays with it until professional help arrives.

There are no countrywide figures available for accidents involving horses, but a survey done in Lancashire showed that one in six riders had been in an accident of some sort involving traffic. As there are nearly two million people riding regularly in this country, if the Lancashire figure was repeated throughout Britain it would produce alarming statistics.

The British Horse Society and the Association of British Riding Schools both hold regular road-safety tests for their members and the B.H.S. has published an excellent booklet called *Ride Safely*, along with car-stickers to push the message home. What we also need is a more conscientious attitude to road safety from some *riders* – and more patience and understanding from some *drivers*.

8 All-day Rides

Pony trekking near Ballachulish, Argyllshire

Sooner or later, someone at the stable is going to suggest an all-day ride, if you are lucky enough to ride in an area surrounded by open countryside. I've found this is one of the most marvellous ways of both seeing and enjoying the country – particularly in the late spring and early autumn. At that time of the year the weather isn't too hot, the flies are not too numerous, and the air is clear. Whereas in the summer, it can be just too sticky and you'll have to compete for space with all the other people who are on holiday in cars, caravans and tents.

Most stable proprietors who can offer a day ride will have their own favourite routes worked out, and be highly organized with stops for lunch and grazing for the horses all planned. But there is no reason why you shouldn't be adventurous and strike out on your own route.

First, get an Ordnance Survey map of the area, and then decide how long you want to be out, rather than how far you want to go. Anything from four to six hours is a good average. More than that might tire the horse unnecessarily (remember it is a stable hack you are riding, not a thoroughbred hunter), and leave you crippled for two days.

Take out an hour for lunch, and reckon on averaging around five miles an hour. So on a five-hour trek you'll cover about twenty-five miles. With your map, work out your route. Stick to bridleways and open spaces where possible. Stay well clear of bogs, quarries and other potential hazards, and try to avoid busy main roads – the whole point of being on a horse is to get *away* from traffic.

At the half-way point, look for a pub or a country hotel for lunch where there is plenty of room for you and somewhere enclosed for the horses so they can't wander off.

In my home county of Devon we've found several pubs and small hotels with a field or paddock attached that are only too happy to accommodate riders at the bar, and their horses in the field. If there is a likely looking place on your route, go to see the landlord and ask if he is happy to accommodate you. Some farmers may be happy to take small parties of riders in a spare field or old barn. Or there may be a Youth Hostel on the route. Unless the horses are used to grazing together, don't turn them loose. They will kick and bite each other and be very difficult to catch. If you draw a blank, then choose a sheltered picnic site away from main roads; and if possible away from crowds of people (not everyone appreciates spending Sunday lunchtime with a herd of horses). It's also good to have some cover under trees in case you don't get the glorious, sunny dry day you hoped for. Riding in the rain can be quite pleasant but eating soggy sandwiches with rain dripping down your neck is not.

Once you've organized your route, and your stop-over point, make sure that someone at the stable knows exactly where you're going. If there is an accident then at least people will know where to start looking for you.

Take with you a map, compass (if you get caught in mist or bad weather it is very easy to lose your bearings) and head-collars for the horses. When you stop for lunch you should remove the bridle so that the animal can graze freely. If you have to take head-collars with you, the horses can wear them over their bridles with the leading rope wound loosely around the neck and tied under the chin. Take note of the weather forecast – that will determine what you wear. And if you are in any doubt include a lightweight waterproof anorak.

Ideally, you should try to get someone from the stable, or a friend or relative to meet you at lunchtime with a car. The driver can bring lunch packs, hot coffee or cold beer, halters and a water carrier, or buckets and possibly a light feed for the horses.

When you set off again after lunch, take it easy for the first twenty minutes or so to give your own food, and the horses' grass, time to settle. And aim to be back at the stable long before it gets dark. It *is* possible to ride at night, wearing a light-coloured or preferably fluorescent jacket and armbands. Your horse should have fluorescent bandages on its legs, and you need small indicator lights on the stirrups. (You'll see them on mounted policemen on winter evenings.) But even with all the right equipment it can still be very dangerous. It is much safer to plan your ride so that you don't have to be out after dark at all.

Trekking

To a lot of people, a pony-trekking holiday is the logical next stage *after* learning to ride. However, many people who embark on a week in the Welsh mountains on a sturdy little native pony have never had a riding lesson in their lives.

Trekking is certainly a pastime that can be enjoyed by people who have learned to ride, or who have spent several week-ends in the saddle. But it is also regarded by people who simply enjoy fresh air and the company of horses as a holiday with a difference that offers a challenge, and an opportunity to get away from the masses.

The national papers carry advertisements for trekking centres throughout the holiday season, and horsy magazines usually devote a whole section of their small ads columns to riding holidays and trekking centres. If you are in any doubt about the qualifications or standards of a particular establishment, then ring the B.H.S. at Kenilworth to check, or better still, get hold of their book, *Where To Ride*, which lists all the B.H.S. approved and recognized stables and trekking centres in the British Isles.

A trekking centre should advise you on what to wear. If they don't, then simply remember that the whole point of your holiday is that you'll spend the larger part of the day out in the open, and the British climate is one of the most unpredictable in the world. You may hope to ride in T-shirts and jeans – you may have to resort to thick sweaters and anoraks. So take a variety of warm, waterproof clothing – enough to give you at least one complete change. If you get soaked to the skin, you cannot rely on getting sweaters and trousers dry overnight.

Liniment and pain-relieving sprays won't appear on any list – but take them just the same. I've never been on a trekking holiday, but I did once spend a day with a trekking party for a programme about holidays. Believe me, *trekking* is not the same as *riding*. You spend a great deal of time just sitting in the saddle at a gentle, easy walk. If you're completely relaxed so that every part of you moves with the horse – that is fine. But most people have a certain amount of stiffness in their bodies and it takes a while to work it out. You may also be lucky and get a saddle that

A tack room should be kept clean and tidy, with saddles and bridles stored on appropriate hooks

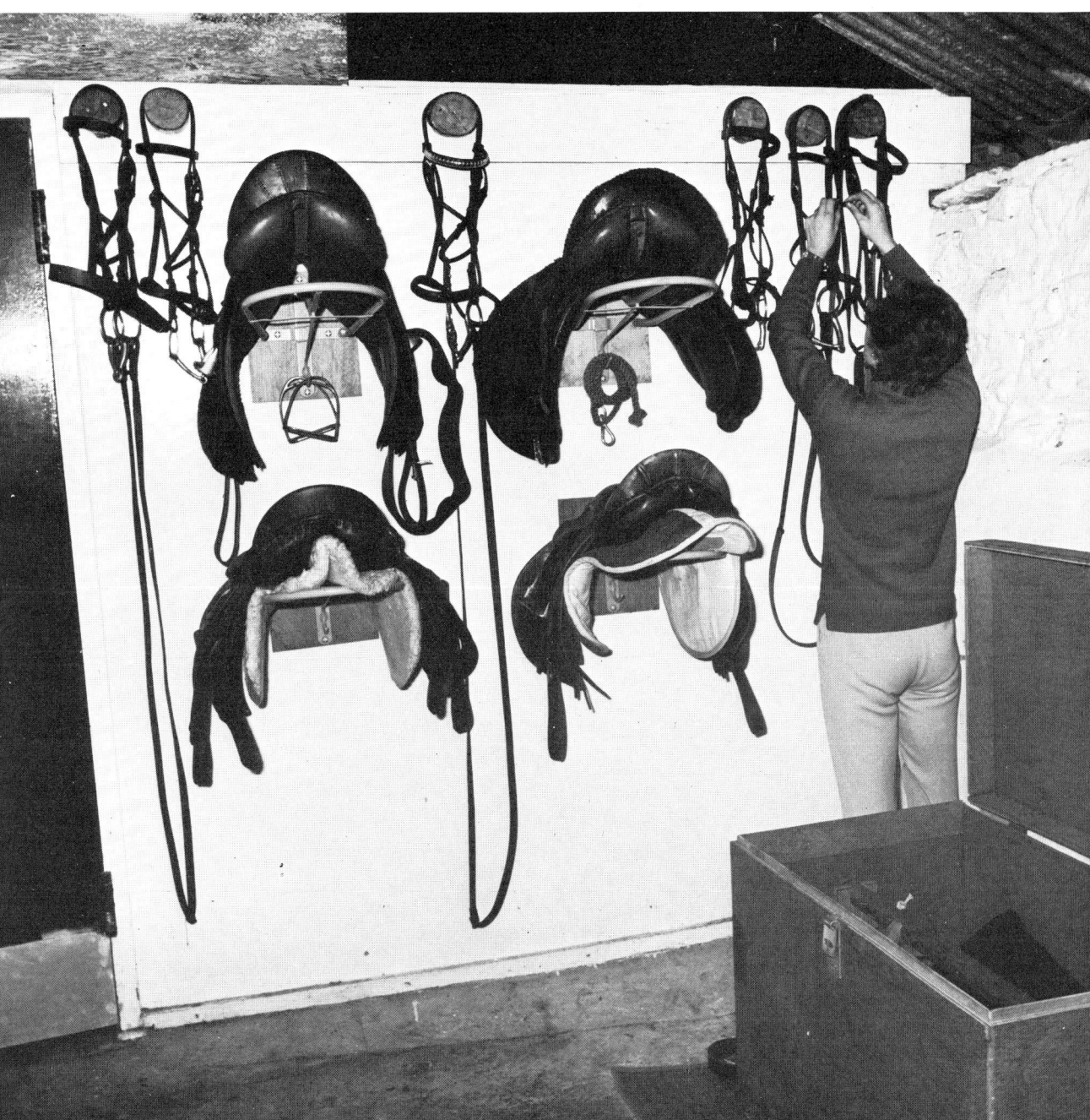

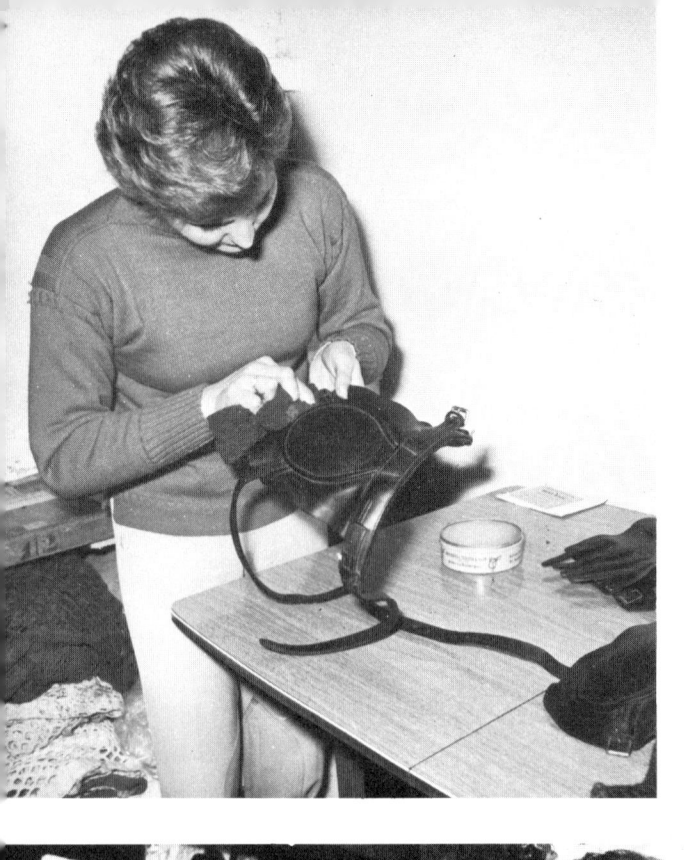

is as comfortable as an old armchair. But some saddles in trekking centres can be old and therefore very uncomfortable as they simply weren't sprung or padded as well as more recent ones. I've sat in a few that feel like solid oak – and the effect can be shattering. After a day's relentless grinding at a steady, non-stop walk, flabby muscles and soft tissue will need all the cosseting you can manage. By the end of the week you'll probably be fighting fit – but the first two days will be purgatory!

One of the bonuses for many people going on trekking holidays is that for the duration of your stay, the centre makes that horse and its welfare your responsibility. There'll be people at the stable to feed, water and help untack. But on the whole, looking after the horse will be seen as part of the holiday activity. You'll be told its stable routine, shown how to groom and bed the horse down, told what quantities of food to give it, and be expected to keep the tack clean.

Ideally, this should be done after every day's riding. That way you don't get a build-up of sweat and grime, and the job isn't too arduous.

To clean the bridle, take it to pieces, wipe off the muck with a cloth wrung out in warm water. Then apply saddle soap to the leather with a sponge, wrung out in warm water until it is almost dry. If you have it too wet with soap it will start to lather and leave soapy smears on the leather. The idea is to work in the glycerine and fat in the soap to keep the leather supple. Wash the bit in clean water. Reassemble the bridle. If you don't know how, get one of the stable staff to show you. Then hang it up with the buckle end of the reins at the top of the bridle over the headband, and the noseband passed round the whole thing to keep it neat on the hook.

To clean the saddle, place it on a saddle 'horse', remove the girth, stirrup irons and leathers. Wash the underside of the saddle first, then go over all the leather with the cloth wrung out in clean, warm water. (If you leave the stirrup irons in the bowl, most of the dirt on *them* will soak off.) Dry the leather, then rub in the saddle soap, making sure that you cover *all* parts of the saddle, and pay equal attention to both sides of the saddle flaps. The oils in the soap are absorbed by both the smooth and rough faces of the leather – and the more you can work in – the more supple you'll keep the saddle.

Clean the stirrup leathers in the same way, and the girth, if it is leather. Webbing, nylon or string girths should be washed if they are really filthy, if not, just rubbed clean. Scrub any mud or dirt off the stirrup irons, then reassemble the stirrups, and lay the girth over the seat of the saddle and return it to its 'peg'.

Incidentally, you won't need to take any of the grooming, or cleaning gear with you, unless you particularly want to use your own. It will all be provided by the stable.

Opposite, above left: Saddle soap and elbow grease keep the tack clean and supple

Opposite, above right: The bridle should be dismantled to be cleaned properly, but sometimes I do a quick job, just hanging it on a stable hook

Opposite, below: A saddle is an expensive item; if you want it to last, remember to clean the underneath bits as well

9 Tack

Some history

A riding instructor once told me, 'The most unfortunate thing that ever happened to a horse was that it had a curve in its back just the right size and shape for a saddle.'

In fact the reason for man's long association with horses is not that mundane, and the saddle was one of the last pieces of tack to be invented. Because no one ever thought to write down, 'Today I domesticated the horse,' it is impossible to say accurately exactly when, or even where the horse first became the 'tool' of man. But a reasonably educated guess would put it somewhere in the eastern Mediterranean about three thousand years before Christ. Originally they were just a good alternative to Shanks's pony for the farmers and herdsmen of the great plains. But the advantages of their speed, stamina and agility in battle, over foot troops, meant that by 1400 BC they were established as a most vital part of the armies of the war-lords who swept across Asia and Europe establishing and demolishing the great empires of our early history.

In the circumstances, it is not surprising that one of the earliest known works on the horse, written around 1400 BC, was the Chariot Training Manual of Kikkulis the Mattanite! Wall paintings and friezes from 1200 BC show the devastating effect on an enemy of hordes of mounted archers, and Mohammed records that he used thousands of mounted cavalry men in his Holy Wars after he saw the superiority of the horse over the camel in battle.

The horse, which is by nature a gentle, grazing creature, more likely to run away from a predator than to attack, was turned into an efficient fighting machine.

Around 356 BC, a Greek military commander called Xenophon, who had turned to writing in retirement, committed his thoughts on horsemanship to paper. He wrote about the breaking and training of a horse, about making it supple and obedient. He encouraged his pupils to treat their horses firmly, but with kindness, and to understand the mind of a horse. His object was to produce an even more efficient, supple and obedient *war-horse,* but he demonstrated a genuine love and respect for the horse, which makes most of his manual of two thousand years ago, totally relevant today.

Xenophon was undoubtedly a great horseman, but even *he* rode without a saddle.

The bridle was an early invention. Even the most primitive of early tribesmen discovered quite quickly that the easiest way to control a horse was to attach some contraption to the head.

The bit probably started life as a leather thong attached to the lower jaw. It gradually became more sophisticated, made of metal, and jointed. We know that the Assyrians were using metal snaffle bits almost identical to those in use today, and they were around seven hundred years before Christ.

As more obedience was required of the horse, the riders didn't look to themselves to improve their own qualities of horsemanship to control the animals. Instead, they produced more severe and harsh bits, some coupled with spiked nosebands, so that the horse would react to pain rather than training. There are some real horrors on show in the White Tower in the Tower of London, all used by European Cavalry.

While the bridle and bit were being developed, still no one got round to inventing a saddle. A cloth or skin might be thrown over the back to take some of the lumps and bumps out of a particularly bony animal with a band around the stomach to hold it in place, but that was all. No wonder Xenophon declared a preference for horses with well muscled backs. He saw no need for a saddle. Bare calf was all that was needed to give good adhesion to the flanks of a sweating horse.

Some historians believe that Nubian mercenaries from the Nile region were the first to employ some kind of saddle in the fourth century. They developed a seat with a high cantle and pommel so that a warrior could brace his back against the cantle when engaged in battle, and would be more difficult to dislodge from the horse's back.

The basic idea was refined and developed, but amazingly no one thought to add stirrups. It was almost another one hundred years before they appeared, and for them the historians point to the Huns of Mongolia as the inventors.

Throughout its long association with man, the horse has truly been a 'workhorse', playing an invaluable role in agriculture, industry, commerce and transportation, not to mention sport and war.

As the horse's role has developed so has its saddlery. When the French knights of the fourteenth century went to meet the English bowmen at Crécy, they and their horses were covered with so much armour they must have looked like lumbering, four-legged tanks. Five centuries later the cavalry horses of Wellington, of the Boers, and of the troops of the First World War, had no protection at all against gunpowder.

Until the establishment of riding as an art form in the Renaissance period in the sixteenth century, horses were schooled with long curb bits, spiked nosebands, rowelled or curved-spike spurs, hot pokers, barbed iron bars, razor-sharp stirrups, and all manner of barbaric tack.

Nowadays, you'll still find curb bits and spurs, but the modern tack room is full of gear designed to give the horse confidence in early training to encourage discipline in its development and ensure that you and it have as comfortable a time 'under saddle' as possible.

Saddles

The saddle is built on a basic frame called a 'tree'. In its simplest form a curved T-shaped piece of laminated wood or, in some cheaper saddles, a man-made fibre. It must be strong enough to stand up to galloping across country, jumping fences but light and flexible enough not to hinder these actions.

It has a well padded lining – the 'cushions' of leather on the underside which ensure that as well as being comfortable on the horse's back, the arch of the saddle is high enough to keep the spine completely free of any pressure or contact with the saddle. The top is usually made of pigskin and fashioned in such a way that the cantle at the rear and pommel at the front will hold the rider in the correct position in the centre of the saddle.

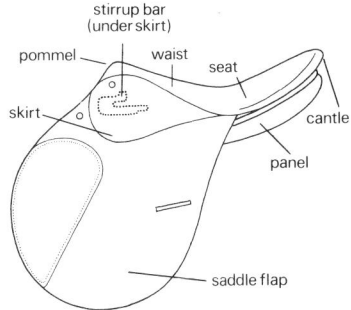

The saddle flap covers the girth straps, the sweat flap and the buckle guard. The skirt covers the stirrup bar. Although all saddles are made up of exactly the same 'components', their overall shapes and outlines differ depending on the needs of the individual horse and rider. The racing saddle has the tiniest of seats and is made to weigh ounces rather than pounds. The flap is very short to avoid contact with the powerful action of the shoulders but cut well forward to accommodate the jockey's knees, drawn up high on the withers by his short stirrups.

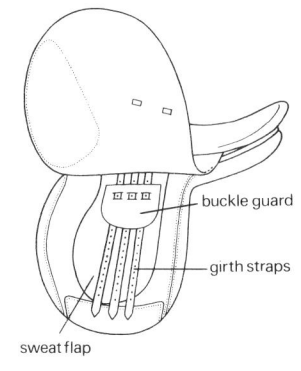

In dressage the rider is required to control the horse through a series of disciplined exercises, displaying as little physical movement as possible. There will be strong impulsion from the horse's hindquarters, the horse will be collected, and the rider will need to sit in the centre of the saddle with no forward movement at all. And so the dressage saddle has been developed with a long, straight saddle flap and deeper seat.

When jumping, a rider needs to be forward in the saddle, pitching his weight over his knees as he follows the action of the horse. And so a jumping saddle is made with the saddle flaps cut on an exaggerated forward line and padded with soft 'knee rolls'.

A general-purpose saddle is exactly that. It is made to accommodate the rider who wants to be comfortable on a long hack, take part in the occasional hunter trial or event, school his horse in elementary dressage, hunt during the season and possibly enter a showing class at a local horse show. It won't have any of the exaggerated lines necessary for the specialist saddles, just enough of each to make it live up to its name.

Girths are made of leather, webbing, string or nylon. Their purpose is quite simply to hold the saddle in place. They should never be so thin that they cut into the horse's flesh, or so tight that the animal can't breathe. A number of girths have elasticated ends to the buckles to allow the horse breathing space.

Stirrup irons – nowadays made from stainless steel for strength (and therefore safety) are like shoes; they come in different sizes to fit different feet.

There are the standard horseshoe-shaped irons, and safety irons which have a release catch of leather and rubber on the outer side. The floor of the stirrup should be serrated to give grip to the rider's foot, but it is also possible to buy stirrup grips made of strong, ridged rubber which fit inside the stirrup and give better grip.

Nosebands

A *cavesson noseband* is one which will sit quite high over the nose and be passed under the cheek-pieces and buckled above the bit.

A *dropped noseband* sits much lower over the nose and is fastened by passing the buckle strap under the bit, and letting it lie in the chin groove. This is a noseband that must be fitted very carefully as it exerts pressure just above the nostrils. If it were too tight or severe it would impede the horse's breathing and be very painful. It is fitted to stop a horse from crossing his jaw or opening his mouth too wide and losing contact with the bit. The reins are attached to the rings at the end of the bit, sometimes fastened with buckles, but usually with hooked studs.

The *Grackle noseband* is so-called after a famous racehorse which wore one. It is also known as the figure of eight and when in position forms a cross of leather over the nose, with a small pad of sheepskin or soft leather to prevent any rubbing on the tender pressure point, just above the nostrils. It's a sort of half-way house, giving more control than either the cavesson or dropped noseband on their own, and slightly less than the double bridle.

Bits

Go into any really good saddlery shop, and you'll find the walls or the shelves festooned with every conceivable shape and size of bit. Every country and discipline has produced its own range of 'ideal' bits to cover everything from the most sensitive-mouthed horse to the most headstrong. But basically, they fall into three main groups, the snaffle, the curb, and the pelham.

But before describing them in detail, it might be worth remembering why the bit was developed, and how it works. Early horsemen recognized that while the horse's head could be harnessed quite easily to give control and direction, the mouth was particularly sensitive. By attaching a bar of some description to the reins, and fixing it in the mouth, they had even greater command over their animals.

The horse has a long horseshoe-shaped jaw. The tongue lies flat in the groove of the jaw, below the level of its teeth. Towards the back of the jaw, at a point just level with the corners of the mouth, there is a gap in the gum between the teeth, known as the bar. When you fit a bit it should lie on top of the tongue and the bars of the mouth, and be wide enough so that it doesn't pinch the skin around the lips, but not so large that it slops in the horse's mouth.

When properly fitted and used, the bridle and bit enable you, through the aids from your hands and fingers, to exert pressure on certain parts of the horse's head. The bridle will control the poll, the nose and the chin groove. The bit will affect the tongue, corners, roof of the mouth and bars. By altering the size, shape and construction of the bit, you can make it soft or severe to exert a lesser or greater pressure.

Nowadays horsemen are sufficiently enlightened to realize that a horse's mouth should never be exposed to pain to produce obedience, which should instead come from steady hands, sensible bitting, and patience. In contrast, our ancestors resorted to methods which produced bits of horrendous proportions looking more like instruments of torture (which they were) than instruments of control.

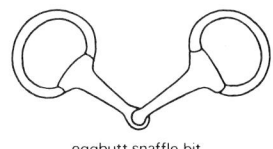

eggbutt snaffle bit

The *snaffle* is the mildest form of bit and can be either jointed or straight. The straight version is called a mullen snaffle, and can be made of rubber, vulcanite, nylon, or stainless steel.

The rubber, vulcanite and nylon mullens are thick, leave plenty of room for the tongue, and are very mild. They would be used on young horses, or horses with sensitive mouths. The metal mullen snaffles are much thinner, and therefore more severe.

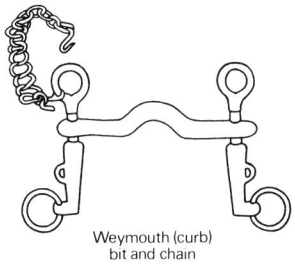

Weymouth (curb) bit and chain

The jointed snaffle is a very mild, comfortable bit for a horse, and therefore the most popular. The joint in the middle allows the bit to bend to the shape of the mouth. It therefore lies comfortably over the tongue, and enables the rider to give independent signals with left and right reins without interfering with the whole bit. The rings, by which the reins are attached to the bit, may be 'loose' – that is, looped into the ends of the bit – or 'fixed' as in an egg-butt snaffle. Then the rings are attached to the bit by means of a fixed broad 'T' bar. The advantage of an egg-butt is that it cuts down the risk of pinching the lips. You may also come across a snaffle bit which has bars or 'cheeks' attached to the ends of the bit in front of the rings. These are usually used on young horses, and are a further aid in keeping their heads straight, especially when they are just learning to jump. It also ensures that if a young horse gets fussy with its mouth, the bit won't slide through.

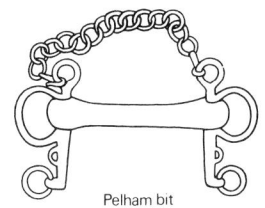

Pelham bit

The *snaffle bridle* is the one you're most likely to come into contact with as a novice rider. It is the simplest, and therefore the safest in inexperienced hands. It has a headpiece which fits over the poll (just behind the ears) and is split into two straps at each end. One set of straps will fasten on to the cheek-pieces which are in turn fastened to the bit. The other strap is cut long and fine and is the throat-latch. The browband is attached to the headpiece by runners and is held in position by being placed just in front of the ears. The noseband has a long fine strap which passes through the runners on the browband, and over the poll to be buckled in place on the left side. The noseband itself will fasten under the horse's jaw.

As the name suggests, the *double bridle* is made of two bits. A bridoon (exactly the same as a snaffle, but when used in a double its name is changed to bridoon – I don't know why), and the curb bit. The curb has a kink in the middle called a port, and both bits are attached to long cheek pieces. A small flat linked chain is attached to the curb which passes under the horse's jaw and lies in the chin groove.

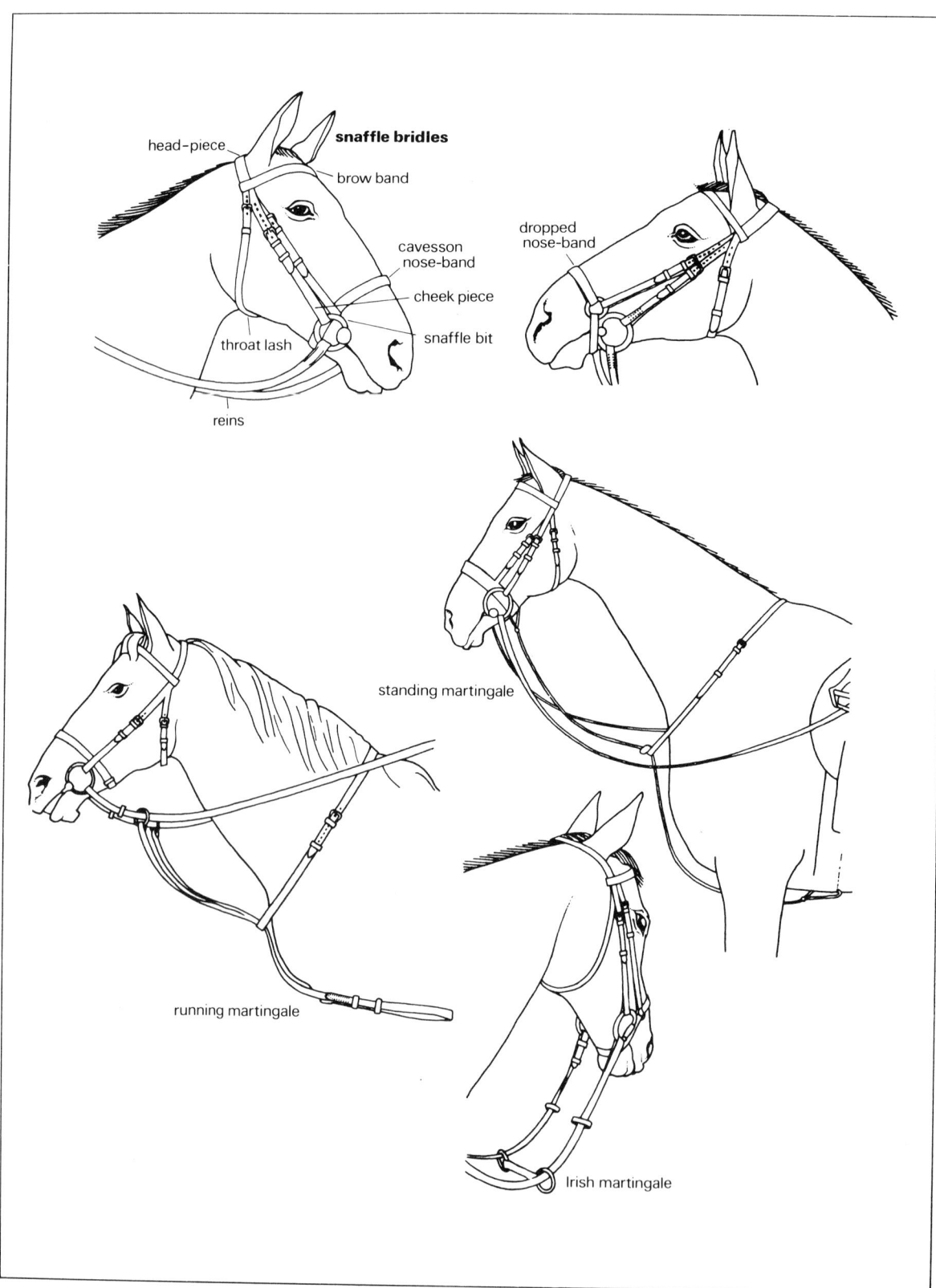

head–piece

snaffle bridles

brow band

cavesson
nose-band

cheek piece

throat lash

snaffle bit

reins

dropped
nose-band

standing martingale

running martingale

Irish martingale

The combined effect of the two bits gives the rider greater control. The bridoon acts on the corners of the mouth and the tongue, and encourages the horse to hold its head up. The curb operates on the bars and roof of the mouth, the poll and chin groove, and encourages the horse to flex its lower jaw and bring the head in. Together they produce the beautifully rounded outline of a collected horse and would be used by riders in the show ring, or for dressage competitions.

To use a double bit effectively, the rider must know *exactly* what he is doing. The reins must be worked with lightness and control. The double should never be used with a drop noseband and should only be used on an experienced horse with an experienced rider.

The *bitless bridle* has been used with some considerable success in the showjumping world. You'll often see it being used by the Irish rider Eddie Macken. Instead of exerting pressure and control through a bit in the mouth, this bridle works on the nose and chin groove, and the mouth is left free. There are two kinds of bitless bridle, the scawbrig and the hackamore. Both are easily identified as the noseband sits low on the horse's face and is very wide and well padded – usually with sheepskin.

In the hands of an expert this is an ideal bridle for a horse with a soft or sensitive mouth. But in rough or careless hands it can be more severe than a strong bit. The bridle acts on the sensitive area above the horse's nostrils, so if badly used it can cause tremendous pain and if incorrectly fitted, will constrict the horse's breathing.

The *pelham* is a half-way house between a snaffle and a double, in an attempt to let one bit do the work of two. It has a single curb bit attached to cheek-pieces. It can be ridden with two reins in which case the bottom rein exerts pressure on the curb action of the bit, while the top rein produces the action of a

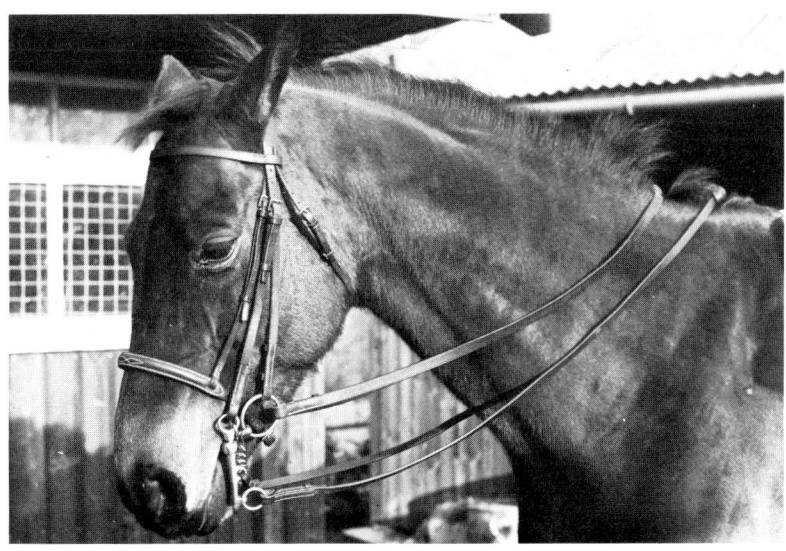

snaffle. You may see this type of bit fitted to children's ponies, when they're considered to be just a little too hot to handle. Then, the bit is often operated with just one rein which is attached to the two rings with a 'rounding', a small leather strap. The idea being that a small child would have greater control, without damaging the horse or pony's mouth.

Martingales
These are straps which give a rider further control over a horse's head, and there are three main types: running, standard and Irish.

The *running martingale* is a Y-shaped strap which is attached to the girth, then runs between the horse's front legs. Each end of the Y has a ring which is slipped over the reins. The reins themselves have small rubber stops fitted at the bit end so that the martingale doesn't slip up the reins towards the horse's mouth and get jammed. Just below the split in the martingale, another strap is fitted at right-angles. This is a neck-strap which loops over the horse's neck, to 'support' it, so that the straps are not flapping around in front of the horse's chest. This combination is commonly used in jumping. It acts on the mouth and stops the horse from carrying its head too high though still allowing it to stretch its neck without restriction.

The *standing martingale,* in contrast, and as the name suggests, doesn't allow the horse to lift its head beyond the limit of the martingale strap. It is a single leather strap, attached at one end to the girth, supported by a neck-strap, then passed up through the front legs and looped over the back of a cavesson noseband. As the object of this martingale is to give the rider control through extra pressure on the nose, it should never be used with a drop noseband as this would be far too severe and restrict the horse's breathing.

The strap might be used on an animal that constantly threw its head, and needed schooling to carry its head in the correct, arched position, and to approach fences without tossing and fussing. To ensure that the strap isn't too tight and restrictive, you should be able to hold the strap in the horse's gullet, and still have enough room for a hand's width between the strap and jaw line.

The *Irish martingale* is the simplest of all, and more usually seen in racing. It's just a strap, around 6 in (150 mm) long with a ring at each end. The reins are passed through it so that the strap lies under the horse's neck, and it is there simply to stop an impetuous horse from throwing the reins along its head.

Breastplates
On some horses you will see a strap passing from the saddle across the front of the horse's chest. It may be a Y-shaped piece of leather attached to either side of the saddle and the girth or a straight piece well padded with sheepskin. Both are breastplates and are used to stop the saddle slipping down the horse's back.

Cloths, boots and bandages

Apart from all the complicated leather saddlery, horses need a sizeable 'wardrobe' of clothes to wear when stabled, exercised, put out in the field, and transported. These are just some of the more common 'outfits'.

Numnahs. Padded cloths in the shape of the saddle which give extra protection to the back. They may be made of sponge, felt, any padded man-made fibre or sheepskin. They are *not* a cover-up for a badly fitting saddle, but they do give extra comfort, and protection, especially when the horse is jumping.

Knee boots. Protective pads made of leather, felt or man-made fibres which protect the kneecap. They should always be fitted when a horse is travelling, and I always use them on my own horse when I'm schooling or hacking. If a horse does stumble and catch his knees he can do really serious damage to the joint which will take weeks to heal. The first time we ever loaded Kate into a horse-box she took a run at the ramp, stumbled and crashed down on one knee. The pad was slashed – but she was fine.

Brushing boots. Leather spats about 8 in (200 mm) deep with a reinforced pad down the centre and three, four, or five buckles and straps at the ends. These are fitted to the front legs with the buckles on the outside and the protective pad on the inside covering the fetlock joint. Their purpose is twofold. They protect cannon-bone – the horse's shin-bone – when a horse is jumping, and they stop the horse from injuring itself by brushing or knocking a fetlock joint with flying hooves.

Back boots. Similarly made, but much longer than the brushing boots, and fitted to the hind legs for the same reason – to protect the cannon-bone and fetlock.

Yorkshire boots. A Yorkshire boot is an oval-shaped piece of felt with a tape sewn across the centre. This is fitted to the hind legs just above the fetlock joint, and folded over. Again, a protection for the fetlock if the horse is inclined to move its hind feet too close together.

Overreaching boots. These are the odd-looking bell-shaped boots, usually made of rubber, but also sometimes of leather, that you'll see flapping around over a horse's front hooves. They are fitted to protect the very tender and vulnerable area of the heel, just above the rear of the front hoof. When a horse is jumping it can bring its hind feet so close to the front on landing that it will 'overreach' and catch the heel. Hooves, flying at speed, can do tremendous damage. To prevent this the boot is fitted to sit in the groove of the pastern and covers the heel.

Travelling bandages. Made usually of felt or wool, they would be used together with a thick protective pad, or piece of gamgee (cotton wool covered in fine cotton stockinet), to protect the horse's legs while travelling. The pad is fitted to cover the area from the knee to the pastern at the front, the hock to the pastern at the rear. The bandages are then wound around the leg, over the fetlock and secured, firmly enough to give support and padding, but not so tight that they restrict the blood. Then, if the horse should stumble, be kicked or knocked in some way while in transit, the bandages will protect the fine and highly vulnerable lower leg bones.

Stable bandages. Made of wool, felt or stockinet and used with extra padding as in travelling bandages. They're fitted in the same way as travelling bandages when the horse is in the stable after a day's hunting, or strenuous exercise in cold wet weather. They keep the legs warm and the circulation going. To a horse, it's the human equivalent of soaking your feet in a bowl of hot water or slipping into warm comfortable slippers or bedsocks.

Exercise bandages. Made of elasticated fabric, these are narrower than travelling bandages and are used to give support to the tendons as well as protection to the legs when a horse is being jumped or exercised. They're fitted over pads or gamgee and are wound to cover the area from the knee or hock joint to just above the fetlock joint. You can't take the bandages below or over the fetlock as this would restrict the horse's movement too much.

Tail bandages. Made from stockinet or crêpe. These are fitted so that they cover the solid, fleshy part of the tail (the dock) from where it emerges from the hindquarters and continuing to a point 1 in (25 mm) below the end of the dock. You can only find the dock by feeling down the bony part of the tail as it is usually completely covered by the thick growth of tail hair.

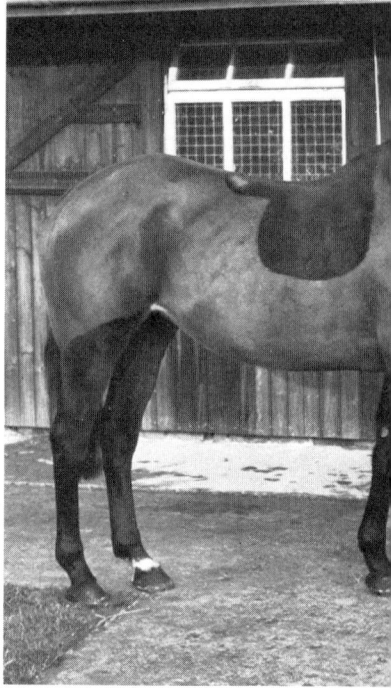

Kate ready for a winter season of hard work, with a hunter clip

When it's travelling, a horse can lean against the box and rub its bottom. In extreme cases this rubs away all the hair at the top of the tail, and instead of having a long, silky swishing tail, you end up with something that looks like a scraggy flue brush. So the bandage is fitted when the horse is travelling, and as an added protection some horses also wear *tail guards* over the bandages. These are leather sheaths held in place by a strap which passes from the top of the tail, along the horse's back and is attached to the roller around the horse's rug. The bandage would also be fitted for a short time in the stable to set the hair into a neat shape. But they're never left on for any great length of time as they can restrict circulation to the dock.

Rugs

Horses are like athletes. If their muscles get cold, they'll seize up, and if their body temperature drops too quickly they'll catch a chill. Left to his own devices the horse would regulate his own temperature throughout the year by having a fine, soft coat in the summer, and growing a thicker woolly coat to give warmth and protection as the temperature drops with the approach of autumn and winter.

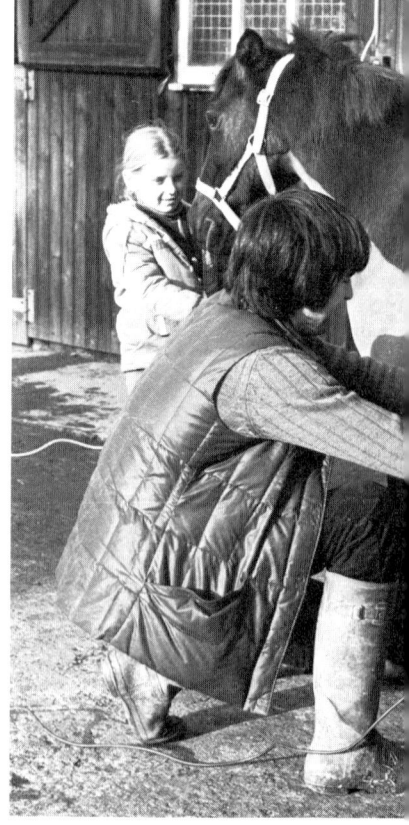

Below: Clipping is a skilled business – and a ticklish one

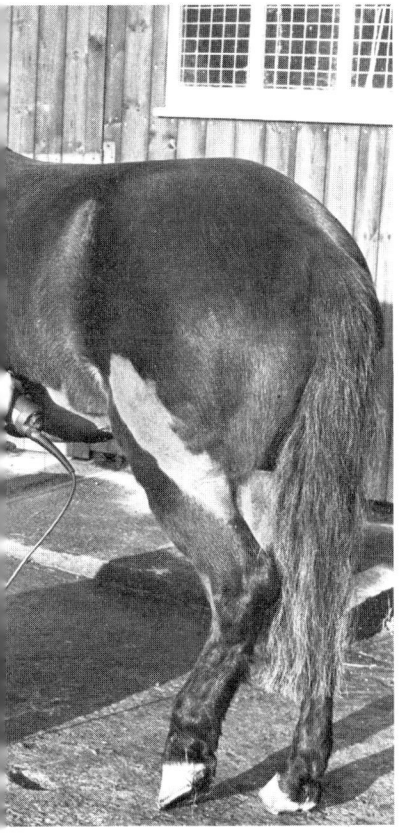

But once a horse is put under saddle, and is asked to work throughout the year as a hack, hunter, showjumper, event horse or whatever, it's going to need help to regulate its temperature, and that means a whole range of fancy haircuts, and artificial overcoats. During the summer, there is not too much of a problem. The horse's own fine coat will cope with the perspiration created by natural body heat and air temperature. The only help it *will* need is in cooling down slowly. But during the winter the problem is one of keeping the animal cool while it's working, and warm when it's not.

If you leave a horse in its natural thick winter coat, and then ask it to perform some strenuous activity, it will sweat, overheat, then loose weight and condition. Imagine yourself running a mile in a fur coat – you'd boil. The effect on the horse is the same. So to help the horse when it is in full work in the winter, the coat is 'clipped out'. When the horse isn't working, but standing in its stable, or a field, it needs some kind of protection to replace its depleted natural coat – and that is when it needs a whole wardrobe of rugs.

Day – or *travelling rug*. Usually of wool and often bearing the owner's initials, this is the horse's track suit. A horse would be dressed in the rug to keep it warm when travelling to or from an event. A day rug is fastened with a strap across the horse's chest, and would be held in place – to stop it slipping off the hindquarters and getting caught up in the horse's legs – by means of a roller or surcingle – a strap passed right around the horse's body and fastened on the near side.

Anti-sweat rug. Looks just like a huge string vest – and works on the same principle. This would be put on a hot or sweating horse to help it cool down slowly so that the body won't chill, and the muscles seize with cramp.

Night rug. Worn by a stabled horse, at night, to keep it warm. The rug is made with two layers: jute on the outside, a woollen blanket fabric on the inside. As the evenings begin to turn cold at the end of September the horse would be 'rugged up' at night in just the night rug, with a roller to keep it in place. As the autumn progresses into winter horses wear their night rugs most of the day when they are standing in the stable, and as the evenings get colder they have an extra one, or possibly two blankets fitted underneath.

The *summer sheet* is made of cotton, and would be put over the horse during hot weather if to give it some relief from the constant, and annoying, nibbling of flies and midges, and to keep the coat clean. It could also be worn for travelling in the summer, when a woollen day rug would be too hot.

New Zealand rugs are usually made of heavy canvas, but sometimes of heavy-duty nylon, to make them waterproof, and are wool lined for warmth. They're worn by horses that are put out in fields by day during the winter to keep them warm and dry. They are held in place with a roller around the girth, with additional straps at the back which fasten around the legs, to stop the rug from slipping off. When horses are left out for any length of time, sooner or later they find a muddy patch and get down for a roll. Unless the rug is fastened securely, it could slip and become lopsided on the body, which is potentially dangerous. The constant flapping of a loose end around a horse's legs can panic it, and a large expanse of canvas waving about just might get tangled in its hooves and bring it down. Any horse dressed in a New Zealand rug has to be checked daily, and have the rug readjusted, so you can be sure it's in place and isn't rubbing, or chafing on the shoulders. If it gets wet it has to be dried out thoroughly and retextured with a dressing otherwise it will go hard and start to crack.

The straps used to keep the rugs in place are called either *rollers* or *surcingles*. A surcingle is usually made of cotton, jute or wool webbing. It's like a long, plain belt with a strap at one end and a buckle at the other. It's important that the horse doesn't have any pressure on its spine, so if a surcingle is used to hold a rug in place, it would be advisable to put a pad of some sort between the strap and the backbone, to give some relief.

A roller is really a surcingle with the protective pad built in. At the point where the strap will pass over the horse's spine it has a hinged pad of leather or some form of cushioning. Some rollers have a leather-covered steel hoop on the top of the hinge. This stops a horse from rolling over on its back in the stable. Usually a horse will roll in the middle of its box, leaving plenty of room for its legs to manoeuvre so that it can right itself and stand up again without doing any damage. But occasionally a horse will roll up close to a wall, or get itself stuck in a corner and be unable to stand up. When that happens it's said to be 'cast'. If the animal isn't found in time so that human helpers can get it up, it can damage its legs, or even worse, twist the inner gut with the constant effort of rolling and heaving, and in severe cases that will kill them.

Clipping

Horses are clipped around the beginning of October. If they do get sweated up, they'll dry out more quickly, and it will be easier to groom them and keep them clean. There are four main styles of clip.

The *full clip* – where the whole of the coat is removed.

The *hunter clip* – not quite as extreme as the full clip – but almost. The only areas left unclipped are the legs, as high as the elbows and thighs, and a saddle patch on the back. The hair on the legs will give a horse protection against thorns and thick mud, and keep him warm. The saddle patch ensures that the back won't become sore and rubbed. You would find this sort of clip on a horse that is hunted or jumped regularly throughout the winter, and kept stabled and rugged up when not in work.

A *blanket clip* – so called because the area left unclipped on the horse's back is in the shape of a blanket. The hair would be left on the legs, and across the back, but completely removed from the head, neck, shoulders and under the stomach. These are the areas where the horse is most likely to perspire when being exercised, or used for fairly light work.

The *trace high clip* – clears the clipped areas of heavy perspiration, but leaves enough coat to keep the animal warm. It's a clip that would be used on an animal left out in the fields during the winter with a New Zealand rug for protection. The hair is *left* on the legs, down the top of the neck and across the back; it's *removed* from the face, the underside of the neck, and under the stomach. That way the horse has protection and warmth while it is in the field, but its skin can still breathe, and it won't become overheated when it's working.

Dealing with crib-biting and wind-sucking

Crib-biting, and wind-sucking are terms you may hear in connection with horses.

Crib biting is usually brought on by boredom and means that the horse starts to bite, or eat away at the wood in its stable. He'll attack any protruding bit of wood, whether it's the top of the stable door, a partition, even the rafters in the roof, and, like a termite, gnaw away at it. With some horses it's just a passing phase, and sometimes you can discourage them by painting the wood with an evil-tasting substance that's supposed to be to horses what similar preventives are to nail-biting humans. If he persists, some owners will fit a sort of muzzle over the nose so that the horse can still breathe freely, and drink – but not nibble.

But a committed crib-biter just keeps on chomping, and this can lead to a more serious habit – wind-sucking. What happens is that when the horse has its teeth gripped on to the wood, it starts to suck in air through its mouth. This gets down into the stomach, and can produce an attack of colic. Some horses go one stage further and become what the vets call professional wind-suckers, which means that they go on sucking in air when they are eating, or just standing in the stable.

You can try fitting an anti-wind-sucking device. They come in various styles, but basically consist of a collar with an arrow-shaped piece of metal attached. This is fitted so that the arrow (with a blunt, not a sharp pointed end) can fit under the horse's chin, towards the gullet. If the horse arches its head, to start wind sucking, the point will jab the gullet, and, with luck, the horse will stop sucking. It may sound a rather severe solution, but remember that colic, at least, is just as uncomfortable and at worst, a killer. And once horses are hooked on the habit, it is almost impossible to stop them, so it can be the ruination of an otherwise sound horse.

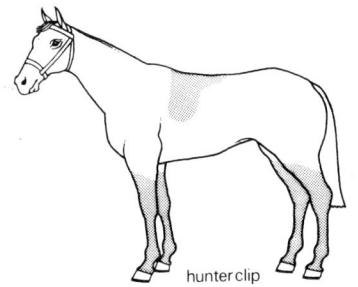
hunter clip

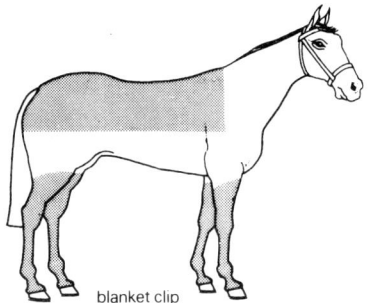
blanket clip

trace high clip

10 Show-jumping

When a group of British prisoners-of-war sat in a German camp in the early 1940s, whiling away their time with the hypothetical problems of jumping horses over obstacles, they could hardly have dreamed that thirty-five years on, 19 million people would be tuned into the telly, hooked on the excitement and spectacle of the Horse of the Year Show or the Royal International.

Show-jumping, like so many other aspects of equestrian sport, grew out of the competitive enthusiasm of a small group of horsemen. If you'd been around in 1865 in Dublin at the Royal Show you'd have witnessed the very first show-jumping competition. Only then it was called 'high' and 'wide' leaping. 'Leaping' competitions were held at the Paris show the following year. The riders launched themselves at full speed over just one or two small obstacles with the sort of gusto and enthusiasm that they would employ when meeting a natural obstacle on the hunting field. Not much skill, very little in the way of tactics – but a lot of fun. Most of which seems to have disappeared in 1923 when the British Show Jumping Association (B.S.J.A.) was formed to 'tidy up' the sport. It immediately went into the doldrums and didn't really emerge until after the second world war.

Colonel Sir Michael Ansell is undoubtedly the man who must take full credit for its emergence as a major national equestrian sport. A committed and highly talented horseman, he found himself in the same P.O.W. camp as Major Bede Cameron and Major Nat Kindersley, all three of them international riders before the war. When they were repatriated they joined forces with the men who had kept the B.S.J.A. going through the doldrums of the war years, and together set out to produce the finest riders in Europe, and give show-jumping a national following.

In 1945 Colonel Ansell organized the first post-war national show-jumping championships with a top prize of £100. Three years later Britain won a bronze medal for show-jumping in the Olympic Games held in London, and we can boast at least one medal for every Olympics since – with the exception of Montreal in 1976.

In the fifties, show-jumping was still drawing the bulk of its following from the established county and horsy set. The real break came in 1950 when the B.S.J.A. persuaded the B.B.C. to televise the Royal International Horse Show from White City. Since then show-jumping as a spectator sport has never looked back.

Riders and horses moved out of the wings of the county shows into the centre stage of the T.V. eye. The riders became television personalities in their own right – and so did their horses. Psalm, Penwood Forge Mill and Mister Softee are still as famous as the people who rode them (Ann Moore, Paddy McMahon and David Broome).

These days a major show-jumping event can guarantee

capacity crowds, and a television audience to compete with the Cup Final. Yet unlike football, a sport with which most of the spectators can identify, as they've probably dribbled a ball down a pitch at *some* time in their lives, with show-jumping, it's unlikely that more than eight per cent of the audience has ever even sat on a horse – let alone jumped one.

The knowledge and understanding that this vast audience has of what is actually happening are restricted to what they glean from the commentary, and a basic realization that horses who knock down poles tend to lose competitions, while horses that jump clear and fast win them.

Apart from that, there is occasionally the hint from viewers that there is more of the circus than sport about show-jumping, and not infrequently, a suggestion that it's really rather cruel to ask horses to jump fences bigger than themselves.

So why do they watch it? Could it be perhaps that jumping, whether it's show-jumping or cross-country, is the one sport in which man and another living creature together pit themselves in competition against what appear to be enormous odds?

I don't know, but the next time you watch a show-jumping competition, either on the box or at a show, it might help to understand not just why and how horses jump, but also the skill that goes into building a course that is designed to test their courage and ability, not break either their spirit or their bones.

Horses are natural jumpers. They have immense power in their hindquarters, and spring in their hocks. In the wild, horses will comfortably clear most obstacles in their path providing they are not *too* high or wide, and owners of domesticated horses are forever making fences higher or thicker to stop their animals 'popping across' from one field to another. So it isn't cruel to ask

a horse to jump, it is just a controlled extension of what he would do naturally.

There's nothing more exciting than to sit on a horse that really enjoys jumping. You can feel its whole body ripple with excitement at the thought of all the fun it is about to have dashing round a ring and leaping over fences.

When I first learned to jump, my schoolmaster was such a horse. A woolly little chestnut who pranced about with such strength that he frightened his owner to death every time they went into a competition arena. He would buck and twirl, throw his head and snort with the excited anticipation of what was to come, and the impatience of being held back. Once let loose on the course he would charge around, literally jumping for joy over everything in his path, and then, his enthusiasm satisfied, return to the collecting ring quite quietly. It took strength, accuracy, not to mention a little courage, to take him round sensibly, but I think I learned more about controlled jumping on that little horse in one ten-fence round, than I would have in six months of careful jumping on a safe old war-horse.

Katie was a delight to jump for the first time. She saw no fear in the coloured poles, decided the whole thing was a marvellous game and looked for any excuse to jump over anything. So much so that asking her to school quietly anywhere near show jumps produced an appalling frustration and the nearest thing to temper she's ever displayed. You could almost hear her demanding, as she stamped her feet and tossed her head, 'Why have I got to do this boring old walking and trotting, when I'd much rather be jumping?' Eventually she learned that the work had to come first – the fun later. But she has never lost her spirit, and although she can now put up a reasonably good showing in a dressage test, she saves her real enthusiasm for jumping. Whether it's show-jumping or cross-country, when she springs off at the start of a course there is a thrill of energy and sheer joy in her that lasts from the first to the last fence, and over the finishing line. If I ever thought for one moment that she hated it, had lost her courage or enthusiasm, I wouldn't ask her to go on. But if I stopped her now, it would be deprivation of the worst kind.

Training a horse to jump

Before you even begin to ask a horse to jump, in the very earliest stages of its training, when it's about four years old, you need to school it at the walk, trot and canter. This will make it supple and obedient, so that it understands fully the aids to quicken its pace, to shorten or lengthen the stride, to give a sudden burst of energy, and then return quietly to a steady control.

All of this is essential at the early stages if you are to have any control and balance at all when you start jumping.

The first 'jumps' will be nothing more than a series of coloured poles laid on the ground at 5–6 ft (1.5–1.8 m) intervals, adjusted to suit the stride of the horse. The rider will ask the horse to trot through the grid at a steady pace. This will introduce the horse to coloured obstacles (which can be startling, even terrifying, to a young horse) and teach the animal to pick its feet up so that it can trot through the obstacles without tripping.

The next stage is the cavalletti: a pole between 10 and 20 in (250–500 mm) off the ground, either on its own or with one or two others as a series with at least one, and sometimes two or three, strides between each. When you consider that a horse's legs measure anything from 2 ft 6 in to 3 ft 6 in (0.75–1 m) long, you can see that at this early stage in the training, the horse could easily step over the poles at the walk. In fact most of the early work, over small obstacles, will be done at the trot. This will give the horse confidence, as it realizes that even if it does knock the pole, it will get out of trouble, simply by picking its feet up and going forward. In the early stages the horse will probably 'rock' over the jump, planting its front two feet firmly on the far side of the pole before taking the back ones off the ground. As it progresses, and gets bolder, it will start to 'jump' taking all four feet off the ground at once.

Even when it reaches that stage, the careful rider will still be trotting the horse into the jumps, so that it remains calm, not over-excited, and keeps 'listening' to the aids from the rider. Once you're confident that the horse is going forward, meeting the jumps in a straight line, and concentrating, you can start to canter slowly up to the obstacle.

Now why – you must be asking – if a horse jumps on its own in the wild, do you need to go through all this palaver just to get it to do what comes naturally? Quite simply, because it's no longer in the wild, but in a contrived environment with the weight of a human on its back.

The whole skill of getting a horse over twelve obstacles of varying heights and shapes in a controlled ring the size of the Wembley arena lies in being able to 'drive' the horse as you would a car. Knowing when to put the throttle on, when to take it off, when to corner, and at what speed, where to take off for a jump, and how to line up for the next. In order to get the best out of the animal's natural ability, the rider must be able to 'read' the course, and pass his instructions on to a horse that's not only willing to jump, but to do so under controlled guidance. To reach *that* stage, you go a step further with the training.

During the very early days of training, the jumps will stay fairly low, probably no more than 2 ft or 2 ft 6 in (0.6–0.75 m) high. This is vital as it will help to build the horse's confidence so that he learns to put trust in both his own and the rider's ability. Once that trust has been established over small jumps, the only limitation as he progresses to bigger, more complicated obstacles will be his own courage and ability.

Types of fences

The obstacles must be uncomplicated in their structure, so that the horse isn't looking at something that's optically confusing. However, a totally 'simple' pole across oil drums with nothing between the pole and the ground, would be wrong. A young horse needs a 'ground line' on the floor – a pole placed on the ground, either level with, or slightly in front of the jumping pole so that, with his limited vision, he can judge the distance between the ground and the height he is being asked to jump. And the space between the ground and the pole should be filled in with other poles either crossed or at a forty-five degree angle. Again so that the horse can see that he is being asked to jump a solid obstacle, not a flimsy bit of fresh air.

The shape of the fence will follow one of three basic outlines which are used for all jumping fences whether at the Pony Club gymkhana or the Olympics. A straightforward upright, or vertical fence; a parallel, where a back pole is fitted exactly level with the front pole with not less than 2 ft (0.6 m) between them; and a staircase, or triple bar where the poles slope away from the ground line to the highest point. Fences may be built as gates or walls and have fancy flowers or bushes incorporated, but they all conform to those three basic shapes.

Pamela Carruthers's show-jumping course for Hickstead in Sussex

A simple upright jump: with three coloured poles set in a vertical line. Kate jumped this with more enthusiasm than style

The different shapes provide horse and rider with different problems. It may look as though show-jumping is just a matter of pointing your horse in the right direction and leaping into the air when you are near enough to the fence, but that's only because the experts make it look easy.

In fact every individual fence needs a different approach, a different speed, and a different take-off point. The paces and strides, take-offs and landings are worked out with as much precision as a formation-dance routine.

When jumping any fence the aim is to produce a perfect arc, or bascule, with the horse's body in mid-air. To make that arc fit neatly over the obstacle you need to know two things. Firstly, the height of the jump, and secondly, the jumping stride of your horse. The jumping stride of a horse usually starts at around 12 ft (3.6 m) from take-off to landing at a steady canter. But the faster the approach, the more powerful and athletic the horse, the longer the stride.

An upright, or vertical fence is the most difficult of all to jump accurately. If you take off too soon, too far away from the fence, you'll hit the pole with the horse's front feet. Take off too late, and get too close to the fence, and you'll hit it with the back feet.

To get it right, your take-off point should be the same distance from the front of the fence, as your landing spot will be on the other side. It is this that gives the impression that a rider is 'standing off' or jumping some distance from the fence

compared to his stride on a spread or parallel. As there's no ground line, or optical aid to help gauge the distance, the rider has to be skilful and accurate in choosing his spot.

When jumping a parallel, the rider has to get much nearer to the fence in order to clear the front and back poles. This is because the highest point of the jumping arc is not in the middle, between the two poles, as you would expect, but just in front of the back marker. If your take-off point and landing are going to be an equal distance from the centre of the arc, then obviously you are going to need to get much closer to the front of the obstacle.

On some parallel fences, the front pole is slightly lower than the back element. In a true parallel, they are exactly the same height. You would never have a parallel where the back marker was lower, as this would give the horse a false eye line. It wouldn't see the back marker, as its attention would be fixed on the first element, and there would be a risk of it dropping its hind legs too soon, and getting them tangled in the poles. If the centre of a parallel is filled in, usually with greenery, then it's called an oxer.

The easiest fence of all to jump is the staircase, or triple bar, also sometimes referred to as a spread. It's easy (or relatively so, compared with the other two) because it forms an inviting barrier to the horse with the ground line clearly defined by the lowest and nearest of the poles, with the rest of the fence – to its highest point – filled in following the natural curve of the horse's leap.

For that reason, a spread would look more inviting and less imposing to a horse than an upright of the same height. However, to a non-riding spectator the spread would appear to be the larger, more difficult fence. When approaching a staircase, the rider would have to make his take-off point much closer to the front marker of the obstacle, as the highest point of the curve will be over the back pole.

Apart from the basic shape of the fence, an obstacle can be made more or less difficult to jump by altering the ground line, and the 'wings' or sides of the jumps. The ground line is quite simply a pole, plank, row of very small trees, or whatever which makes a positive line at the bottom of the fence and tells the horse, with its limited vision, 'the bottom of the fence starts here'. When that line is in position, it helps the horse to judge the scope of the obstacle ahead. Take it away, and it is optically more difficult for the horse to assess the height. The wings are structures which support the poles, whether they are traditional triangular wood sections, as you would see at any 'proper' show-jumping event, or the oil drums in the field.

To make the jump easier for the horse, the wings should be

angled in some way so that it gets the impression of riding into an enclosed area, and will be less likely to 'run out' or dodge to the side and avoid jumping. You can achieve this effect either by 'dressing' the wings, (as would be done in a large well financed show) with small conifers or banks of potted plants, or using bales of straw and poles. To increase the degree of difficulty, you reduce the angle on the wings, until the 'dressing' is in direct line with the face of the fence, or taken away altogether.

Bearing that in mind, the easiest of fences should be a staircase with well defined, angled wings, a slightly more difficult fence would be a curved wall and the most difficult of all would be a vertical fence, say a gate, with no ground line, and no wings.

If a show-jumping course consisted of a series of individual jumps, placed in a straight line with plenty of room between each for the rider to canter on, and in a leisurely fashion size up his approach and tactics for the next obstacle, then show-jumping would not only be fairly easy, it would be very boring.

The international rules governing the sport say in chapter 1, paragraph 1, 'A jumping competition is one in which the combination of horse and rider is tested under various conditions, over a course of obstacles. It is a test intended to demonstrate the horse's freedom, its energy, its skill and its obedience in jumping, and the competitor's horsemanship.' To achieve that test of horse and rider, the course is built in an enclosed arena with fences up and down the sides and across the centre, so that the rider has to follow a path over a variety of obstacles, has to turn sharp corners, negotiate awkward angles, and frequently has to ask the horse to lengthen or shorten its stride. And, of course, the fences don't come as single obstacles.

They're built as combinations, with two obstacles making a double, three a treble. Each of the fences in a combination is a different shape, and between each there may be one or two strides, or what's known as a bounce, where the horse lands between the fences, then immediately takes off for the next fence without putting a stride in between.

Controlling and instructing the horse
So that the rider knows precisely how he must ride into each fence, and what he must ask of the horse, he will always 'walk the course' before the competition.

This means walking exactly the same route that he intends to ride, working out as he goes how he will approach the fence, where he will take off, where he needs to turn to get his approach right for the next obstacle, how many strides he must ask the horse for between the elements of a combination, how fast he can afford to go, and where, if at all, he can cut corners.

With the route and tactics firmly in his mind, the rider must then be able to convey his needs to the horse – who hasn't had the advantage of seeing the course beforehand, and so, unlike the rider, doesn't know what's coming next.

Before going into even the smallest show-jumping competition a rider will spend hours not just teaching the horse to jump the various obstacles, but getting it fit, supple and obedient to the aids. In order to negotiate a series of fences in the confines of an arena a horse must be so fit and supple that it bounces like a rubber ball, so athletic and obedient that it can explode and then recoil like a loaded spring.

As the rider approaches a fence, he'll be asking the horse for a short, bouncy stride while he lines his mount up to the centre of the fence and gauges the exact point of take-off. Although short, it will be a stride full of energy with the rider holding the horse like a coiled spring. At the appropriate moment, the rider will ask the horse for a surge of power – he'll let the spring go so that the horse can jump with maximum strength and energy over the fence, and, on landing, return to the rider's control so that he can once again gather up the power ready for the next fence.

When approaching an upright the rider should maintain that short powerful stride to the last moment to get the horse up and over the vertical in a short curve. With a spread, he would probably uncoil the spring two strides out so that the horse would stretch over the fence and make a much longer 'bascule'.

Where the fences are placed individually, this explosion and containment of power from one fence to the next is relatively simple for a trained horse and reasonably experienced rider. It gets much more difficult when riding through combination fences, with only one stride between the elements. The easiest double combination is a spread followed by an upright. Bearing in mind that the rider will ask the horse to 'ride on' at the spread, he should then be able to collect the horse on landing, take one stride and make a clean up-and-over jump to clear the upright.

Slightly more difficult is two uprights. The rider must be able to contain the horse's energy on the approach to the first element, and then gather up the horse quickly and produce another surge of energy immediately to clear the second upright element.

The most difficult double is an upright followed by a spread. The rider will have to ask the horse to be gathered for the first element on a short bouncy stride. Chances are that the horse will land not far from the back of the fence, so he'll have to take a long stride in the middle, and then really stretch to clear the spread.

The risk is that the rider and horse will put so much effort into the first element and the landing, that all the energy will disappear as the horse stretches at the front. To prevent this the rider must allow the horse to stretch without losing contact and keep revving up the back by using his seat and legs.

On a triple combination there is usually just one stride between each element, but the fence can be made easier by putting two strides between the second and third elements.

The easiest combination would be a spread followed by two uprights. After lengthening the horse's stride to clear the spread, the rider should be able to gather up the horse to jump the two uprights.

When the combination goes spread, parallel, upright, the rider can take a good long leap at the spread, begin to gather the horse for the parallel and have it right back on a short bounce for the upright. But the combination of upright, parallel, staircase (spread) is the most difficult of all because the pattern of the jump changes from high, to wide, to very wide and the rider must have a horse so perfectly balanced, so athletic and powerful that it can bounce over the first element, lengthen its stride without losing energy to take the second, and really stretch out without any loss of impulsion to take the third.

Show-jumping classes
At a small local show in the novice classes any young horse meeting a difficult combination would be able to 'fiddle' its way out of trouble, as the fences probably wouldn't be more than 2 ft 9 in to 3 ft (0.85–0.9 m).

But once the fences get up above 4 ft (1.2 m) it is almost impossible to 'fiddle' your way out of trouble on any fence unless you have a remarkably intelligent and athletic horse. Which is why the British Show Jumping Association have strict rules about maximum fence heights for horses of varying abilities and a grading system to ensure that horses are given plenty of time and opportunity to develop and find their own level.

You wouldn't expect someone who jogs around the block every morning just to keep fit, suddenly to find himself representing Britain at the Olympics in the 1,500 m. Equally, horses that show some potential as novice jumpers in riding-club competitions don't get thrown in at the deep end to tackle the Horse of the Year Show.

Horses, like athletes, need time to build their stamina and muscle power, and experience to prepare them for major competitions. Those that don't have the ability, the courage, the flair, will only reach a certain level and never improve beyond it. For every thousand amateur athletes there is only one Steve Ovett or Mary Peters. For every thousand horses there is only one Psalm or Penwood Forge Mill.

When a novice horse sets out on its career, if it has any potential at all then it will be entered into a British Show Jumping Association competition at any one of the B.S.J.A. affiliated shows around the country, and there are over a thousand of them.

A horse begins in a newcomers' competition where, in the first round the fences would be not less than 3 ft 3 in (1 m) or more than 3 ft 6 in (1.05 m) high, with only one combination – a double made up of upright obstacles. In a newcomers' jump-off the fence would not go above 4 ft (1.24 m).

A horse cannot be entered in a newcomers' competition after it has won more than £25 in prize-money. Then it will be entered for a foxhunter competition. In foxhunter competitions nothing is higher than 4 ft (1.20 m), but to test the horses' ability, the spreads are made bigger, up to 4 ft 6 in (1.35 m), and there could be a water jump with a spread of not more than 12 ft (3.65 m). In the jump-off the highest fence on the course must not exceed 4 ft 3 in (1.30 m).

In order to enter a B.S.J.A. competition, a horse must be registered with the association and is graded according to how much prize-money it has won. A horse starts in grade C and stays with that grading until it has won £200 when it moves into grade B. It becomes a grade A show-jumper when its total winnings are £500 or more.

Prize-money in show-jumping is pretty meagre, especially in the more novice classes. So it can take years to build up enough prize-money to move from one grade to another unless you keep entering competitions and have a horse that wins consistently.

The grading system ensures that no horse can be pushed beyond the limits of its own ability. If it can't jump, it won't win, and will remain ineligible for the bigger competitions. Every class in a show-jumping competition states quite clearly which horses are eligible to take part, be it novice, foxhunter, grade C, B, or A. There is no risk of an unqualified horse slipping through the net. So you can be sure that the show-jumpers that thrill and delight the television audience in major competitions are right at the top of their profession, and well qualified to tackle any of the problems that the course-builder sets. Because, make no mistake about it, once a horse has reached grade A and proved that it has the ability and skill to jump clear over big fences, the real test of its own potential, and its rider's horsemanship, lies with the course-builder. It's up to him to design a sequence of fences that will demand perfection from horse and rider, and turn a mere talented individual into a superstar.

Course design
There is possibly no one in Britain more aware of the importance of course design than Alan Ball, the B.S.J.A.'s senior course-builder, and the man we see in the middle of our television screens at almost every major event, walking from fence to fence between rounds carrying a long measuring stick and wearing a wide grin.

Alan has been building courses since he came out of the Army in 1955, taking it on as a full-time job in 1972 and covering everything from the World Championships and Royal and Dublin Shows to the B.S.J.A. Pony Club Championships and the major telly spectaculars at Wembley and Olympia. He admits to having neither the skill, nor the desire, to jump any of the courses he builds, but he has the 'mechanics' of course-building, the distances, the strides, the heights and the optical illusions, down to such a fine art that he can build a course indoors, or out, for any class of competitor, that will get the best out of horse and rider. Spend half an hour talking to him about building courses, and you learn an awful lot about how to jump it.

The first thing a course-builder needs to know is the location of his course – whether it is indoors, or out. An outdoor arena will usually be quite large. The minimum recommended by the B.S.J.A. is 100 yards by 80 yards. This gives the builder plenty of scope for placing his jumps.

In an indoor ring, the surface is man-made so the builder can keep it even. Outdoors, where the arena may be just a field converted for the day, the builder will need to look closely at the condition of the surface immediately in front of a jump. If it is uneven or has a bad slope, then the fence can be moved a few feet to a spot where the ground is flat.

Outdoors, horses tend to ride on a longer stride, and like to canter on between fences. So the builder can allow plenty of room between obstacles, without worrying too much about 'related distances' from one fence to another – a point that is crucial when building indoor courses.

An indoor arena is much smaller. For the Horse of the Year Show, for instance, the Wembley arena is just 205 ft (62.5 m) long by 83 ft 6 in (25.5 m) wide. So fitting in twelve big fences for a major competition is a mathematical puzzle.

There must be at least 45 ft (13.7 m) from the landing point after a jump to the end of the arena to give the horse enough room to land, collect himself, and turn the corner. Similarly, the take-off point for a jump should be not less than 50 ft (15 m) from the end of the arena so that the horse has enough room to turn a corner, straighten up and approach the obstacle on a straight line.

It may sound a lot, but when a horse is cantering around a show-jumping course, each stride eats up between 14 and 16 ft (4.3–4.9 m) at a time, which means he'd have just about three strides either into or out of a fence placed the minimum distance from the end of the arena. That length of jumping stride is the critical factor when designing an indoor course. As Alan Ball says, 'You have to construct a course that is a test for the rider, and a sporting spectacle for the audience – but you can't have the fences so close that you don't give the horse a chance.'

So, like all builders, he works to a table of 'related distances'. In three strides a horse will cover 48 ft, in four, 60 ft, on five strides 72 ft and on six 84 ft. Knowing that, and being aware of how many strides a rider will need to get sufficient impulsion to clear an upright, parallel or staircase, he can place the fences in relation to each other in a pattern that will keep the rider on his toes and give the audience a gasp every five seconds, but never demand a physical impossibility from the horse. Alan's philosophy is simple. 'I never build a course to bring down horses – just to test the riders' skill.'

There are several other things he needs to consider when deciding on the layout of the course. Never bunch all the fences in one part of the arena – it's a bad use of space, and very unattractive visually for the spectators. Whenever possible, place the first fence so that it can be jumped going towards the collecting ring. Horses are gregarious creatures, and novices especially will jump more willingly going towards home, than away from it.

Space the fences so that the rider can maintain a steady rhythm around the ring and not muddle around in fits and starts. Always ask for at least two changes of direction, and in a major competition, aim for four or five. A change of direction doesn't just mean moving physically from left to right, it means that the horse has to 'change legs'. When a horse is cantering in a circle to the left, it 'leads' with the left leg (just as children do when they are imitating galloping horses – try and go left with the right leg leading and you'll probably fall over). When it is asked to turn to the right, it has to change legs and lead off with the right. You'll see that a really experienced horse will change leg, not on the ground when it lands, but in mid-air as it is going over the jump. It may go into the jump with the left leg taking the lead, and come out of it, right leg leading ready to take the next bend.

The big wall for the puissance competition. How big? Well, those fellas are all six feet!

Alan Ball usually works on a series of patterns that follow a figure of eight, so that the horse can swing around the corners in rhythm, without having to make sharp, right-angled, and unbalanced turns.

So having decided on the position of each fence, and the question he is going to pose the rider by the shape of the obstacle, he turns to their construction.

Alan Ball is a joiner by trade. That is how he got into building courses in the first place. (That and the fact that the family haulage business kept sixty horses at one time, so he had a natural interest in, and love of horses from the start.)

Knowing how to construct fences means not only that he's developed some of the best and most inexpensive fences on the European circuit, it also means that if a rider goes crashing through them, Alan can mend them on the spot.

The standard construction of a show jump starts with the wings. Made of wood, they stand anything up to 5 ft 6 in (2 m) high and are mounted on bases that give them stability on the ground. The inside strut on the wing has a series of holes at 3 in (75 mm) intervals. Each hole accommodates a pin which holds in place the shallow cup that will support the pole at the required height. The poles are plywood and 4 in (100 mm) in diameter. The cups are $1\frac{3}{8}$ in (35 mm) deep, which is just enough to ensure that any horse that raps the pole hard will knock it clear out of the cups. Less than that and they would allow the pole to roll off at the least brush or puff of wind – more than that and the pole would stay rooted no matter how hard you hit it.

An incredible burst of energy from horse and rider as they climb over the wall. Although the rider is slightly out of balance in the saddle, he's not interfering with the forward action of the horse, and never loses contact with the front end

There must never be any nails, or sharp jagged edges on which a horse or rider could be injured. Safety is paramount and that goes for the 'dressing' as well as the jumps themselves. On one occasion Alan ordered small Christmas trees to fill in a big parallel to make it into an oxer. When they arrived, they'd been cut to the height he specified. So instead of having a tapering, harmless top to the trees, each one had a sawn-off jagged stump. If a horse had come down in between the poles it would have ripped its legs to pieces. So the trees were abandoned.

I am sure that many people who see show-jumping on television assume that all the strategically placed conifers, banks of flowers and shrubs around and in front of the fences are put there just to make the place look attractive for the spectators.

Up to a point, that is true, but, as I've already said, as far as the horses and riders are concerned, those flowers and trees are not *just* set dressing, they are as much a part of the fence as the poles, planks and gates. Colour is important too. All sorts of experiments have been done to determine whether or not horses really do distinguish between colours, or if, as many people suspect, they are largely colour blind. The fact is, regardless of experiments, that people like Alan Oliver, a leading British rider turned course-builder, won't ever use green in fences outdoors, because the poles would disappear into the colour of the grass surface, and Alan Ball always tries to get his colours to blend. He'd certainly never introduce wild colours or patterns on any of the fences in a combination, like adding a wall with a jazzy black and yellow stripe in between two more soberly coloured elements. And one fence where he has found that colour really does make a difference, is on the big wall in the puissance competition.

The puissance is the competition that most people love to hate. I've lost count of the number of times I've heard people say, 'It's unnatural,' referring to the fact that the horse is being asked to jump what looks like a solid wall, so high that if you stand on the far side, you can't even see the horse making its approach!

When Alan Ball builds the fence, he does it in such a way that it will be inviting to the horse, and completely safe. The wall stands 21 ft (6.4 m) across, with two 5 ft (1.5 m) square pillars at each end. And it has a ground line – usually a sloping plank – on the take-off side. It is constructed with light, individually made, hollow wooden bricks. There are no solid bits in it anywhere. And the bricks are laid one on top of each other in tram-lines, not overlapped as you would with a real brick wall. This means that if a horse crashes through the wall, or just knocks off the top bricks, the whole thing will collapse without causing injury to horse or rider.

The wall at Olympia has been jumped at 7 ft 2 in (2.18 m). (Think of any tall, six-footer of your acquaintance and add another fourteen inches – frightening.)

Only the very fittest, the very strongest, and the very bravest of horses are ever entered for the 'big' competition, but Alan Ball has found that, whatever the scope of the horse, they all jumped better when the wall was red! Next time you watch the puissance, look at the wall. On the approach side it is red, on the landing side, yellow. At one time he had the yellow bricks facing the approach. One year he changed them round – and he reckons the horses jumped better.

What is worth remembering is that the fences leading up to the big wall are no mean test of ability either. In 1979's competition, the spread, the fence immediately before the wall, stood at 6 ft 3 in (1.9 m) with a spread of 7 ft 6 in (2.29 m)!

In fact it is often difficult to gauge the size of obstacles on a televised competition. Most of the cameras are above the arena, which gives excellent coverage of the action, but tends to scale down the bulk and height of the fences. For many people, the puissance is one of the less interesting television competitions. They see it as an equine variation on the high jump, and much prefer the excitement and spectacle of the speed and precision competitions where horse and rider pit their skill over their rivals, against the fences and the clock. One of the classic tests at the Royal International Horse Show is the battle for the King George V Cup open to leading men riders in Europe. A traditional feature of the course is that it always includes two gates 5 ft (1.52 m) high. Apart from that, as Alan Ball describes it, it's a competition that must pose 'difficult questions over big fences'.

For the 1979 competition Alan designed a course with twelve fences including the double gate and one treble. So there were fifteen elements to clear, with five changes of direction.

He didn't need to take a horse over the jumps to know how the course should be ridden. On paper, the perfect round would go like this.

Down the side of the arena to the first fence, a good inviting spread 4 ft 8 in (1.4 m) high and 4 ft 8 in (1.4 m) wide. Fence number two a 4 ft 9 in (1.42 m) upright straight ahead, but only five strong bouncy strides away from the first. On landing, turn right across the centre of the arena to number three, a set of cross poles with a spread of 5 ft 5 in (1.62 m). The rider would have to jump the fence dead centre to be right in line for the next two fences. Just four bouncy strides after the cross poles was fence number four, a 5 ft (1.5 m) high wall. Three longer strides on from the wall, fence number five, a true parallel at 5 ft (1.5 m) high with a 5 ft 3 in (1.57 m) spread. These three fences across the centre of the arena would be a sure test of horsemanship. If they met the crossed poles badly, they'd have to fiddle to get straight and be on the right stride to meet the wall. Get the wall wrong, and land too short, and the three long strides into the parallel would need an enormous effort from the horse to jump cleanly out over such a big fence.

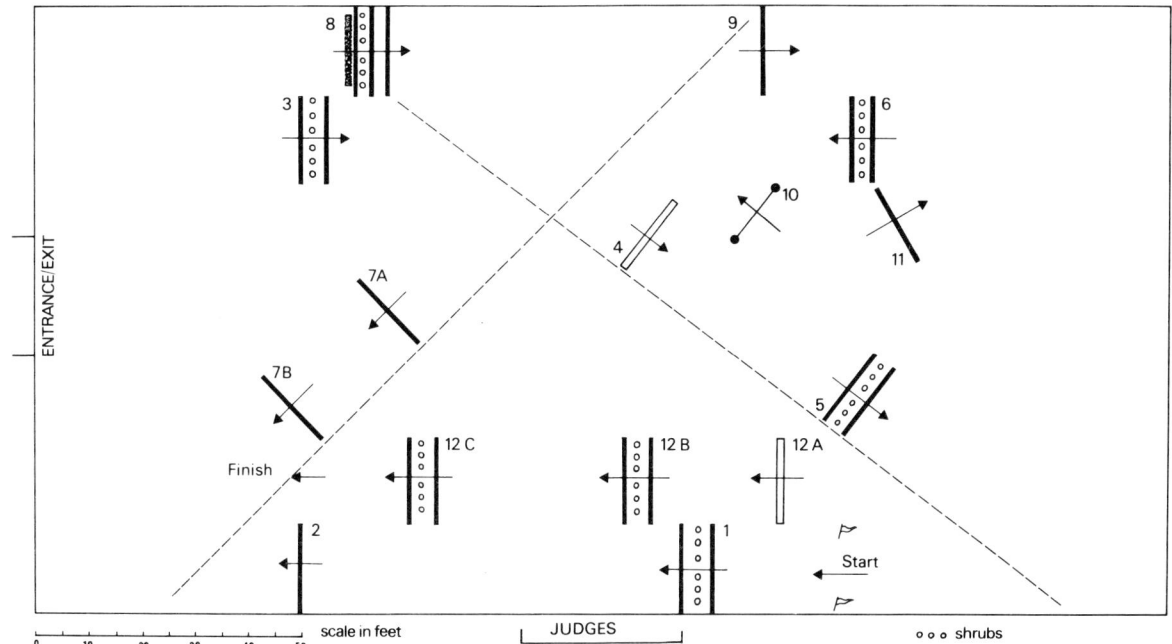

scale in feet   JUDGES   o o o shrubs

0 10 20 30 40 50

After the parallel, turn left (the second change of leg) into fence number six, a spread of five rustic (not painted) rails standing 5 ft (1.5 m) high, and 5 ft 3 in (1.57 m) across. The rider would need to ask the horse to lengthen his stride before the spread, then come back to a short powerful bouncy stride into number seven, the 5 ft (1.5 m) high double gates with one stride in between.

After that, another change of leg and a right-hand turn, into fence number eight, a 5 ft 2 in (1.55 m) staircase with a 6 ft 6 in (1.95 m) spread. On landing, pick up the horse after the spread for just five short, powerful strides into fence nine, a 5 ft 3 in (1.57 m) upright of coloured poles.

Fence ten was a curved gate 8 ft (2.30 m) wide and 5 ft (1.5 m) high – a true vertical with no ground line. It was placed at the end of the arena, off a right-hand turn. The riders would have to negotiate the bend, using every inch of the arena, then produce tremendous impulsion for just three strong strides into the fence.

On landing, take a left-hand bend to fence eleven, another upright with poles at 5 ft 3 in (1.57 m), then right handed to fence twelve down the centre of the arena.

This final obstacle was a triple combination starting with a wall at 5 ft (1.5 m), then after one stride a spread of 5 ft (1.5 m), then two strides into a parallel of 5 ft (1.5 m) with a 5 ft 3 in (1.57 m) spread. This combination needed accuracy and an obedient, athletic horse to meet the demands of the three 'problems'.

After the first round the fastest of the clear rounds was 92 seconds. In the jump-off, Robert Smith cleared the course in 63 seconds. According to Alan Ball – it was a copy-book round. Which is presumably why he won!

King George V Gold Cup
Royal International Horse Show, 1979
Plan of Course

1 Coloured red. Small arched wall underneath shrubs in centre
4 ft 8 in spread, 4 ft 8 in back pole, 4 ft 4 in front pole.

2 Red planks and poles, with pole on top
4 ft 9 in high.

3 Brown and stone, 2 cross-poles in front from top of wing-stands, 2 poles 5 ft high at back,
5 ft spread.

4 Viaduct wall, flowers in openings
5 ft high.

5 True oxer, with red and white poles
5 ft high, 5 ft 3 in spread.

6 55 feet in from end. Varnished rustic poles, 5/6 poles at front, 1 behind,
4 ft 9 in front, 5 ft back, 5 ft 3 in spread.

7 Double, both white railway gates with disc in centre
4 ft 9 in – 5 ft high, 25 ft between each gate.

8 Triple bar with small bush in front
front 3 ft 3 in, centre 4 ft 4 in, back 5 ft, overall 6 ft 6 in.

9 Upright blue, white and red poles
5 ft 3 in high.

10 8 ft wide curved gate standing on brown pillars
6 ft high.

11 Upright blue and white poles with blue hurdles
5 ft 1 in high.

12A Green wall with round toppers
5 ft high.

12B Green and white poles over green and white solid panel
4 ft 10 in at front, 5 ft back, 5 ft spread.

12C Green and white poles
5 ft front, 5 ft back, 5 ft spread.

11 Eventing

The very first time I went to the site of the Badminton three-day event in the spring of 1973 and indulged in the ritual of walking the course the day before the cross-country, I wondered to myself what sort of lunatic would want to hurl himself and half a ton of horseflesh over what seemed to be totally unjumpable fences, for they were big, imposing, solid, and positively terrifying.

My reaction, I think, was fairly typical of most people seeing for the first time a sort of giant commando obstacle course, that looked as though it should be swung over on ropes, not jumped over on horseback. A reaction that's confirmed every time you see a horse and rider fall foul of the obstacles. But one that turns from disbelief, to amazement, to unadulterated admiration when an expert horseman on a bold, fit horse, defies the laws of gravity, and makes it look both effortless and simple. It is neither, of course, but then that's the skill.

Eventing began as a military riding contest. Indeed for many years it was referred to as 'the military'. The French were the pioneers, and in 1902 organized the Championnat du Cheval d'Armes, for military horses and competitors only, which was divided into four sections: a dressage test, a steeplechase course, 3 miles (5 km) of roads and tracks followed by show-jumping. Even in 1912 when the three-day event became the first equestrian event ever to be held in the modern Olympic Games it was military combinations that came from each of the ten competing nations.

Britain really didn't take the sport at all seriously. Any horse capable of riding fast across country got all the 'sport' it needed on the hunting field, where neither horse nor rider had to worry about the niceties and discipline of the dressage test. In 1936 we won the bronze medal in the team event, but if national pride was stirred by this it was short lived. We had to wait another twenty years before we took the gold medal at the 1956 Olympics in Stockholm.

We were first again at Mexico City in 1968, and four years later at Munich pulled off the double of team and individual gold medals – the individual honours going to Richard Meade riding Laurieston.

To a certain extent eventing at a national and international level still has an air of exclusivity, of being open to only the élite, county set. But as a spectator sport, it's a winner with people from every walk of life. And among the quarter of a million or so people who turn up every year for the cross-country section of the Badminton Horse Trials, you'll find hopeful young riders, townies, countryfolk, really anyone with a genuine love of competition, and horseflesh.

As with show-jumping, television has brought the 'event scene' into the living-room of every television family in the country. But I'm sure that most of the people who tune in for the recorded highlights, or turn up in their hundreds of thousands

Kate and I at our first event – I was terrified, she had a ball

Clearing the last fence at the Cornwood Hunter Trial

just for the cross-country day or any major national three-day event, assume that while there may be a bit of show-jumping involved somewhere, eventing is really all about a fast gallop across country punctuated by heart-stopping leaps over mighty fences. Well yes – it's partly that. But there's a whole lot more besides.

The sections of a three-day event

To begin with – let's get the definitions right. *Horse trial* is the generic title used to describe any 'event' that includes, or involves a timed course over open country, jumping 'natural' obstacles, known as the *cross-country*. The simplest form of the horse trial is the *hunter trial*, and this consists solely of a cross-country competition. The day may be split into various classes to accommodate restricted novice, novice, junior, intermediate or open riders and horses, with the height and difficulty of the fences altered to suit the ability of each class.

Combined training is the term used when a horse is asked to complete three disciplines: a show-jumping course, and a dressage test as well as the cross-country course. Though just to confuse the issue, it is also used as a synonym for 'eventing' and to describe the two disciplines, show-jumping and dressage.

When all three, cross-country, show-jumping and dressage, are put together in a contest covering one day, it's called a *one-day event*, or *one-day horse trial*. There are nearly ninety official British Horse Society one-day events held throughout Britain in the spring and autumn, and countless competitions organized by local riding clubs. They are held during those seasons mainly because many 'eventing' horses would be hunted during the winter, and turned out to grass during the summer, when it would be too hot anyway for anything that involved sustained galloping.

The *three-day event* is a really major undertaking, for competitors and organizers alike. It is the ultimate trial of skill, courage, obedience and horsemanship designed to test the combination of horse and rider, and, as such, is reserved for major national and international events, including the Olympics.

There are just five three-day event venues in Britain. At Bramham in West Yorkshire, Windsor in Windsor Great Park just outside London, Wylye in Wiltshire, and, perhaps the country's two most famous locations, Burghley, at Stamford in Lincolnshire where the Marquess of Exeter is host every September, and Badminton in Avon, which is the setting for the first major event of the year in April where the Duke of Beaufort organized the first British three-day events after the Second World War.

The basic ingredients for the three-day event have always been: dressage on day one, show-jumping on the final day, with the cross-country sandwiched in between on the second day.

The cross-country ride is nowadays part of the much longer, more testing section known as the speed and endurance test, which is itself divided into four sections.

Phase A is a speed test over a set distance when the rider may walk, trot or canter to finish in the allotted time. Phase B involves riding around a steeplechase course. Phase C is the second part of the speed test when again the rider has to cover a fixed distance in an allotted time. Then there is a break of ten minutes before the start of phase D – the ride over the cross-country course.

These are the components of a three-day event, but to understand *why* it's such a major test of both horse and rider, we need to start with day one.

Day one

The dressage test in the three-day event is included to ensure that the horse is well balanced and obedient, and that there is a rapport between horse and rider. Dressage grew out of the training given to military horses to make them obedient, supple, manoeuvrable and athletic in war. The capriole, for instance, when the horse leaps in the air off all four feet at once, kicking out with the hind legs, originates from the movement taught to war-horses to get their masters out of trouble in close combat, kicking out at the enemy in the rear.

At its most refined and disciplined level dressage is an equestrian art in its own right with the horse performing a sequence of movements with balletic precision to show the harmony between mount and rider. And such is the total concentration and discipline required that the horse would probably do nothing but dressage.

An event horse isn't asked for such single-minded dedication, nor is it expected to reach the giddy heights of *haute école,* or high school, dressage. But it must be able to show that, whatever power, speed and jumping ability it may possess in order to explode into action on the second and third days of the competition, on the first day it's able to suppress its natural volatile instincts, and perform a test to prove its mental discipline, physical agility, and willingness to be controlled by the rider.

To the untrained eye, a dressage test may look like a circus act, with the horse doing fancy steps and tricks. In fact, each movement is specifically designed to stretch and flex muscles, make the spine more supple, the horse more responsive and agile. A ballet dancer performs exercises at the bar, to become supple and strong and then builds up his or her repertoire with a series of steps and movements which eventually become a routine. When dancers perform, their agility comes from a body that is perfectly tuned, like a racing car, and their effortless movement and grace comes from the strength of firm, toned muscles. So it is with the horse. In training the rider will try to achieve a 'rounded' outline to the horse. By flexing the horse's jaw through his fingers, and producing energy in the hindquarters with strong aids from his legs, the rider can compress all the horse's energy so that he has, in effect, a rounded, light flexible spring in his hands, ready to be compressed or let out as needed.

Imagine that you have a crop, or some other whippy stick in your hands. If you hold each end, and start to push inwards on both hands at once, the whip will bend in the middle. The more energy you compress, the more springy the stick becomes. If you suddenly let go with either hand, there's nothing to 'push' against any more, so all the energy will just disappear and the stick will flatten out.

A dressage rider will spend hours on a flat piece of ground just going round and round in circles, up and down the sides of an oblong to achieve this springy, rounded shape. At the same time, he'll introduce the horse to some of the individual movements that will make him supple and strong, before plunging him into the disciplines of a complete dressage test with numerous changes of direction, speed and length of stride. When the test is performed at a competition it must be done from memory, and within the allotted time of seven and half minutes. Mistakes are penalized on a sliding scale with two penalty marks for the first error, five for the second, eight for the third, and elimination after the fourth.

So the test must be practised over and over again, to ensure that each movement is done with precision, and that the complete routine is firmly planted in the rider's mind. But in practice, the rider has to be careful. Horses are clever and soon learn the test as well as their riders, and if you are not careful, they will start to anticipate your directions and move from one sequence into another when *they* think they've reached the right point, not when you ask them. To avoid this, riders will often practice small pieces of the test, and try to 'loose' the sequence in the middle of a set of other, unconnected exercises.

The dressage arena for an advanced competition measures 196 ft 10 in by 65 ft 7 in (60 m by 20 m) and is divided into sections with the use of markers, each of which is identified by a letter of the alphabet. There are five markers down each long side of the arena, five through the centre and one at each end. They bear no relation to any alphabetical sequence, and I cannot find anyone who knows how the pattern evolved.

The dressage test in a riding-club event or competition would be of novice standard in an arena of 40 m by 20 m (131 ft 3 in by 65 ft 7 in) and have fewer markers – one at each end and three down the long side and the centre. Each movement must begin or end at one of the markers and the rider's accuracy is judged by the position of his body in relation to the marker. It's the rider who must be level with the marker, not the front or rear end of the horse.

The 'clothes' worn in a dressage competition, by both the

horse and rider, are clearly defined in the rule books of the British Horse Society, and the Fédération Équestre Internationale (F.E.I.), who are responsible for all national and international competitions. For the horse, the keynote is simplicity. It mustn't be tacked up in anything that will either disguise the fluidity of movement, or support and help the rider to achieve control.

It would therefore wear an English general-purpose or dressage saddle, a snaffle bit with a cavesson, dropped or Grackle noseband (which must be made entirely of leather), or

The F.E.I. Three-Day Event Dressage Test (1975)

To be ridden in a snaffle or double bridle

Time allowed: 7½ minutes

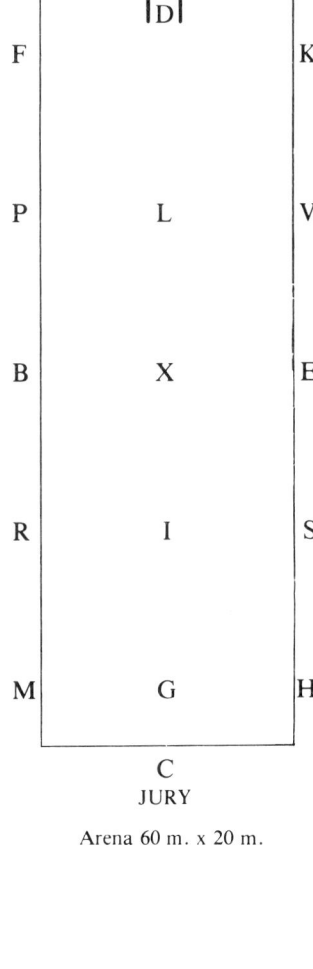

Arena 60 m. x 20 m.

		TEST	MAX. MARKS
1	A	Enter at working canter	
	X	Halt—Immobility—Salute	
		Proceed at working trot	10
2	C	Track to the left	
	S	Medium trot	
	EBE	Circle to the left 20 metres diameter	
	EV	Medium trot	10
3	V	Working trot	
	A	Down centre line	
	L	Circle to the left 10 metres diameter	10
4	LS	Half-pass (left)	10
5	C	Halt—Rein back 5 steps—Proceed at working trot	
		without halting	10
6	R	Medium trot	
	BEB	Circle to the right 20 metres diameter	
	BP	Medium trot	10
7	P	Working trot	
	A	Down centre line	
	L	Circle to the right 10 metres diameter	10
8	LR	Half-pass (right)	10
9	C	Halt—Immobility 5 seconds—	
		Proceed at working trot	10
10	HXF	Change rein at extended trot (rising)	
	F	Working trot	10
11	KXM	Change rein at extended trot	
	M	Working trot	10
12	C	Medium walk	
	HSXPF	Change rein at extended walk	
	F	Medium walk	10
13	A	Working canter—Circle to the right 10 metres diameter ..	10
14	AC	Serpentine 3 loops, the first and the third true canter, the	
		second counter canter	10
15	MXK	Change rein at extended canter	
	K	Working trot	10
16	A	Working Canter—Circle to the left 10 metres diameter ..	10
17	AC	Serpentine 3 loops, the first and the third true canter, the	
		second counter canter	10
18	HXF	Change rein at extended canter	
	F	Working trot	10
19	A	Down centre line	
	L	Working canter to the right	10
20	G	Halt—Immobility—Salute	10
	A	Leave arena on a long rein	

Collective Marks

1.	Paces (freedom and regularity)		10
2.	Impulsion (desire to move forward, elasticity of the steps and engagement of the hind quarters)		10
3.	Submission (attention and obedience, lightness and ease of movements, acceptance of the bit)		10
4.	Position, seat of the rider, correct use of the aids		10

MAXIMUM TOTAL MARKS	240

(except in novice classes) a simple double bridle. Martingales, bearing, side or running reins are forbidden, as are bandages, boots and any kind of blinkers.

As for the rider, if he's a military competitor then he must wear his uniform, with regulation headgear, and spurs. The 'civilian' riders, men and women, can wear a hunting jacket, with either a tie or white stock, white breeches and a velvet cap; or the full dressage kit of tail coat, waistcoat, breeches, stock and top hat. Spurs are compulsory but whips are forbidden. At a riding-club or pony-club competition you wouldn't see the formality of the top hat, but apart from that, the general principles of dress would be much the same. But let's assume that we're at Badminton or Burghley and day one is about to begin.

The judges will sit at the end of the arena beyond the C marker. There will be three of them marking independently, each marking every one of the twenty separate movements in the test out of a maximum of ten.

When the test has been completed they will then allot what are called the collective marks, a further score out of ten for each of four further headings: (a) paces of the horse, (b) impulsion (the desire to move forward, the elasticity of the steps and engagement of the hindquarters), (c) submission (attention and obedience, lightness and freedom of the movements and acceptance of the bit), (d) position (seat of the rider, correct use of the aids).

This means that a rider can collect a maximum of 240 points. Any penalties incurred by taking longer than the specified $7\frac{1}{2}$ minutes, or for errors, are subtracted from each of the three sets of marks. The marks are totalled, then averaged by dividing by three. That figure – referred to as the good marks – is then subtracted from the maximum 240. The resultant total expresses the score in penalty points.

Janet Hodgson on Gretna Green, riding in the pre-dressage test at Badminton

Opposite: Emerging from the stable with my tack

Left: Kate and I under instruction from Sue Armstrong

Below: Jumping a staircase or spread

Before going into the arena the rider will have spent some time working the horse in to get him supple, and in the right frame of mind. The rider himself will need total, undivided concentration. (I am sure that is why so many people think of some riders as being haughty or snobbish, but the fact is that if you're concentrating your whole mind and body on achieving the right sort of harmony you simply don't see or hear anyone else!) The concentration is absolute.

From my own humble attempts at dressage, I know that if you stop working, either physically or mentally, for just one second, then the test starts to fall to pieces. You have to concentrate on remembering the test, and making sure that every muscle in your body is giving the right aid, at the right moment, and at the right strength, to get the horse to respond instantly, but fluidly. Part of the skill of dressage is to do all that, while sitting as still as possible so that it *looks* as though there is no physical effort involved. The effort on the rider is exhausting. I usually leave the arena with my back dripping, sweating buckets and my shirt sticking to me.

Dressage tests are compiled by the B.H.S. and (at national and international level) the F.E.I. It is possible to follow the test movement by movement, as it's always printed in full in the official programme at horse trials. The number of the exercise is in the far left column, the markers at which the movement should begin and end, in the second column. (By following these, you can work out the route that the rider will take.) In the middle, there is a description of the exercise setting out in detail what the rider will be expected to do, and in the final column, the maximum marks.

Each section of a three-day event runs to a strict timetable, so riders know at exactly what time they will be called. They will be summoned into the main arena by a steward and allowed to circle the actual dressage arena until the judges are ready. When they are, a bell or hooter will sound, and the rider must make his way to the entrance at marker A. From the second they enter that sixty by twenty oblong, they will be under the judges' scrutiny.

The judges want to see straight lines, square halts, and round circles, and clearly defined changes in pace occurring exactly when specified in the test sheet. To give you some idea of a few of the things they'll be looking at, let's go through some of the movements from the F.E.I. three-day event test first set in 1975.

The rider enters at A travelling down the centre line at a working canter. The judges will want to see that the horse has steady, controlled paces, and that it's going absolutely straight, not swinging off the central line, which isn't as easy as it sounds! At X, in the centre, the horse will stop – all four legs must be square like the legs on a table – if they're not, the rider will lose points. Having stopped, the rider must salute the judges. While he does so, the horse must not fidget. When he is ready, the rider

Opposite: Riding across Dartmoor

Torrance Watkins on Poltroon
during the three-day event at
Burghley, 1979

can 'collect' the horse, and prepare to begin the first movement. The whole of the first half of the test, up to movement nine, is done at the working, and medium trot. The first is a stride full of energy and spring, with the horse taking relatively short steps. The second calls for a slightly longer stride, with just as much energy, but no increase in speed. Indeed, throughout the test, regardless of change of direction or pace, the judges will be looking to see if the horse can maintain the same steady, controlled rhythm, without hiccuping around the arena in fits and starts.

Figures two and three call for circles of 20 and 10 metres. These will show the judges that the horse is on the bit, supporting his own weight and can bend without 'motorbiking' around the corners, or letting his shoulder fall in. It will also show that the spine has strength and flexion, as will the half pass at figures four and eight.

The fifth movement is a halt, followed by a rein-back for five steps. The halt must be square and positive, the rein-back perfectly straight and without any resistance from the horse. When once the fifth step has been completed the horse must be pushed straight into a working trot. It must be a positive action, the judges won't want to see the horse falling, or slopping into the action, nor will they want to see the head fly up in resistance.

At the half-way point, there is another halt. This time at the bottom of the arena at marker C. The horse must be square, and not fussing. It must not anticipate its rider's command to move off. The extended trot, diagonally across the centre of the arena (movements ten and eleven), can be the most stunning display of balance and 'style'.

I remember watching Torrance Watkins of the United States competing in the 1979 competition at Burghley. Her horse, the eleven-year-old Poltroon, stuck out like a sore thumb among the dark bay, grey and chestnut horses of the rest of the competitors. Poltroon is a diminutive 15 hands 2 in (1.57 m) skewbald – a coloured pony of brown and white splodges. There are those who think that coloured ponies are rather 'common' compared to the thoroughbred mono-coloured horses we usually see at competitions, and certainly Poltroon did not command too much interest when he first entered the dressage ring. But in her warm-up, Miss Watkins put the horse into an extended trot – and a gasp of appreciation went round the arena. It was magnificent. The horse floated over the ground with long, bouncy elegant strides, throwing out its front feet with the grace and verve of a real showman. Her mark in the subsequent test, eight out of ten, reflected her horse's achievement, and the judges' satisfaction.

Movement twelve is a long walk from marker C, a third of the way along one side of the arena, across the centre, and down the final third of the opposite side. It's not a rest for the horse, or rider – the walk is one of the most difficult of all strides for a horse to maintain at a rhythmic, active pace. If the rider lets go, the horse will flop. If he pushes too hard, it will probably 'break' into a trot. Getting it just right requires considerable control from both halves of the partnership.

Straight out of the walk at the top end of the arena the horse is pushed into movement thirteen, the canter. If the rider doesn't have the horse completely on the bit and the hocks well underneath him, like the proverbial coiled spring, when he asks for the canter, the horse won't have either the energy or impulsion to oblige.

The serpentine, at figures fourteen and seventeen, is done at the canter, with the rider tracing three loops across the centre of the arena. The horse must be flexible to make the three changes of direction within such a limited space, but more than that, there must be total obedience, because on the second loop the horse will be cantering on the 'wrong' leg. As he turns out of the left-hand bend into the right, the temptation will be to change legs – and vice versa when the exercise is repeated in the opposite direction. What the judges will be looking for is that, despite its natural inclinations, the horse is so supple, so well trained and obedient, that it performs the three loops of the exercise without changing legs and maintaining a bend around the left leg.

Towards the end of the test, the horse is asked for the nearest thing it will ever get to a full-blown 'gallop' in a dressage test, the extended canter diagonally across the arena. But once it reaches the far side of the arena, it must resist the temptation to dash off. Instead, it must come right back into the rider's hands to a steady working trot, followed by a controlled canter straight down the centre line to the judges. The rider will halt, salute, and then leave the arena on a long rein. Still the judges' eyes will be on him.

The salute is marked as part of the test. I once forgot to salute the judge because I was so mad at myself for doing a rotten test, and I was penalized on the score sheet. And when the rider lets out the reins for the horse to walk out of the arena, the judges will want to see the horse stretching its neck to release the tension in the muscles, as proof that the horse was bending and 'using' itself throughout the test.

Dressage does not have the crash-bang-wallop appeal of show-jumping or cross-country. It is far too subtle, too intricate and controlled to produce the same, instant audience reaction that you get from a horse leaping a mighty fence. But once you begin to get an inkling of the complexities, and demands of the subject – you're hooked. You don't have to be an expert. Just by watching a series of tests you can soon see whether or not A is good, bad or indifferent compared with B or C, and while three-day events are not exactly won in the dressage arena, the performance by horse and rider can have a fundamental effect on the overall result.

Torrance Watkins was in fourth position at the end of the 1979 Burghley dressage section, and went on to finish second overall after a fast, agile and accurate round on both the cross-country, and show-jumping courses. Karl Schultz, the West German maestro, with his horse Madrigal gave an exhibition performance of dressage on the first day of the 1977 European Championships, and then went on to do a blistering cross-country round, and faultless show-jumping phase.

Their horses were not just fit, agile, fast and explosive. They were obedient, supple, and disciplined. And these are the qualities that the three-day event puts to the test. Though arguably, day two is the greatest test of all.

Day two

Day two of the competition is always referred to as the speed and endurance section – aptly named, as horse and rider will have to complete something like 16 miles (25 km) in an hour and a half.

The riders are not allowed to have a practice ride around the course, but they can – and do – walk it as often as they like.

The purpose of walking the course is to fix in your mind the route you have to take, the way you will approach the obstacles, and the speed at which you'll ride each section.

This is important because each of the four sections that make up the speed and endurance test have an optimum time. Any competitor going over the time limit will incur penalty points. So these days you'll often see competitors riding with stop-watches and small time sheets strapped to their wrists, so that they can keep checking their pace at every stage of the day.

The two sections of roads and tracks, phases A and C, total about 8 miles (13 km). The rider will need to walk the course, not only to make sure he doesn't lose his way, but also to decide how and where to 'pace' the horse at the walk, trot and canter so that he'll finish the phase within the time, but not wear the horse out in the process.

The steeplechase course has to feature the sort of fences used on national hunt racecourses in the country hosting the competition, which in Britain means large, solid brush fences, some with an open ditch in front. When riding the course, the competitor will be asking for speed and fluency from the horse, just as if he were riding in a race. He won't want to 'check' the horse on its approach to a fence and upset the rhythm. Bertie Hill, an Olympic team gold medallist and national trainer, believes that the steeplechase section is one of the most important in the competition. 'You can see from the way the combination ride the steeplechase course how they are likely to attack the cross-country,' he says.

Any horse that has to be driven into the fences, makes heavy weather of the fast going, and looks generally disunited, isn't going to fare too well over the fixed obstacles in phase D. The repeated breaks in rhythm will lose valuable time, and probably drain some of the horse's energy. So what trainers, spectators and riders will be looking for is a horse with strong fluent strides, meeting the fences just right and sailing over and on without any interruption to his flow, at a steady speed that will enable the course to be completed just under the time limit.

Riders do an awful lot of walking. Apart from the roads, tracks and steeplechase, they'll probably walk the 3 miles (5 km) or so of the cross-country course at least three times. I know of one competitor who walks the course the first time just to familiarize herself with the route, and the fences themselves, and to make a preliminary decision on how to approach and jump each obstacle. Then she walks the course in reverse on the principle that if you start from where you hope to land – that may give you a whole new perspective on the place you should be taking off from and your approach line. Then she walks again – the right way round – to set quite firmly in her mind her exact route, her take-off position, where she intends to jump the fence, and which route she'll take through the combinations. That's the least she'll do. If there is time, she will walk the entire course again and again. If not, then she will be going back to the fences that set special problems to look at them individually, right up to the morning of the competition.

The point of all this is to help the rider to solve the problem that's been set by the course designer. Some fences are quite straightforward. All you have to do is work out how fast you'll approach, from what direction, and at what point you'll ask the horse for maximum effort and take-off.

At others the speed at which you approach will be critical. And on the combinations you need to work out not only which route will suit both your own and the horse's boldness and ability, but also, which alternative easier route to jump if you come unstuck and get a refusal.

The 1979 Badminton three-day event had a particularly nasty-looking fence at number eighteen. A Z-shaped bridge over a stream. There were three alternative routes over the bridge, with two 'emergency' routes. Lucinda Prior-Palmer was the first to go, and I watched her take one of the easier routes on the far left-hand side of the bridge. This meant jumping the stream, going up the bank on the other side and clearing a 3 ft 8 in (1.12 m) rail at the top. As the horse stretched to jump the rail, its hindquarters slipped on the bank and the pair of them slid down into the stream. Lucinda gathered up the reins, rode sharply round to the right-hand side of the fence, popped over the stream and out the other side. Because she'd worked out every single alternative available to her she didn't waste a second wondering how to get herself out of a mess – and in championship competitions, every second is vital.

I know there are people who look at cross-country fences and dismiss the whole thing as cruel, or believe that the course-builders and designers are asking too much of the horses.

Admittedly, if you compared the fences at pre-war Olympic three-day events with those at present-day Badmintons and Burghleys, the former look like novice, pony-club jumps. Over the past twenty years, course-builders and designers have produced fences that demand more and more of horse and rider. But riders and trainers have responded by being much more technical in their own approach to jumping, and have produced horses that are so fit and bold that they can take the fences, quite literally, in their stride. Let's face it, you and I wouldn't dream of attempting to run a mile for a bus in four minutes but Sebastian Coe could do it in his wellies – simply because his body is geared for that sort of performance.

You can't just enter a big competition because you ride and

SPEED AND ENDURANCE
Steeplechase and Cross-Country

CROSS-COUNTRY FENCES

1	Timber Wagon	15	Sunken Wall
2	Flower Bed	16A D	Steps Down and Up
3	Lambert's Sofa	17	Crush Barrier
4	Fisherman's Corner	18	The Malting Rails
5	Palisade	19	Trout Hatchery
6	Lower Trout Hatchery	20	Open Water
7	Water Troughs	21	Waterloo Rails
8	Capability's Cutting	22A-C	The Folds
9		23	Trakener
10	Double Gates	24	Chabonel Rails
11	Flight Butt	25A-D	Double Coffin
12	Pardubice	26	Zig Zag
13	The Tunnel	27	Oxer
14	Beehives	28	Log Pile

think you might like to 'have a go'. Competitions are graded into novice, intermediate, open intermediate and advanced classes and only horses that have gained sufficient points appropriate to the class can enter. Every horse starts at grade three. When a horse has won ten points it becomes grade two. When it reaches forty points it is upgraded to grade one and only then can it take part in open intermediate and advanced classes.

As with every form of competition, the points are not easy to come by. Only the very best will be placed consistently and so tot up enough points to pass from one grade to another. If they're not good enough they'll fall by the wayside long before they're overstretched. So by the time they reach national advanced championships they've proved themselves to be bold, fit and capable all-round athletes.

Course-builders and designers are not sadists, trying to push rider and horse to the limits of endurance, and even if any of them ever were tempted to ask just that little bit extra of a horse – they wouldn't be able to. The F.E.I. have a 116-page set of rules in which they state clearly the maximum height, spread, drop and width of every conceivable style of fence. Plus their location, construction and the *number* of obstacles on a course – an overall average of four fences for every 1,000 metres. Rules are essential if the sport is to have world-wide standards. Though even without them, I doubt that designers would make ludicrous demands on competitors.

Bill Thompson is the man who largely pioneered course-building in this country. He's built countless championship courses around Europe, and been responsible for the competition at Burghley since 1950 – a vet by profession, he says quite simply, 'I set problems for riders, not horses. I want to encourage horses to jump – not hurt them.' He's an expert who's observed horses jumping and dropping over things for more than thirty years. He started just after the Second World War with a small riding establishment which had an old gravel pit nearby. He admits, 'I became fascinated with what you could teach a very moderate horse to jump,' and he believes that, even these days, very few people fully appreciate just how much a *really* fit horse is capable of.

His fences are solid, made with timbers at least 8 in (200 mm) in diameter. 'Horses respect solid fences,' he says. 'Those flimsy little four-inch-wide poles on top of oil drums just make me scream. They encourage ponies to be careless – and riders too. But solid fences need respect and horses don't take chances going over them.'

Every fence is made so that it can be demolished quickly if a horse gets into trouble. The top poles are lashed into place with rope, and every fence judge has a small hatchet to slash through the rope and dismantle the fence if it is necessary. Thompson also rests any lower poles on chocks, so that should a horse get a leg jammed, the poled can be released quickly.

'I know I've saved the lives of at least four horses by doing that,' he says, with more satisfaction than ego. The location of the fence is vital. The F.E.I. rules state that fences should be fixed, imposing in shape and appearance, and left, as far as possible, in their natural state, following the natural contours of the land. The Double Coffin and Trout Hatchery at Burghley and the Quarry and Lake at Badminton are perfect examples of this rule in action.

Natural contours in the land, when used as part of the obstacle can make all the difference in the world to the difficulty of the test. A fence like a post and rails that would be relatively simple placed in the centre of open flat land, becomes far more difficult when built on the top of a slope, in a hollow, or with a ditch or water in front of it as part of a combination. The skill of the designer is to plan a course that will be demanding, without being destructive, on the horse, and make the rider think about every stride from start to finish.

Which is why walking the course, and trying to get inside the mind of the designer to anticipate and solve the problems he has set, is just as important as riding the course on the second day.

As with the dressage test, every rider is given a specific time at which to start the speed and endurance phase, with competitors being sent off at intervals of not less than four minutes.

Karl Schulz and Madrigal at Burghley, 1977

As soon as they start on phase A the clock begins. In 1976 at the Burghley Horse Trials, phase A was 2 miles 1,595 yards (4,677 m) and had to be completed in 19 minutes 30 seconds. Every second over that incurred one penalty point. The end of phase A is the starting box for the steeplechase. Most riders will try to arrive at the start of the steeplechase with at least two minutes in hand. The steeplechase at Burghley in 1976 was 2 miles 250 yards (3,447 m) long and had to be ridden in five minutes dead – that meant a constant speed of 754 yards (689 m) a minute – or around 26 m.p.h. (41 km an hour). Phase C begins immediately the rider crosses the finish line of the steeplechase – without any stop. So winding down slowly with a gentle canter then a steady trot after the burst of speed over the steeplechase fences is a good way of covering the first mile or so of phase C.

The third phase is always the longest, at something in excess of 5 miles (8 km). It's a phase that needs to be ridden more considerately than the previous two to leave the horse with plenty of energy in reserve for the cross-country. Between the end of phase C and the start of phase D there is a compulsory stop of ten minutes – though if a rider can arrive in the starter's 'box' with time in hand, it is to his, and the horse's, advantage. During the compulsory stop the horse is examined by a veterinary panel to make sure that it is fit enough to go on. Any doubt and the horse is withdrawn.

Once it's passed fit, if the rider is lucky he'll be able to take a breather, and leave the horse to a team of willing helpers, who will start checking the saddlery to make sure that nothing has moved, or broken. They'll be cooling the horse down, removing any excess sweat, and covering the front legs with a thick layer of grease to give extra protection, and help it slide over the solid obstacles.

A few minutes before his scheduled start, the rider will re-mount, tighten the girth and walk the horse around gently in preparation for the start. Anyone who thinks that the horse is being pushed into an unnatural competition against his will should stand for a while at the start and watch the horses as they prepare for the cross-country. I don't think I'll ever forget watching that great horse, Cornishman V at the start of the 1973 Badminton cross-country. He was plunging backwards and forwards like a giant rocking-horse, ears pricked, nostrils blowing. He was an old hand at cross-country with two Olympic gold medals and a world championship to his credit. So he knew exactly what lay ahead. As far as he was concerned, it was the best part of the day and he couldn't start soon enough. Mary Gordon-Watson, his diminutive rider, was perched on top of this 17 hands (1.73 m) powder keg just holding him in check as the starter counted down, three – two – one. She let him go, and he shot off like a rocket. It would have been cruel *not* to let him go!

Once on the course, riders should stick to the route they've

Mary Gordon-Watson on Cornishman V at Badminton, 1973

decided on, and aim to maintain a rhythmic, steady canter. A pace that will eat up the ground, and ensure that the horse is balanced and responsive when approaching a jump. Asking the horse for a flat-out gallop on all the runs between fences, then checking him and interfering with his stride on the approach to a jump, is a sure way of breaking his rhythm and sapping his energy.

Each fence has a number, and a set of marker flags, red on the right, white on the left, and is surrounded by a penalty zone that extends 33 ft (10 m) either side of the fence, 33 ft (10 m) in front and 66 ft (20 m) beyond. If a rider has a fall or stop outside the penalty zone, it doesn't count – but once you enter the zone, any error starts clocking up the penalty points like this:

First refusal, run out, circle of horse at obstacle:
20 penalties.
Second refusal, run out, circle of horse:
40 penalties.
Third refusal, run out, circle of horse:
elimination.
Fall of horse and/or rider:
60 penalties.

131

Leaving penalty zone without jumping obstacle:
20 penalties.
Second fall of horse and/or rider at obstacle during steeplechase:
elimination.
Third fall of horse and/or rider at obstacle during cross-country:
elimination.
Missing out an obstacle, or passing on the wrong side of either the red or white flag:
elimination.
Retaking an obstacle already jumped:
elimination.
Jumping obstacles in the wrong order:
elimination.

Riders are not allowed any assistance while they are on the course – like people shouting instructions to them about fences, or standing in a position where they can encourage a horse to jump. But if a rider falls off, then he is allowed assistance to catch his horse, and remount.

Assuming that the rider doesn't fall off, that the horse doesn't refuse, and together they sail over high fences and wide spreads, drop into sunken roads, and climb out over banks with the power and agility of Pegasus, they'll make a flat-out gallop for the finishing line to complete the course in the fastest time possible. Both horse and rider will then have at least twelve hours to recover, reflect on the day's performance, and prepare for the final test – the show-jumping.

Day three

Day three begins with a veterinary inspection early in the morning. During a three-day event there are three such inspections by a panel of international vets. The first inspection takes place before the competition actually begins, so that the panel can decide from the start, whether or not a horse has been brought up to a peak of fitness that makes it eligible to compete. Horses are rarely found to be unfit at that stage – but it has been known. And regardless of how far a competitor has travelled, even from overseas, how long they've worked, or how confident they are that they should be allowed to compete, the panel's decision is final. The second inspection is carried out during the speed and endurance test between phases C and D.

This third and final inspection, on the morning of the show-jumping competition, ensures that the horse has not suffered unduly from the previous day's exertions, and is able to carry on.

The horses are paraded by their riders on a flat firm surface, without bandages, boots, or tack of any kind – just a plain head-collar. The horse is led into the ring, and presented to the judges for a 'static' inspection. Bereft of any 'clothing' the judges can see at once if there are any lumps, bumps, cuts or grazes. The horse is walked away from the judges, and then trotted back. On a perfectly level surface the judges can see at once if the horse shows any signs of being stiff, lame, sore or unsound in any way. If there is any doubt, then the horse is not passed 'fit to continue'. Those that are, can return to their stables in preparation for the show-jumping phase.

Professional show-jumpers can look at the course on the final day of a three-day event, and consider it very small fry. Nothing will be higher than 3 ft 11 in (1.19 m) or wider than 11 ft 6 in (3.5 m) for a spread. There won't be any difficult combinations, or tricky stride patterns to contend with. But then, this isn't a test of style and ability to show what a good show-jumper the horse is. It's there to prove that the horse is still supple, and has the energy and obedience necessary to continue after the previous day's severe test of endurance.

In a proper show-jumping competition the penalties awarded are three for a refusal, four for a knock-down, and elimination after the third refusal. In the three-day event, ten penalties are awarded for a refusal, or knocking down a pole, twenty penalties for a second refusal, and elimination after the third.

For horse and rider this phase of the competition is as much a trial of mental discipline as physical effort.

On the previous day the horse will have enjoyed its release from the straightjacket of the dressage test, and galloped at full tilt over thirty or so fences strung out on a $3\frac{1}{2}$ mile (5.6 m) course. On day three, in the show-jumping ring, it must come back to a disciplined, steady stride to negotiate between ten and twelve fences covering around $\frac{1}{2}$ mile (800 m) in an enclosed arena – and as with every other phase in the competition, it must be done within the time allowed.

The order of jumping is decided by the position the combination have gained at the end of the first two phases. They are ridden in reverse order so that the rider and horse in the lead at the end of the dressage and cross-country are always the last to go. As the marking is usually very close, and the penalty points awarded in the show-jumping phase are so high, the positions at the end of the last day can change dramatically if a rider has a bad show-jumping round, by knocking down fences, having a refusal or going too slow and clocking up time penalty points. For the riders, it can be the most exciting and frustrating day of the competition. Especially for those in the top six placings. They have to overcome their tensions, stay cool, and go clear.

At the very end of the competition, whether it's a major national or international three-day event, a world or European championship, or the Olympics, the horses that win the rosettes and the medals will be acclaimed as champions. But every horse that takes part in, and completes, a three-day event course will have displayed outstanding qualities of discipline, athletic ability and courage. And they are qualities that are unequalled in any other sphere of equine sport.

12 Fox-hunting

Hunting is an area of equestrian activity that doesn't necessarily go hand in hand with riding for pleasure.

I know scores of people who own their own horses, and ride regularly, who've never been near a pack of hounds in their lives. Others, from dockyard workers and farmers to television personalities and bankers, regard hunting as the only worth-while way to spend a day sitting on a horse.

Hunting is a subject that is fraught with controversy and myth, but it isn't my job, or intention, in a book of this type, to give a detailed, balanced argument either for or against field sports. Anyone with any serious doubts about the moral or social aspects of hunting should contact the League against Cruel Sports, who will give you their case and the British Field Sports Association who will give you theirs – after that, you're on your own. But if you have already decided *you* do want to hunt, then the only questions are how, where, and how much.

The first rule is: don't even consider hunting unless you're confident that you really can cope with a long hard day's riding, and that means up to four or five hours in the saddle riding about thirty miles, though it can be less or more! Take a good look at the countryside over which you normally ride at a fairly leisurely Sunday morning pace, and consider whether or not you can ride the same hills, banks, roads and wide open spaces, at full gallop in a crowded field. If you think you can – the next move is to ensure that you can hire a horse.

Getting a horse
Some hacking stables do hire out horses for hunting, and if you've been riding regularly at one stable then the owner will be able to judge which animal will carry you safely through the day. A huge, fit hunter may look very elegant at the meet, but will be a real handful to control in a fast and furious chase – so don't be too ambitious on your first outing. Be prepared to settle for something sure-footed and sensible to give you a comfortable, safe ride. If your regular riding stable won't hire you a horse, they should be able to recommend one that will. And in many keen hunting areas there are stables that operate only during the season, and keep horses for hunting and nothing else.

You'll be charged a daily hire fee. In early 1980, fees ranged from as little as £5 up to £25 or even more. The fee may include transporting the horse to and from the meet if it is too far away for you to hack. The stable will usually prepare the horse for you – but check on whether or not they expect you to help in grooming the horse, plaiting its mane and cleaning the tack until it gleams. If so, allow enough time to do that *and* get yourself ready when you're planning the day's timetable.

Where can you hunt?
Once you've established that you can get a *horse*, you must then find whether or not you'll be *able* to hunt. The whole of the

Setting off at the head of a keen pack and field, Mr Bertie Hill, joint master and huntsman of the Dulverton West Hunt.

Mr T. F. Ryan, master and huntsman of the Black and Tans, working his hounds in open country in Co. Limerick

British Isles is divided into hunting areas called 'countries', with the boundaries clearly defined. There are 197 recognized hunting packs in the country where the followers are mounted rather than on foot. Over ninety per cent hunt foxes – the remainder, stags. And while there are *slight* differences in rules and terminology between stag- and fox-hunting, the basics are much the same, and as most people are likely to be involved with the latter – for the purposes of this chapter, I'll be talking about *fox* hunting.

In effect, the local hunt is a private club, with members paying an annual subscription to hunt anything from one to five days a week. One of the cheapest subscriptions I know of is £30 to hunt one day a week, but in the larger, more exclusive hunts it can run up to £500. And while many hunts wouldn't mind if you just turned up on the day, at others, people hunt 'by invitation' only. So it's as well to ring the hunt secretary and check before you set out. It's also considered the polite thing to do!

Your riding stable will give you the name of the local hunt, and the name, address and telephone number of the secretary. Or you can look them up in *Baily's Hunting Directory* (there'll be a copy at the local library), and every November the *Horse and Hound* magazine has a special hunting issue giving the location and details of every pack in the country. In some areas you'll even find them in the Yellow Pages, listed under H for Hunt Kennels.

By ringing the secretary you can establish if you can hunt, where they meet, and when, and, (very important) how much it is going to cost. As a casual member you'll be expected to pay 'cap' money – a sort of temporary membership fee. You would be accepted as a temporary member on up to four, or maybe five outings – after that, you would be considered a regular hunter, and be expected to pay the full annual subscription fees the same as everyone else.

What to wear

What you wear depends on when you hunt. The cubbing season begins in mid-August and is a much more relaxed affair than the main hunting season which starts around 1 November and goes through to March or April the following year. During the eight or so weeks up to 1 November, young hounds are introduced to quarry for the first time and taught to hunt foxes, and nothing else; it disperses the cubs, so that farmers don't have to contend with too many foxes in one area, and it culls the population. It also gives new hunt employees an opportunity to get to know the countryside and terrain, and young cubs the experience of knowing that when hounds are out they should make themselves scarce. Cubbing usually begins very early in the morning when the scent is still strong on the ground which helps young hounds with identification. The huntsman, master and hunt 'servants', or employees, would not wear hunting pink – their red jackets, and the field – the riders – would also be less formally dressed in what's called 'ratcatcher'. In other words, hacking jacket with collar and tie and, traditionally, a bowler. Although, nowadays, most people wear velvet caps.

On 1 November – for the opening meet – everything becomes very formal. The 'correct' hunting dress for a man is black tailcoat, white stock, black silk top hat, and black boots and white breeches. Or they can wear a modified version of the ladies' dress, of black hunting jacket, white stock and breeches, and a black bowler. Women should also always wear a hairnet to stop flyaway locks. Velvet caps should really only be worn by hunt servants and farmers. But these days very few people would object if you turned up wearing a black or blue jacket, white stock and velvet cap. You *can* carry an ordinary riding crop, but a proper hunting whip has an L-shaped bone handle, for hitching and unhitching gates, and a long leather thong used mainly to keep the hounds away from the horses' feet.

Anyone hunting for the first time needn't go to the enormous expense of buying a complete outfit. The breeches, boots and cap you would wear for hacking would be totally acceptable, and you could possibly borrow or even buy a second-hand hunting jacket. The 'stock' – the white necktie – will cost about £5 and someone at the stable will be happy to show you how to tie it, although most now come with a small instruction leaflet! Hunting isn't cheap by any standards, but it needn't cost a fortune.

It's worth remembering that hunting is a *winter* activity, but some of the *clothes* you can wear when hunting aren't necessarily warm. So do equip yourself with a full set of really warm underwear, thick warm socks, a quilted waistcoat and warm gloves. If it is going to rain, wear a proper riding mac. They're made of a rubber-lined fabric with double 'storm' cuffs to keep draughts out of your arms, and straps to hold the front panels to your legs so that they won't flap about and distract the horse.

Both you and your horse should always be properly 'turned out', as a compliment to the master. But don't let fashion get in the way of comfort. There is nothing more miserable than being stuck on a horse in the middle of nowhere soaked to the skin, or with toes and fingers so cold they ache, and the prospect of a very long ride home before you reach a warm stable and dry clothes.

Hunting for the first time
As soon as you arrive at the meet, make yourself known to the master. If you're a stranger he'll want to know who you are and where you've come from. Don't trample on the hounds, and don't be tardy in paying up. If necessary, go in search of the secretary to pay your cap, don't wait to be asked. Aim to arrive at least five minutes before the hunt moves off. It is considered very bad manners to join in once the hounds have started working. Identifying officials of the hunt is fairly straight-

forward. The master will be wearing a red jacket, properly called hunting pink, with a black velvet cap. The master is the commanding officer, and has overall command of the hunt servants and the pack of hounds, and you are his guest for the day. The huntsman is the man who will work the hounds. The master may double as huntsman, or there may be a separate professional huntsman – either way he'll be the one in hunting pink, with a black velvet cap, carrying a horn.

The whippers-in also wear hunting pink and caps, and will be responsible for keeping the pack together once they're on a scent. In a few hunts, the hunt servants don't wear pink at all but a personal livery. In the Duke of Beaufort's hunt, for instance, the servants wear blue jackets with a white flash. The field master will be wearing hunting pink and a black silk top hat. Once the hunt moves off, he will be in charge of the field. So if it's your first time out, get someone to point him out to you, and try not to lose sight of him during the day.

When the hounds and huntsman move off, don't follow *them*, follow the field master. The hounds may be taken to an area to draw – or flush out – a fox, and the huntsman won't want a gaggle of riders in his way or distracting the hounds. The field master will decide *where* the field should wait, and *when* they should move off in pursuit of the hounds.

Once you do move off, if you're new to an area then stay fairly close to the bulk of the field, but not *too* close. Leave yourself room to manoeuvre in case you have to suddenly stop, change direction or jump an obstacle. But you don't have to stay with the bulk of the riders. You can take your own line providing you don't *ever* get in front of the master, huntsman, or hounds. Don't ever ride across fields, always round the edges, and always close gates after you've gone through, or hold the gate for the rider following. Remember you are guests on private land – don't ever abuse the farmers' or landowners' hospitality.

Communication in the field
A hunting field is a little like a public library, talking in a normal voice is fine – but not shouting. Don't ever raise your voice, burst into loud, raucous laughter, or generally distract the master, huntsman or hounds, and remember, some women's voices carry a long way in still air.

If hounds lose the scent, and you see the fox, don't shout wildly. Hounds work with their noses close to the ground. If they are distracted by any shouting they raise their heads and stop working. If you are in the sight line of either the master or huntsman, raise your hat above your head to arm's length, and 'point' your horse in the direction you last saw the fox. If you're out of sight, ride to the field master or one of the hunt servants and tell them. When hounds (always hounds – never dogs) start to work as a pack, they're said to be 'drawing a scent', which means that they get busy sniffing around in a likely spot until they get a 'find', and pick up a trail.

As soon as hounds find, they begin 'speaking', letting out that wild, high-pitched baying that signals to the huntsman, and the rest of the pack, that they've picked up the scent. 'Following a line' is what they do once they've picked up a strong scent, and set off in pursuit. If they lose the scent, and have to start searching around to pick it up again, they're said to be 'casting'.

All the time the huntsman must keep his pack in sight and together. He does this with his voice – knowing every hound by name and calling instructions to them individually, and also by the hunting horn. Some huntsmen have their own code of messages which they pass on to hunt servants or the master via the horn – like a jungle telegraph. But on the whole, riders should be familiar with five main calls.

The huntsman will repeat a long, single note while hounds are drawing or casting so that they'll know where he is, and not get lost. When they find, he'll let the field know by 'doubling' on the horn – blowing a continuous 'ripple' with the single note of the instrument. 'Gone away' says that the hounds have picked up a fox scent and taken off at speed. It beats out a rhythmic semaphore of a sharp one-two-three and longer one – two, and is a signal for the field to follow hounds. 'Gone to ground' sounds like a low rattle and tells the field that the fox has gone to ground and that everyone can relax for a while.

'Going home' is as you'd expect, a long, single mournful note and signals to the field that the day's hunting is over and everyone can go home. You don't, of course, have to stay all day. You can leave the hunting field when you like – but it's polite to find the master or the field master before you leave to thank them for your day's hunting.

Caring for your horse
If you do stay the course, remember to hop off your horse and loosen the girth whenever there's a long pause in the proceedings. This will rest the horse and help to keep it fresh throughout the day.

If hounds do find, and kill, the chances of you being on the spot are very rare indeed, and whatever you may have heard about 'blooding', the ritual of rubbing a new member's face with blood from the fox, it simply doesn't happen nowadays. Some masters might agree if a rider was particularly insistent – but it's not a regular feature of modern hunting.

Once the fox has been killed, the huntsman will remove the mask (the head), and the brush (the tail), and the four pads (the feet). These can be awarded by the master as trophies to those who have distinguished themselves by their riding throughout the day – and are much prized.

When your day's hunting is over, and you return to the stable your first priority must be the horse. It must be dried off, rugged up, fed, watered and made comfortable for the night. Then you can see to yourself!

13 Riding for the Disabled

Because riding is generally accepted as being an energetic sport,
it's easy for most people to assume that it's something to be
taken on only by the hale and hearty. But that's not strictly true.

One of the most exciting, and rewarding, developments in the
riding world over the past thirty years has been in riding for the
disabled – both children and adults.

Because a horse is a living, breathing creature, it can become
the eyes of the blind, the ears of the deaf, and the legs of the
physically disabled.

In the early 1920s one or two orthopaedic pioneers were
introducing riding as a physical and mental therapy to men
whose minds and bodies had been savaged by the First World
War. In the 1950s efforts to help victims of the polio epidemics
of that time, were given a tremendous boost when Madame Lis
Hartel of Denmark won the silver medal for dressage in the 1952
and 1956 Olympic Games. She was partially paralysed in both
legs after an attack of polio and could only walk a few steps, with
the aid of crutches.

After that, riding as therapy grew rapidly. At first, there were
just eight groups in Britain where the skill and theory of riding
instructors, doctors and physiotherapists were put into practice.
By 1969, it had grown to eighty. It was then that the Riding for
the Disabled Association (R.D.A.) was formed, and now, ten
years later, there are nearly 500 groups in the British Isles, with
similar work being done in almost every country throughout the
world.

The horses are carefully chosen so that they won't do anything
unpredictable or startling to frighten a disabled or handicapped
rider. Special saddles have been developed to help riders who
find it difficult to balance or grip. Games and exercises make
each session more interesting and stimulating, but are carefully
geared to strengthen muscles, make immobile joints work and
improve coordination. Every rider has one, sometimes two,
helpers running beside the horse to give moral as well as
physical support to those who need it.

In 1976 I was made a national vice-president of the
Association. I'd known of their work for sometime, but it
wasn't until I started visiting groups in various parts of the
country, that I realized what a marvellous 'medical machine' the
horse is.

If you've ever sat on a horse you'll know that as soon as the
horse starts to move, you move. Your arms follow the action of
the head through the reins, your back pivots backwards and
forwards with the movement from the horse's hindquarters.
You need to flex and grip with your leg muscles to stay on, and
sooner or later you find yourself talking to the horse. Everyone
of these actions, when applied to the disabled rider, becomes an
extension of whatever therapy they may be receiving from a
specialist.

For instance, some of the mentally handicapped find it

141

difficult to communicate with other people. Autistic children particularly can withdraw into their own private, silent world and refuse to talk to anyone. I recently met a little girl in Cornwall who had done just that. After a few weeks at a riding group she began to talk to her pony. Quietly and secretly at first, until eventually the pony got a complete run-down on everything she'd done that week – though none of the 'humans' got a word out of her. She's now started talking, just occasionally, to one of the instructors.

The R.D.A. don't ever claim to work miracles, but they do have quite a few minor triumphs. Like the young army officer caught in the blast of a bomb in Northern Ireland. He was left disfigured, partially maimed, and a shuffling, withdrawn shadow of his former self. Once he sits on a horse, his self-confidence comes flooding back. And the remarkable sixty-year-old former G.P. who was paralysed down his left side by a stroke, and now gives riding demonstrations for the R.D.A. His left shoulder is completely immobile, but to keep it working he wears a special glove that is attached to the reins. The constant action of the horse's head ensures that his shoulder and arm are being exercised for about an hour. No physiotherapist would work that long on one joint. 'And besides', he says 'riding is much more fun.'

That's really the key to much of the R.D.A.'s success. Go to any group, especially one where the riders are children, and the noise you'll hear above the sound of the instructor's voice is that

142

of laughter. Whatever the medical benefits and improvements that become visible to their teachers and doctors, the children, for the most part, will be quite happy to progress from the walk, to trot and canter, with perhaps a small jump over cavalletti – as long as they go on having fun. Though for some, riding has become much more of a challenge. A seventeen-year-old boy who was born without legs, developed such perfect balance in the saddle that he started taking part in dressage competitions. A girl born without arms goes hunting regularly, does dressage and show-jumping, by controlling the reins with her feet, in the stirrups. An American soldier who lost both legs in Vietnam, now runs an Arabian Stud in California, though before the war he'd never sat on a horse in his life. And I recently met a young blind woman who had ridden round a show-jumping course with the jumps at 3 ft 6 in (1.07 m) – She put her faith in the horse, and listened to every detailed instruction from her teacher. She admitted that if she'd been able to see the height of the fences she probably wouldn't have had the nerve to jump, but that takes nothing away from her courage.

Riding isn't just about galloping over the countryside at breakneck speed and leaping over fences. As much as anything, it's about building a relationship with another living creature, and enjoying the freedom and mobility offered by that animal's strength, four legs and independent brain. It may be more difficult for the disabled to take advantage of those freedoms – but it isn't impossible.

14 Careers with Horses

It's not unusual to hear people who enjoy a once-a-week contact with horses and riding and the great outdoors say, 'I wouldn't mind doing this for a living.' Certainly, from a casual involvement it can look like an ideal life. But I know of no one who has ever made a fortune out of horses, a few who make a comfortable income, but many who just make a living wage.

Horses are expensive to buy, feed, clothe and house. They demand round-the-clock attention, whatever the weather, and in pure business terms, give a very low return for an enormous outlay. Which is presumably why very few people who work with horses are in it for the money. Most accept that working with animals, doing a job they love, in the open air, is, in the long term, worth more than a flash salary. And if those are your criteria when looking for a job there are endless possibilities and these are just a few.

Instructors

To become a *riding instructor* you need to pass the professional examinations set by the British Horse Society. The first of these is the Assistant Instructors Certificate. The minimum age for taking the test is $17\frac{1}{2}$ and candidates must have G.C.E. O level grade A, B, or C, or C.S.E. grade 1 in four subjects, including either English language, English literature or spoken English. That qualification will enable you to work as an assistant at a stable or riding school. To become a teacher in your own right you need to go on to take the Intermediate Instructors Certificate, the Intermediate Teaching Certificate, and then the B.H.S. Instructors Certificate. The apprenticeship has to be served at an officially recognized B.H.S. riding school, and the test taken at a B.H.S. examination centre.

Young people going into a stable straight from school are unlikely to earn a great deal of money, and in cases of real need some local education authorities will make discretionary grants. But grant aid is not easy to get, so check well in advance of leaving school whether or not your own local education authority has the funds.

For mature students – those who've left school for more than three years, and intend to make a complete change in their careers by working with horses – there is a Training Opportunities Scheme run by the Training Services Agency. This enables a student to receive a grant covering six months training at a B.H.S. centre before taking one of the instructors' examinations.

The British Horse Society have a full-time careers officer at their headquarters in Kenilworth, and have produced a booklet called *Training for a Career with Horses* which gives full details of grant aid schemes, and the standards and qualifications required for each stage of the instructors' certificates, plus lots of other useful information.

Opposite above: Schooling a horse on the lunge at the National Equestrian Centre, Stoneleigh

Opposite below: Six magnificent teams of working shires in full regalia at the Horse of the Year Show

The racing game

For many young people the prospect of working with elegant, expensive racehorses suggests a glamorous life. For some it may be – for most it's just darn hard work. Any boy or girl over sixteen and weighing less than 7 stone 7 lb (47.6 kg) can apply for a job as an apprentice jockey. Those weighing up to 9 stone (57.2 kg) would be taken on as stable hands. Part of every day in a racing yard certainly is spent exercising the horses in your care, but most of it is taken up with mucking out, grooming, cleaning tack and feeding. However, if you are convinced that the turf is the life for you, the Jockey Club Registry Office at 42 Portman Square, London W1H 0EN, will let you have the names and addresses of registered trainers, and details of apprenticeships.

Heavy horses

There are a few farms in Britain where horses are still used on the land. But there the major qualification would be one in agriculture, not horsemanship. A number of breweries still find horse-drawn wagons much cheaper to run than lorries, and expect their draymen to know as much about horse management, care and driving (not to mention cleaning the harness and brasses), as they do about loading barrels of beer. The Brewers Society at 42 Portman Square, London, W1H 0BB or the Shire Horse Society at the East of England Show Ground, Oundle Road, Alwalton, Peterborough PE2 0XE, can let you have relevant names and addresses.

The police have mounted divisions for men and women in the Metropolitan and some provincial divisions. Any police station can let you have the relevant career leaflet.

A hunting stable will keep anything from three to forty horses, depending on the size of the hunt, and number of days in a week that the hounds are out. *Baily's Hunting Directory* has the name and address of every pack in the country, but jobs are few and far between, so persistence and patience are essential qualifications.

And there is always the Cavalry! Any Army Careers Office will be able to tell you how to join the battalions of the British Army that are still mounted: the Kings Troop Royal Horse Artillery, the Coldstream Guards and the Life Guards.

Horse management and business studies

There are a few courses available at technical colleges in Britain that deal specifically with the commercial aspects of running a stable or equine establishment. They are aimed at people who want either to run a yard of their own, or to work for a major business concern, where understanding land management, staffing and accountancy are as important as riding itself.

The Warwickshire College of Agriculture at Moreton Hall, Moreton Morrell, Warwick, CV35 9BL, and West Oxfordshire Technical College, Holloway Road, Witney, Oxfordshire OX8 7EE, can let you have details of their year-long syllabus.

Just working with horses

A lot of people don't want the bother of studying for qualifications and official titles. They just want to be able to work with and look after horses. The situations vacant column of the *Horse and Hound* magazine, or, if you live in the country, your local county newspaper, can provide no end of opportunities for just that sort of work. Breeding establishments, riding schools, show-jumpers, and farmers who keep horses as part of their stock, are always advertising for stable hands and grooms. But experience, good references and a willingness to learn are essential.

There are also a number of opportunities to work with horses on a part-time, unpaid, or voluntary basis. Many stables welcome people who want to help with the chores at week-ends in return for free riding and lessons. Organizations like the Riding for the Disabled Association depend on volunteers who are prepared to help with grooming and feeding the horses, and, most importantly, to walk beside the horses to steady them, and their disabled riders.

Every year the B.H.S. receive over ten thousand letters asking about job opportunities in the horse world. The Worshipful Company of Farriers, and the Society of Master Saddlers are over-subscribed with people wanting to serve a craft apprenticeship. And the youngsters itching to become champion jockeys are legion.

Horses may have been replaced on the farm and the roads by tractors, cars and lorries, but as a source of leisure they are on the increase. And as the interest in horses and riding expands, so do the opportunities for working with them.

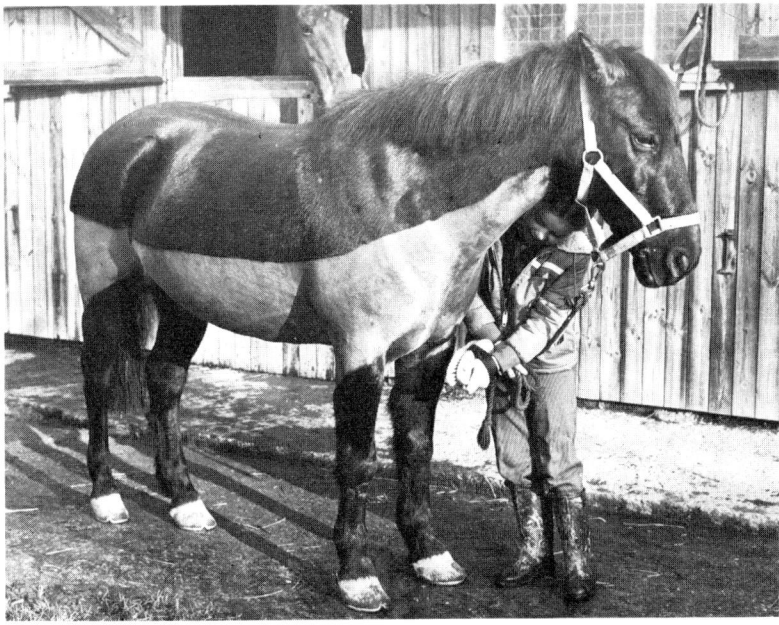

15 *A Horse of Your Own*

I suppose that sooner or later everyone who rides regularly at week-ends, and gets more and more involved in the horse scene, is going to think about the possibility of owning their own horse. Fortunately, most stop there at just thinking about it. For there's a world of difference between turning up at the stable when the horse has been fed, watered, groomed and saddled up ready for you, and doing the whole lot yourself. The determined converts are usually blind to the practicalities – seeing only the prospect of endless riding when and where they choose.

In reality it isn't quite like that, so, for once, let me be the voice of caution.

The first thing to remember is that horses are expensive, both in time and money. If you aren't prepared to spend at least five times the amount you devote to 'hobby' week-end riding – forget it.

Where to keep it

Before you even begin to look at what sort of horse you might like, consider how and where you're going to keep it.

The easiest, least difficult and least time-consuming way is to put the horse straight into a livery stable, where qualified people will see to the feeding, grooming, tack-cleaning and general well-being of the horse. As the owner, you can get involved as little, or as much, as you like, and even if you don't know the first thing about stable management or equine care, your horse won't suffer as the result. Your pocket will, though, as this is undoubtedly the most expensive way of keeping a horse, with fees ranging, at the time of writing, from £18 as an absolute minimum, to around £35 or £40 (or even more) for an establishment where an indoor school, show jumps, cross-country fences and so on are included in the facilities.

In some livery yards, the horse owners have an arrangement with the proprietor whereby they allow their horses to be ridden by other people and have a percentage of the income earned by the horse deducted from the weekly keep. It can cut the cost of ownership, but it does increase the risk of the horse being 'spoiled' by inexperienced or bad riders. The owner has to decide whether the risk is worth taking.

If you're going to stable the horse yourself you must have some open land on which to turn the horse out on days when it isn't ridden, somewhere to dispose of the soiled bedding, and enough *time* to feed the horse three times a day, groom it, muck out the stable, 'dress' the horse in rugs (when needed in winter) and stable bandages, and clean the tack, not to mention finding anything up to an hour for daily schooling or hacking to keep the animal fit and supple.

If you can regard your own time and labour as 'free' then your costs, when compared to a full livery charge, are limited to bedding and feed.

Bedding and feed costs vary enormously depending on the

A horse box gives you the freedom to travel, but it's one of the extra expenses size of your animal, and the amount of work it's being asked to do (obviously a horse or pony that hunts regularly or is taking part in jumping competitions is going to need a greater intake of energy foods than one who does fairly light hacking duties). It is almost impossible to pin any corn merchant down on 'average' prices because bedding straw and hay can vary dramatically in price depending on the time of year, supply and demand, and whether or not you collect the stuff or have it delivered. So at one end of a good year you might be able to buy hay at £35 a tonne, but a long wet winter, and short supply of feed stuffs could send the price up to £90 a tonne. Pony cubes, oats, corn and other supplementary foods also vary slightly in price, but over a year you can reckon on a stabled horse eating its way through about £10 to £15 worth of food a week.

At the other end of the scale, the cheapest way to keep a horse is out at grass. This means not bringing it into a stable at night, but letting it live in the open all the year round. The area available to you should be not less than 4 acres (1.6 ha), preferably made up of two or three separate fields so that you can move the animal around from one location to another. This way the ground won't be over-grazed and, in the winter particularly, the ground won't be churned into a mud-bath.

It will also help if you can put the horse into a field where sheep or cattle are grazing as this helps to keep the ground clear of worms and parasites. I won't go into detail to explain the technicalities of the 'worm cycle', as it's called – if you really want to know the mysteries of that particular miracle of nature you'll find it in any veterinary handbook. Suffice to say that multi-grazing keeps the grass sweet, and provides better grazing.

Don't think that you can work a horse and expect it to live on grass and nothing else – it can't. Grass will fatten a horse up, but the muscles will remain slack. To give a horse stamina you have to feed it 'hard' foods – especially in the winter – and that means supplementing the diet with sugar-beet, barley, bran and possibly oats. Although you're not going to stable the horse, you must provide it with some sort of shelter where the animal can get out of the wind – at best a barn or lean-to or, at least a stout hedge. Some breeds are so hardy and tough they seem impervious to anything the elements throw at them. Their thick, woolly, winter coats can shed rain and keep out the wind, but when wind and rain combine allowing the cold and wet to get through to the skin then they do suffer. Finally the field must also have a constant supply of fresh water – unless, that is, you're prepared to keep running backwards and forwards with buckets!

As you'll have gathered, there's much more to feeding a horse than just sticking it in a field and letting it eat its head off. Feeding is a complex and important part of horse management. If you don't know how to go about it – find out by asking your

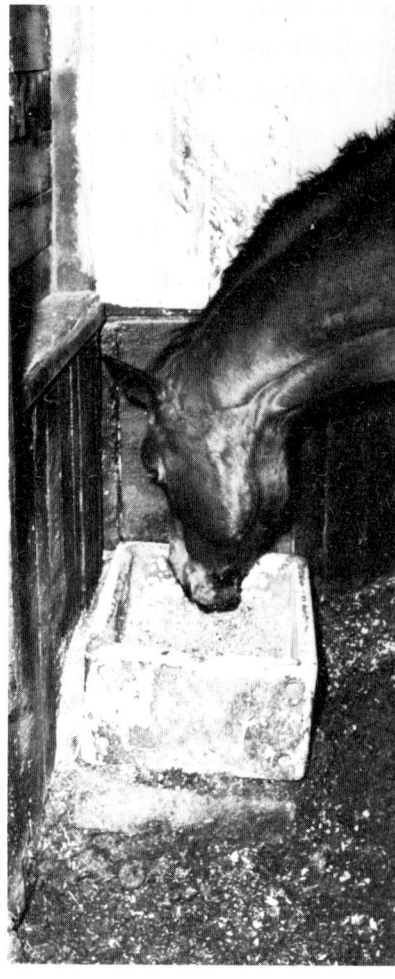

The activity Kate enjoys most: eating. Usually conducted on three legs with the fourth digging a huge pit in the stable floor

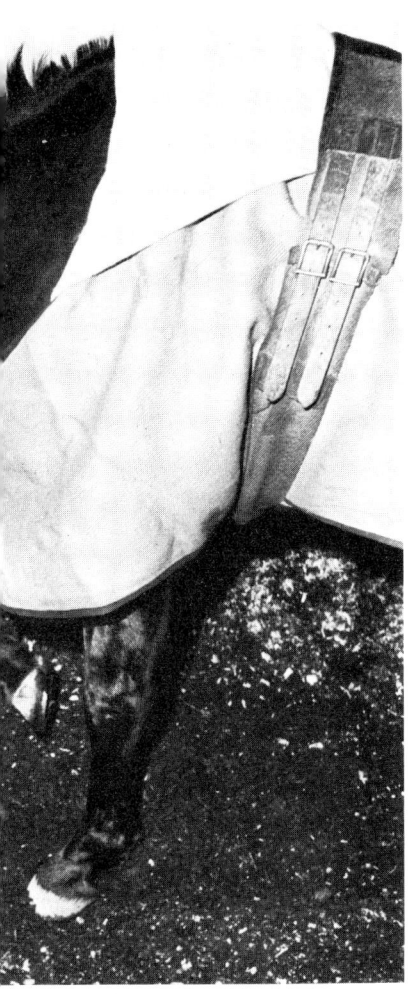

vet or instructor. Some things in the horse world you can pick up as you go along – feeding isn't one of them. And the next time you see a poor, ribby, half-starved horse, remember, there's as much cruelty caused by ignorance as ever there was by brute force!

Don't be afraid to ask for help or advice. Even if you think you're doing things properly, while you're still learning it will pay to get someone experienced to check your routine and methods occasionally just in case you're doing something wrong that you're not aware of.

More expenses

Whichever way you decide to keep your horse, and the supply of grazing land and livery stables may be as much of a deciding factor as the money involved, there are other, constant costs that can't be cheese-pared.

You may be able to keep the total down to about £15 to £20 a week by doing much of the work yourself, but even that doesn't give a realistic picture of the total financial outlay involved. Regular shoeing, insurance and vets' bills will all add to the overall weekly cost.

When you hire a horse, you hire the lot – horse, saddle and bridle. Until you walk into a saddlery and pick up a few price tags you're unlikely to have any idea of the sort of money invested in all that gear.

A saddle can cost anything from £100 if it's second-hand, to £300 if it's new. The girth, stirrup leathers and stirrup irons are all bought separately: they are not included in the saddle price. An English leather bridle starts at about £16. Sometimes the reins have to be bought separately, and the bit is always extra.

Don't ever be palmed off by someone trying to sell you second-hand or inexpensive saddlery claiming that it's a bargain. It may well be, but it could just as well be rubbish. So always get someone who's independent, and really knows what to look for, to help and advise you. Any saddler worth his salt will let you either take a saddle on approval, to make sure that it fits you and the horse, or come to the stable with a selection for you to try.

So now you have a saddle and bridle – but those are just the basics – the spending hasn't stopped yet.

A sweat rug is a good buy (though you could make do with a layer of straw under sacking). Depending on whether you keep the horse in or out, you'll probably also need one or more of: a night rug, stable blankets, a day rug or a New Zealand rug. A quick look at Chapter 9 will also show that depending on your horse and what you intend to do with it, you could run up a sizeable bill buying 'extras' like brushing boots, knee pads, exercise bandages, stable bandages, travelling bandages, tail bandages, protector pads for travelling and so on. I won't quote prices, because they vary dramatically depending on the quantity and quality of the items you buy. But you don't need a degree in mathematics to realize that we're talking about a lot of money. And don't forget that while you just ride the horse for pleasure in the vicinity of the stable it's only going to cost you the replacement value of worn-out shoes. As soon as you start thinking about entering shows, gymkhanas, hunter trials and the like you're probably going to have to add to that list transportation to the site, either in someone else's lorry (minimum cost of a shared journey £5) or your own horse trailer (anything from £300 to £1,100), entry fees, clipping charges, and possibly B.H.S. or B.S.J.A. registration fees.

And if we're really going to be practical we can't forget the cost of a wheelbarrow, grooming kit, tack-cleaning kit, stable brushes, forks, shovels and buckets.

All this – and you haven't even got the horse yet!

What kind of horse?

If you have weighed up what's involved, and you're still determined to go ahead, next – catch your horse.

Start by taking advice on the sort of animal that's going to suit you.

It's no good being stuck with a breedy, fiery thoroughbred if all you want to do is plonk around the lanes at week-ends, any more than a safe steady plodding cob will suit the rider who has aspirations to compete in one-day events and hunter trials.

Enlist the help of either your instructor or someone from your regular riding stable. If they know your capabilities and potential as a rider they'll be in an ideal position to advise you on the sort of horse to look for – they might even be prepared to go with you to look at likely buys.

There are no hard-and-fast rules about types, but a few basic things to remember are these.

Ponies are never more than 14 hands 2 in (1.47 m) high. A hand is a measurement of four inches, so 14 hands 2 in – which can be written as 14.2 hh ('hands high') means fourteen sets of four inches, plus two inches. Horses and ponies are measured without shoes from the base of the hoof to the tip of the wither – the highest point just in front of the saddle. If the animal is wearing shoes, you have to make an allowance of $\frac{1}{2}$ inch (10 mm). Any horse that has a 'life certificate' is one that has been measured at an age when it's stopped growing, and has a certificate which establishes its height for the rest of its life. The certificate is not very important if all you want to do is ride the pony for pleasure, but it is essential if you decide to start entering the horse or pony in measured showing classes.

Ponies *can* be ridden by adults, but just by looking at them you can see that they have a height and weight limit – so they're a better buy for children and youngsters than grown-ups.

A *cob* type is a stocky, sturdy animal. They're rarely bigger than 15 hands 3 in (1.60 m) but have a tremendous capacity for carrying weight. They're a hardy bunch and would be ideal for the owner who wanted to keep his animal 'out' rather than face the expense of stabling.

A *half-* or *three-quarter-bred* horse is an animal that has half or three-quarter-thoroughbred breeding from its sire (father) with the rest – probably cob – from its dam (mother). You rarely see a horse advertised as half- or three-quarter-bred – it would probably say 'good jumper' or 'has hunter trial and eventing potential'. Indeed, most of Britain's top event horses are three-quarter-bred. It brings out the best qualities of stamina and temperament from both parents – but it does mean that the horse is less likely to stand up to the rigours of an outside existence. As soon as you have any thoroughbred breeding in a horse, you have an animal that has to be pampered – which means stabling.

A *thoroughbred* is an animal bred from the purest lines in the stud book on both the male and female sides – the Rolls-Royce if you like of the equine world. They're fine limbed, highly strung, and definitely not suited to the rigours of an English climate. Most thoroughbreds are reared for racing. I mention them only because many people dream of owning an ex-racehorse. It is possible – but it's not the ideal mount for a novice, and they will need expensive cosseting all their lives.

Now I admit that it may seem as though I've been pouring cold water on the whole idea of ownership by spending so much time talking about money and costs. But it is a *vital* consideration, and one that people too often minimize in their enthusiasm to buy. How much you can afford on 'keep' should be the first thing to consider in detail, because it's bound to influence the sort of animal that you'll eventually buy. And it doesn't matter how much you may fall in love with a particular horse, if you can't afford the money and time it's going to demand of you, it simply isn't worth going into debt – not for a hobby!

Where to buy
How you eventually find your horse is very much a matter of personal choice. The columns of a county newspaper are quite a good place to start, and by asking the newsagents you'll find out which day is the 'horse' day for the classifieds (in our area it is always Saturday, and includes notice for horse events, sales of tack and trailers, and lots of other useful information – it's also a good guide to local prices). Horse fairs are held regularly at market towns around the country, again the local paper will have details of dates and locations, and all the national horse magazines have columns of animals for sale.

For a first-time buyer, it is probably best to get something that has been recommended. In the horse world there is always someone who knows of someone else with a horse to sell. If it's

A Dartmoor pony

A cob

A thoroughbred

A half-bred

local to you, the chances are that you'll be able to see it in action at a local show, or find someone who has, and thereby get a fairly good idea of how it rides, and its potential.

Advertisements make all sorts of claims. That the animal is bomb-proof, quiet to shoe and box, good in traffic and an ideal first horse/pony. That may all be true, but as a first-time buyer you're a sitting target for the unscrupulous. So just in case, take someone with you who can cut through the compliments and see the real horse. Ideally, your adviser should be someone who has a higher standard of riding than you so that he can ride the animal to judge whether or not it's been properly trained and schooled to the level the owner claims. For instance, a horse advertised as an 'ideal first ride' but presented wearing a standing martingale and pelham, 'because he likes the sound of the chain jingling under his chin, dearie', might look fine to your untrained eye – but wouldn't fool an expert for a moment.

Don't be tempted to take the first horse you see – there will be others. If you're looking for a good partnership it's worth waiting to make the right choice.

Even when you do find what you want, don't rush into a purchase without considering certain basic safeguards.

Horse fairs and local livestock auctions are not particularly good hunting grounds for novices. There are rarely adequate facilities for trying out horses, and competition from the meat trade (a sad but inescapable fact) may inflate the price of some animals to their value on the hook as opposed to on the hoof.

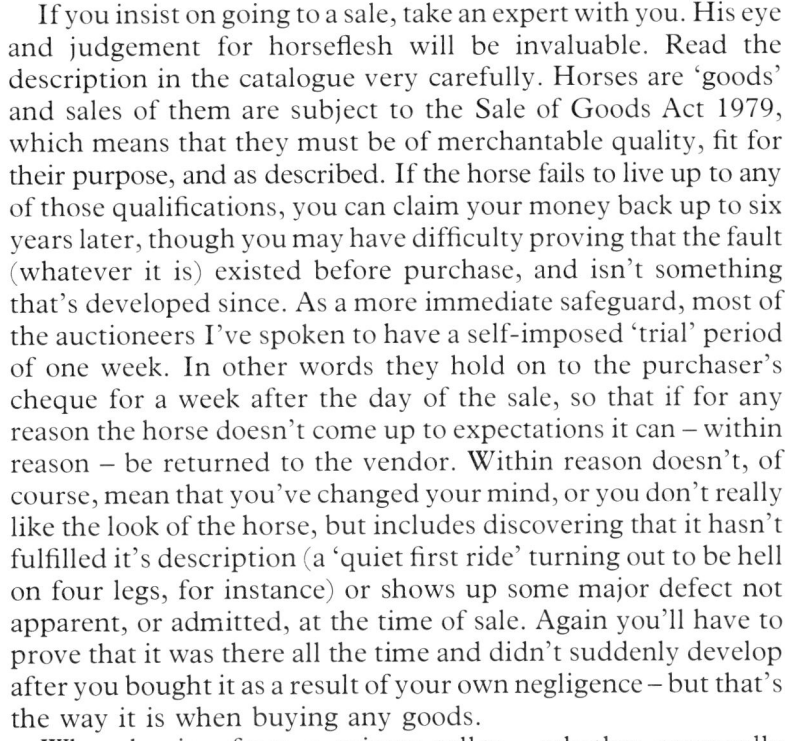

If you insist on going to a sale, take an expert with you. His eye and judgement for horseflesh will be invaluable. Read the description in the catalogue very carefully. Horses are 'goods' and sales of them are subject to the Sale of Goods Act 1979, which means that they must be of merchantable quality, fit for their purpose, and as described. If the horse fails to live up to any of those qualifications, you can claim your money back up to six years later, though you may have difficulty proving that the fault (whatever it is) existed before purchase, and isn't something that's developed since. As a more immediate safeguard, most of the auctioneers I've spoken to have a self-imposed 'trial' period of one week. In other words they hold on to the purchaser's cheque for a week after the day of the sale, so that if for any reason the horse doesn't come up to expectations it can – within reason – be returned to the vendor. Within reason doesn't, of course, mean that you've changed your mind, or you don't really like the look of the horse, but includes discovering that it hasn't fulfilled it's description (a 'quiet first ride' turning out to be hell on four legs, for instance) or shows up some major defect not apparent, or admitted, at the time of sale. Again you'll have to prove that it was there all the time and didn't suddenly develop after you bought it as a result of your own negligence – but that's the way it is when buying any goods.

When buying from a private seller – whether personally recommended, or gleaned from the classifieds – the Sale of Goods Act still applies. But unlike a 'business sale', a private seller is not required to supply something 'fit for its purpose', or even of 'merchantable quality', though it must be as described by the seller. Again, you can take the animal back up to six years later with your complaint, and proof, but there are less painful ways of horse-dealing for the first-time buyer.

Very occasionally a private seller will allow his horse out on a week's trial, but even when they aren't that generous, it should always be possible for a potential buyer, or someone experienced representing him, to ride a horse being offered for sale to see that it lives up to its description, and will be suitable.

You might get the vendor to agree to a post-dated cheque, giving you two or three days in which to try the horse at home, or the vendor may take a deposit with the balance payable within an agreed period of time. Someone who has nothing to hide will be happy to make the sale as uncomplicated as possible so that both parties end up satisfied. But don't forget that the honest vendor will want to make sure that you are an honest purchaser, so be prepared to provide proof of intent and ability to pay.

Finally, the golden rule is: always have the animal vetted. The vet will do a thorough medical check on the animal. Tell him what you intend to use the horse for – it's no good letting him think that the horse will just be trotting round the lanes when you intend to enter every hunter trial and event in the area. He will tell you whether or not the horse is medically and physically

157

suited to your needs. It doesn't matter how much you may have fallen for the animal – if it isn't sound, you're buying nothing but the privilege of keeping the vet in business, and yourself out of the saddle.

Or borrow

These days you can pay anything from £500 to £1,000 and beyond for a 'hobby' horse (not to be confused with the sort we see on the telly which cost more than a semi-detached). However, it is possible to have a horse for less. To start with, you can occasionally buy a good riding horse from one of the horse charities. Although most of them exist to rescue horses from slaughter and ill use and to allow them to live out their days in retirement, it is sometimes possible to buy a 'rescue' riding horse considerably cheaper than you might otherwise.

The charities always think of these arrangements as 'permanent loans' rather than sales, as they part with the horse on the strict understanding, that when you want to get rid of it, you return it to the charity. They will from time to time check that you're looking after it properly, and if they find you lacking the horse will be taken away. If you'd like more details of how the scheme works write to The R.S.P.C.A. at Manor House, The Causeway, Horsham, West Sussex (telephone Horsham 64181), the Horses' and Ponies' Protection Association at Greenbank Farm, Wheatley Lane Road, Burnley, Lancashire (telephone Nelson 65909) or the International League for the Protection of Horses at 67a Camden High Street, London NW1 (telephone 01–388 1449).

You might consider sharing a horse with someone. This can be a simple fifty-fifty arrangement with a friend (two is a comfortable number – more than that usually ends in squabbles). Together you buy and equip a horse and pay for its keep, in return for an equal share in the riding. But make sure that the 'equality' is carefully worked out, with plans for what happens when the animal goes lame and it's your day to ride – and so on. You may think that the quickest way to lose a friend is to go on holiday together – but you try sharing a horse. It calls for a very special kind of relationship! The other way of sharing involves sharing only the cost of the keep with someone who's already bought a horse and its tack, and simply needs help to meet the weekly livery bill.

It's also possible to have a horse on loan. You'll often see advertisements from people offering to 'lend' their horses for a limited period to someone who's prepared to take on the full responsibility of keep and exercise without getting involved in the massive outlay of actually buying a horse. Last, but not least, you can always offer to ride other people's horses. I have a friend who once put an ad in the local paper offering to exercise horses for people 'under pressure of time'. She got replies from a small-time racehorse trainer, parents whose daughter had gone off to university leaving a lively novice event horse, and a lady in the last months of pregnancy with a much loved pony who was getting nearly as fat as her, through lack of exercise. As a result, my friend got as much riding as she could cope with – and it was free!

Clubs for owners

So, you've taken the plunge and bought your horse; now what are you going to do with it?

Frankly, if your riding is going to be confined to going out on Sunday morning with the stable string, then you might as well not have bothered to go to the expense and trouble of buying a horse in the first place, but should have stayed as a paying customer.

Once you have your own horse, your aim should be to try to improve your own standards and those of the horse, and the best way of doing this is to join either the Pony Club (if you're under seventeen) or a riding club (for riders over seventeen). You can in fact join either organization even if you don't have a horse of your own, but can hire or borrow one, so it's not a bad idea to join one of the two clubs before you buy your own horse, as you'll learn much that will make life easier for you when you finally become an owner.

Paragraph 1 of the Pony Club Rule Book states the objects of the organization. They are, 'To encourage young people to ride and to learn to enjoy all kinds of sport connected with horses and riding; to provide instruction in riding and horsemastership and to instil in members the proper care of their animals; to promote the highest ideals of sportsmanship, citizenship and loyalty, thereby cultivating strength of character and self-discipline.'

I once heard a tiny tot wailing with disappointment at her mother, 'But he won't jump, mummy.' 'Don't worry, dear,' said the mother, 'Daddy will make him jump for you.' The mind boggles. Daddy of course couldn't 'make' the horse jump, but the Pony Club probably could have helped both the young rider and her horse to develop together.

As for riding clubs, well each branch is as different as the people that run them. But on the whole their activities include a list of things that will help any rider gain a better understanding of his horse, and of equestrian sport. They will organize various forms of riding instruction to cover most levels of competence, in all three disciplines. They have competitions, demonstrations,lectures, social events, and so on.

Both clubs have their headquarters at the National Equestrian Centre, Stoneleigh Park, Kenilworth, Warwickshire CV8 2LR (telephone Coventry 52241), and will be happy to send you details of membership, and your nearest branch.

You can, of course, exist quite happily without the bother of joining any kind of club. But you'll probably learn more, and get more fun out of your sport with them than without.

16 Some Horses I've Ridden

Kate and a country cousin: an
encounter on Dartmoor

Skippy

'Skippy by name – skippy by nature.' That's how I was
introduced to one of the first really exciting ponies I've ever
ridden and how I always think of him. I'd been riding for about
two years or so, mostly on safe, steady week-end plodders.
Skippy was something special. A small 14 hands 2 in (1.47 m),
grey gelding, he'd done some pony racing as a four-year-old and
had the reputation of being the fastest, nimblest horse in the
stable. Being allowed to ride him was a bit like being given a
proficiency certificate. He had the short, light, bouncy step of a
small racehorse, and the sight of a long open piece of moorland
was the signal for a flat-out gallop – and nothing less.

In a less well mannered horse it would have been a dangerous
tendency. But Skippy had perfect manners, coupled with a real
joy of being out in open country which made him a remarkable
and delightful week-end companion. His responses to the aids
for walk and trot were always sharp and willing, and no matter
how much his feet may have itched to eat up the turf on a
favourite long stretch, if you asked him to walk or trot instead,
he would do so ungrudgingly. But indicate by the slightest
movement of body or reins that you'd like to canter or gallop –
and he'd be off like a rocket. His line would be true, his footfall
strong and sure. He loved every stride.

Although the wind would whistle past my ears, and the
bushes merge into a streaky blur with the speed, I never once felt
unsafe or frightened on his back. You didn't have to ask for
speed or power – he just gave it with every fibre in his body. He
was enjoying himself, doing what he wanted to do most, and just
taking me along for the ride. Once we stopped you could feel the
satisfaction welling through his body. He didn't need words to
express himself – you just knew he was thinking, 'I *did* enjoy
that.'

Only once did we both come a cropper, when we rode, full tilt,
into a Dartmoor bog. Most bogs on the moor are well defined –
the moorland grass is a brighter green, a different texture to that
around it and the ground is spongy or soggy in the vicinity. But
at this one there were no warning signs. Indeed while Skippy
and I were sinking in the mire, my father and his horse were
standing just a few yards away on solid ground. It happened
very quickly, and very silently. One second we'd been cantering
over dry springy tussocks, the next we were swallowed up by the
ground – no splashing, no squelching of mud – just a shocked,
immobile silence, while we both took in what had happened.
Then I felt sick and Skippy panicked. The mud was up to his
stomach and he started plunging to get his front legs free. With
each burst of effort from the front, his hindquarters were
sinking lower and lower. Every time he moved I could hear the
mud sucking and rattling as he churned and dragged on his legs,
and I was convinced that the next noise I'd hear would be the
sickening crack of a bone. He made one enormous effort, almost

161

standing up right in the mud – I fell off backwards and started to sink. But Skippy had got his front end free. He thrashed out of the sticking cloying mud and his front feet hit solid ground. He heaved himself out, and dragged me with him as I'd had the sense to hang on to the reins. We were both plastered in slimy, black, freezing cold Dartmoor bog mud. I trotted him up and down to make sure he was sound – he was. So Father and I started rubbing him dry with handfuls of grass, to get the mud off, and keep his circulation going. I was shaking from head to foot, more from fear of what might have happened than from cold. We took the long road home at a steady walk, in case he had strained his legs, with the occasional trot to keep us both warm.

The next day Skippy was as right as rain, but I've never forgotten the experience. My father says the whole thing took less than fifteen seconds – if so, then fifteen seconds is a lifetime, as it remains in my mind as one of the most frightening things that's ever happened to me on a horse.

Skippy is quite an old gentleman now. His smooth grey coat is almost white, and very furry. His legs are a little stiff with age, and he takes life generally at a much more leisurely pace. I rode him regularly at week-ends for almost three years and together we discovered remote bits of Dartmoor, watched buzzards hunting, and saw at least one spring lamb born in the shelter of a rough granite boulder outcrop. I've ridden many horses since – some faster, many grander – but Skippy and I had a lot of fun together – and that makes him rather special.

Red Rum

I've lost count of the number of times people have asked me, 'What was it like to ride Red Rum?' And I know that the question is asked more out of affection and admiration for the Champ than it is out of curiosity for my own feelings.

Red Rum is a remarkable horse. Three times winner of the Grand National, subject of a biography, switcher-on of the Blackpool illuminations, opener of fêtes and supermarkets and generally much loved and respected all round.

Who but the British would make national heroes out of horses, and who but Red Rum is better equipped to cope with the fuss and adoration?

In 1978, after having won the National three times already, Rummy was back in training at Southport, and Ginger McCain was fairly confident that come 1 April, the horse would be lining up with the starters at Aintree.

A week before the race there were rumblings that Rummy had a bruised heel and his fitness was in doubt. Three days before the race I was sent up to the training stables at Southport to do a progress report for the Nine O'Clock News. 'Take your riding kit,' I was told. 'McCain has agreed to let you ride him.'

The McCain training yard is right in the middle of the seaside town of Southport, just a few yards from the railway line that slices through the town, and behind the forecourt where Ginger carries on his other business – dealing in second-hand cars.

There are no long rolling green downs or gallops as at Lambourn or Newmarket. Instead, when the tide goes out, it exposes miles of flat, hard sand – providing a newly washed, perfectly surfaced training ground twice a day. And the sea itself is like a giant, free swimming-pool, where the horses can 'paddle', and have any heat or swelling taken out of their legs by the cooling, pummelling action of the water.

This was where Red Rum had been nurtured – where his muscles were hardened, his legs strengthened to carry that huge heart around the most formidable steeplechase course in the world.

When I arrived at the stable his hind leg was bandaged. 'Ominous!' I asked. 'Not necessarily,' I was told. The plan was to give him light exercise on the sand, then a paddle through the breakers, to reduce the swelling. The day after he'd have a sharp gallop, and after that they'd know whether or not he'd be fit to run.

Rummy's stable lad, Billy Beardwood, saddled him up, and rode him in a string with other horses from the yard, out through the used cars, over the level crossing, through the town to the beach where a huge crowd of fans had gathered for a glimpse of the horse.

There was also a whole gang of press photographers, so while Billy rode the horse into the surf, the camera crew and I made for the far end of the beach in an attempt to do our film without too much of a crowd jostling around the camera and the horse. Red Rum came out of the surf – and the crowd came too – Billy hopped off, and Ginger gave me a leg-up into the saddle. My first impressions were that he was much smaller than I'd expected. I'd assumed there would be huge muscular shoulders and a thick powerful neck. In fact he was quite narrow across the withers and the neck was long and fine.

His head was held high – eyes alert and ears pricked as cameras clicked and cameramen shouted instructions. Neither Rummy nor I took much notice of them. He took them all in, his head moving in a steady arc from left to right, like an orator appraising his audience before launching into his speech. I was far too busy adjusting my stirrups and putting on my crash-helmet.

'Oh, Gawd,' said Billy Beardwood, 'she's got it on back to front.' He had a great affection for the horse, and quite obviously hated a lot of the fuss that went with looking after a 'personality'. And having someone who wasn't even a bona fide

jockey sitting on his back was the last straw – especially when she didn't put the crash-helmet on properly.

I readjusted the cap, picked up the reins, and turned the horse towards the relative quiet and privacy of the open sea. Visions of the old chap pounding around Aintree unchecked by the size of the fences or length of the course, meant that I was prepared to be tossed and jogged by a strong, impatient prima donna. In fact he was calm and responsive – a perfect gentleman. I could feel the strength and purpose in every stride, and regretted that I wouldn't be able to ride him at speed across the sand. Instead we walked and trotted. Rummy responded well to light hand and leg aids, stopping, turning, and going forward when asked, moving with the light springy action that makes a racehorse unlike any other. 'Is he always as calm as this?' I asked Billy, who'd remounted another horse and joined me in the surf. After the hat episode he wasn't letting me out of his sight with his precious Rummy for a second!

'He's a fantastic animal,' he said. 'He seems to know just when

he's going to need his maximum burst of energy. Until then he saves himself. He loves people, he loves all the fuss and attention, the crowds patting him and cheering him. He doesn't get at all upset by all this publicity lark – in fact he's got a lot more sense than some people I know.'

Rummy was a real pro. I delivered my report sitting on his back and walking towards the camera. He stopped on exactly the right mark, stood still while I dismounted, looked intelligently at the camera while I went on talking and whispered his 'tip' for the National in my ear right on cue. I had felt a strange lightheadedness, a mixture of excitement and apprehension, sitting on the back of one of the most famous and courageous horses in the world. He was obviously not at all impressed by *me* sitting on *his* back, or by anyone else for that matter. I got the distinct impression that Red Rum had worked out years ago who the real star of the show was – and he loved it.

He didn't run in the National that year, or ever again. His stable lad walked him down the course to say farewell to the punters and anyone who saw him on television couldn't fail to see the confusion and frustration in his whole body as he walked past the jumps and wasn't allowed to jump them.

I met him again some months later, at the Royal Agricultural Show where he was making a personality appearance. He was standing in the collecting ring with a whole crowd of show-jumpers waiting to make his entrance. I went across to give him the obligatory pat and peppermint sweet. Suddenly a whole crowd of hot-air balloons swooshed into the air and every horse in the place went bananas. Even the super-cool Rummy backed off and reared slightly at the unexpected and unfamiliar noise. But he calmed down and waited for another mint then stood right on my foot. I don't suppose for one minute that there's a sign on his saddle saying 'Angela Rippon sat here', but there's definitely a lump on my foot to which I can point and say, 'Red Rum stood there.'

Cornishman V

You may have already gathered in reading this book that I reserve the greatest admiration for the horses and riders involved in the three-day event. So when rider Mary Gordon-Watson offered to let me ride the legendary Cornishman V, I could hardly believe my luck. Cornishman V had the most humble of beginnings. He was bred on a Cornish farm out of a working mare called Polly. But he went on to be European champion in 1969, world champion in 1970, and winner of two Olympic gold medals in 1968 and 1972. When I first rode him in October of 1979 he was twenty years old and still had the sort of fire and exuberance that made him a testing ride.

On a previous occasion when I'd hoped to ride him I arrived at the stable to find him rugged up and munching on a hay net. Mary had ridden him out in Windsor Great Park that morning

Red Rum going past the winning post to win the 1977 Grand National

to 'quieten him down before you came', she said – but he'd taken off on a wild gallop so it was considered safer all round if he ate while I rode something else. So I admit to feeling slight trepidation as he was walked out of his stable that morning in October all saddled up and ready for me to ride. 'You'll be fine,' said Mary, reading my expression. 'I took him drag-hunting yesterday so he should be fairly subdued.'

No horse with such a distinguished international career is going to be taken in by a rank amateur, and as we sized each other up, I knew which half of the partnership reckoned it was going to be in control! He stands 17 hands (1.73 m) high – which is big. But then everything about Cornishman V is big. The size of his heart and his courage are beyond question. When he moves his long stride is full of grace and power as it eats up the ground, and looking along his neck and between his ears is a bit like looking down the bonnet of a Rolls-Royce. It's strong and beautiful and it doesn't half make you feel safe!

Working with him in an indoor school I went through one or two schooling exercises and pieces from a few dressage tests. To begin with he resisted. He'd already decided that I was a soft touch and wasn't going to ask him to work too hard, so he gave just as much as he wanted, and no more. To get the beautifully rounded shape, and lightness in step I knew he was capable of I had to work really hard and convince him that I *did* mean business. Eventually he was 'giving' to me and it was fantastic. We floated around the school, made beautiful bends, easy transitions from walk to trot to canter, and perfect, square halts.

It took only the lightest aid from leg or hand, the slightest shift in weight and balance for him to respond. I felt I would only have to think 'turn' and he would. After forty minutes we'd both had enough. Cornishman V is a marvellous schoolmaster, but to get the best out of *him* you must give the best of *yourself*. I was exhausted, and a horse that's proved himself the greatest in the world, become a national hero, not to mention the star of at least one full-length cinema film, doesn't want to be bothered at his age with a rider who's still wearing L-plates. I had worked hard and ridden as well as I knew how but Mary's verdict was that I had a stiff back, stiff arms, stiff wrists, and forward shoulders and was generally considered to be in need of some fairly concentrated tuition. In other words, *I* was rubbish – but the horse was great!

The Robber

Show-jumping in private, in the seclusion of the practice field behind the stables, is one thing. Doing it in public in front of a paying audience is something else.

Until 1976 I'd managed to keep my riding at a very private level, and very few people besides a few friends and regular week-end hacking companions, had ever seen me even sitting on a horse, let alone attempting to show-jump. In that year I'd been made a national vice-president of the Riding for the Disabled Association, and one morning received a phone call from fellow vice-president, Jimmy Hill. He'd been asked to get a team of four vice-presidents together to jump at a fund-raising effort to be held at the National Equestrian Centre at Stoneleigh. Jimmy had already recruited former jockey Richard Pitman, and Ann Moore had agreed to bring Psalm out of retirement for the day. So would I be the fourth member of the team. 'How big are the jumps Jim?' was all I wanted to know. 'Oh, nothing more than about three foot I should think.' Three foot was about my limit, so I said, 'Yes, I'd love to,' and got down to some serious jumping lessons with my trainer.

When we arrived at the Centre we walked past the warm-up paddock at the rear of the building and saw two whacking great fences of crossed and parallel poles. 'After you, Jim,' I said. 'No, after *you*', he said, and without saying as much we each assumed that the practice jumps were there for riders taking part in one of the advanced lessons being given at the school that week-end. We strode into the arena to walk the course – and were both stopped dead in our tracks. The fences were *enormous*. With hindsight, I'm sure they weren't really any bigger than about 3 ft 6 in, but they looked at least 4 ft 6 in. I walked from fence to fence working out strides and approach, trying to look as though I knew what I was doing, but every upright, parallel and spread made me think, 'What have I let myself in for?'

At which point, enter the horse. The Robber had been raced, hunted and show-jumped, and was being kindly loaned to me for the afternoon. When I sat on his back I thought he was the biggest, strongest thing I'd ever ridden. It took me several circuits of the practice ring to get the feel of his stride and spring before I felt I had enough confidence to go near the jumps. When I finally decided to risk it, he bounced over the poles like a rubber ball and threw me clean out of the saddle. Inexperienced as I was, I tried too hard to get his pace and my position absolutely right. It was a waste of time. That horse was such an expert that in the end I just headed him at the jump and left the rest to him.

I know that in really top-class show-jumping or equestrian sport of any kind, both halves of the partnership – horse and rider – have to be confident and competent, if they're going to be successful. But lower down the scale a good rider can make all the difference in the world to an inexperienced horse, and certainly I was about to prove that a really good horse would not only teach an inexperienced rider a great deal about jumping, but manage perfectly well on his own providing the jockey sat still and didn't interfere.

On The Robber's back I was jumping higher, wider and faster than I'd ever done in my life. He had all the skill and confidence I lacked, so by the time we rode into the main arena with the rest of the team I was ready to sit back and enjoy myself.

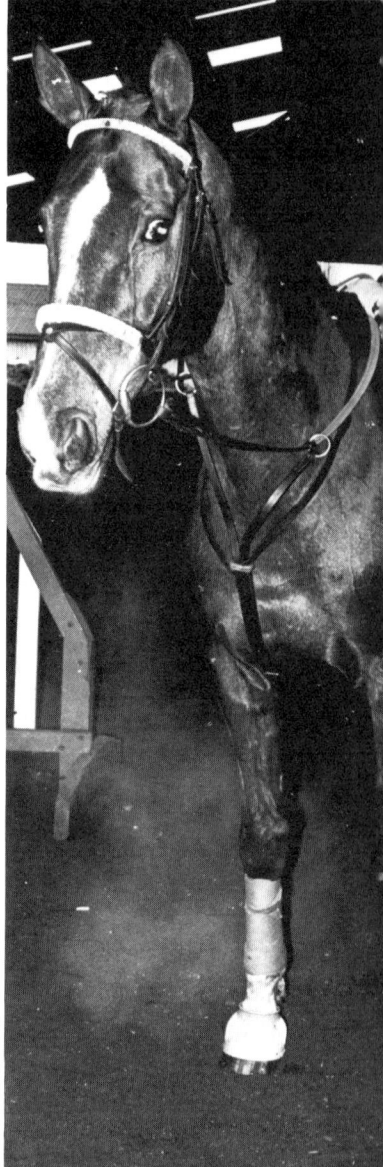

A leg-up on to The Robber from Jimmy Hill

There were twelve teams taking part, made up of local farmers, huntsmen, lady jockeys, local vets and so on. Each team rode a relay with the first rider completing the eight-fence course, then passing on a 'baton' – in this case a riding whip – to the next rider, and so on.

Jimmy Hill was the first to go. He rode clear, and passed the baton on to me. We pinged over the first two fences down the long left-hand side of the arena, turned right and cleared the two on the opposite side. Another right-hand turn took us in a figure-of-eight pattern across the centre of the arena, over another two fences, then left-hand down for the parallel and the wall across the centre – and the finish line.

Show-jumping is exhausting work – and half-way round I realized that I was no match for the powerhouse that was carrying me around the ring. The first four fences were fine, but as I went into number five I started to weaken. On the strides between five and six I gathered my wits and remembered that I'd have to make a sharp turn at the bottom after going over number six to get a good approach for the last two obstacles.

We were clear over number six, and as we landed I thought 'Turn', so the horse did – about two strides earlier than I'd expected. So he went left and I went straight on. I still don't remember how I stayed on. All I do remember is finding myself staring at the floor of the arena with my hand around his neck, my left leg somewhere up in the air, my hat skew-whiff over my eyes and an awful lot of shouting, laughing and screaming in the crowd.

As I've said before, ego is a wonderful self-preservative. I was determined not to fall off. My stomach muscles worked overtime and I heaved with arms and legs to right myself. And while I gave a public demonstration of very inadequate acrobatics, The Robber stood absolutely still. He didn't turn, walk backwards or fuss at all. He just waited until I'd stopped clambering all over him and, as soon as I got back into an upright position and pointed him at the fence, he took off almost from a standstill and cleared the poles with room to spare.

We popped over the wall at the end, and passed the baton to a relieved Richard Pitman. He had a refusal, which left Ann Moore and Psalm with the job of mopping up some of the precious seconds we'd wasted. Needless to say, Psalm leaped like a gazelle, turned on a sixpence, and recorded the fastest time of the day.

Later, Ann gave a demonstration round on Psalm, clearing a spread set at 5 ft 2 in (1.57 m). He made it look effortless, and left the little tots from the pony club agog with admiration. As for me – I'd jumped a clear round of eight fences at 3 ft 6 in (1.07 m). It may not sound much – but it took me nearly three years before I had the courage to jump that height again, which says a lot for The Robber – who had courage enough for both of us.

17 Kate

In 1970 when Chelsea and Leeds United were battling it out at Wembley for the winner's trophy in the Cup Final, a mare called Bold Venture, who'd been mated to the stallion Cintrist, stood in a stable in Sussex on the verge of giving birth to a foal. The full-time whistle went with the score at two all, and the game went into extra time. Chelsea were finally to win the Cup in a replay, while the mare delivered a beautiful bay filly foal called Extra Time.

She grew into a sleek, 15 hands 2 in (1.57 m) ladies' hunter and had a successful run of seasons in the show ring as a small hunter. But when I first clapped eyes on her in June 1978 she had a huge stomach, a concave back, her coat was dull and matted, and her tail and mane rubbed away to a mangy stubble. She looked a mess.

The beautiful Extra Time had been mated. The result was twins but unfortunately they were born dead. For a while she'd been quite ill, but when she recovered, her owner, Anne Sizmur, gave her time off, out in the fields on their Devon farm where she could relax and build up her strength. So when she was brought into the yard for me to see, her flabby muscles indicated that she'd been a lady of leisure for over a year, and judging from the state of her coat, her main delight for the last month had been to roll in every patch of mud she could find.

The mare was ready to start work again, but the Sizmurs already had a full complement of horses in training, so Extra Time would have to be got fit, schooled and worked by someone else. She was not for sale – they were too fond of her to part with her for good. What they proposed was that I should borrow her for three years.

While my riding instructor looked at her legs and back, prodded her sagging muscles and declared that she had marvellous potential, I stood at the front end with her head cupped in my hands. I·could feel the soft velvet of her muzzle and the warmth of her breath on my palms. I'm sure that gauging her potential was important, but I just knew that I liked her, and said yes to the deal without hesitation.

The plan was that we should get her fit and then start training her to jump. She'd never been near a jump of any kind in her life, so it would be a bit like taking on a newly broken four-year-old. The first thing we did on getting her back to the stables was stop calling·her Extra Time. That name would be brought out for special occasions and used on official entry forms for competitions, but in the stable and among the family she was Katie.

It was appropriate. What Katie did, and what Katie did next became familiar topics of conversation among friends and family. What Katie actually did was take life very easily for the first few weeks. She hadn't been ridden for nearly two years so we had to start by 'backing' her – that is just lying across her back gently until she got used to the sensation and balance of carrying a human body. Then we had her shod, and for the first

171

day she walked about with feet swinging, just like a baby who'd been introduced to real shoes for the first time after months of weightless woolly bootees.

Her training programme was strict. For the first few days she was walked gently for half an hour, then forty-five minutes, then an hour. She was taken up and down hills to strengthen her legs, build her muscles, and help improve her balance and coordination. Eventually we started to trot her, gently and just for a few minutes a day to start with, then building up to a steady constant rhythm. At the end of a month her coat was beginning to shine, her backbone and stomach had lifted as the muscles along her spine tightened up, and in the schooling ring she was showing a willingness to work and ability to learn.

Training to jump
Kate's introduction to jumping was a quiet affair. My instructor laid a set of coloured jumping poles on the ground leaving enough room for one stride between each pole. I walked Katie up the centre of the school and over the poles. She could have shied. She could have stopped and taken a good, suspicious look at them. But she didn't. She just kept on walking as if they weren't there. When I took her round the school again and asked her to trot over the poles, she picked her feet up and trotted through them perfectly without any fuss. It was a good sign, and I was delighted.

Slowly we introduced her to the low cavalletti poles and other small jumps, each a different colour and construction from the last. To begin with she just trotted over the fences. As she became more confident and eager to go, I'd leave her to break into a gentle canter for the last few strides into the jump and she would pop over without showing any of the fear that some young horses have of taking all four feet off the ground at once.

In the fields around the riding school there were a number of 'natural' jumps over ditches, hedges, tree trunks and rustic poles. As she got stronger, and more familiar with the demands of jumping in the school, we introduced her to the small, uncomplicated fences in open country. And she blossomed. She obviously decided that whatever had gone before had been a dull and boring waste of eight years. Introducing her to jumping was like taking the lid off a jack-in-the-box. It was all she wanted to do. Which was fine while jumping was what she was supposed to be doing but totally disruptive if I wanted to school her on the flat. The merest sight of a jump would get her excited and it would take ages to get her to concentrate. It was a good lesson in discipline for us both, but it took nearly a year for Katie to come to terms with the fact that schooling work must come first – pleasure later.

Her enjoyment of jumping was so obvious that I was completely unprepared for the first time she stopped dead on me. We were both learning together, and I suppose I thought that if I was prepared to tackle something a little bigger, or more complicated, then she would be too. It wasn't quite like that. She was beginning to put her trust in me, so when I gave only the slightest hint that I wasn't totally sure about a fence, she wouldn't jump. I had a lot to learn about jumping – even more to learn about schooling and understanding my horse. But gradually we started to work together, and by late summer I felt we had the beginnings of a real partnership.

Our first event
In October the local riding club was holding a two-day event. There was a class for novice horses and riders, and my instructor, Sue Armstrong, decided that it would be a good goal for us both to work towards. Because I worked for most of the week in London, I could only get down to Devon, and Kate, on two or three days a week at the most. At least an hour of every day at home was spent in the saddle, working on sections of the dressage test, improving our work over show-jumps and coping with bigger more complex obstacles on the cross-country course. And we did two small jumping and dressage tests to get us used to the atmosphere and discipline of a competition.

While I was working in London someone else would ride Kate, so her fitness wasn't a problem. Mine was. Riding a horse around a cross-country course is almost as much of a strain as running the course – you need plenty of muscle power and puff. I had very little of either. 'You're going to have to run,' said Sue. 'Twenty minutes every day to build up your muscles and your lungs.' That was fine while I was home. With acres of woodland and open moorland on our doorstep, and at least one dog that needed plenty of exercise, I could slot the run into my daily routine without too much difficulty. When I was in London it was more difficult. I'd read somewhere that Jane Bullen had trained for the Olympics when she was a nurse in London by running up to the roof of the hospital and doing 300 skips with a skipping-rope twice a day. Well I wasn't exactly training for the Olympics – but my husband Chris bought me a rope and I managed at least 100 skips a day in my dressing-room at Television Centre, and I took to walking up the six flights of stairs to our office, rather than riding in the lift.

We were having an extension built on our house that summer, and I'm sure that the builders thought I was mad. I'd disappear off through the woods with the dog every afternoon looking reasonably hale and hearty and return twenty minutes later scarlet in the face, dripping wet, and gasping for air like a fish out of water. Muffin, the dog, thought it was wonderful – *I* was beginning to have my doubts. But it paid off. By the end of September I was pale pink rather than scarlet, could hold a reasonable conversation within thirty seconds of my run, and the walk to the sixth floor didn't leave my legs quaking with fatigue.

October loomed, and on the first day of the two-day competition, various family and friends came with me for moral support, though I was so preoccupied I must have been a cheerless companion.

Katie was in high spirits. It was her first outing to a location with *hordes* of other horses, horse-boxes and people, and predictably she took ages to calm down. With horses all things are relative. By the time we had to perform our dressage test she was certainly calmer than she had been – but she had by no means reached that placid, responsive state that ensures total concentration. She was in fact explosive. There were two cross-country jumps between us and the warm-up area next to the dressage arena. She caught sight of them, crabbed sideways to have a better look, and spent the next two minutes arguing with me. *She* wanted to jump. *I* wanted to do a dressage test. The judges' hooter decided the issue, though as we entered the arena her ladyship was even prepared to argue the issue with the dressage judge as well. So instead of making a straight entry and a square halt, we did a sort of slalom down the centre line and stopped at a forty-five-degree angle.

We began the test. Kate grudgingly took the first bend and grumbled her way through the first few movements. I stiffened up like a ramrod. I was convinced that if I let go she'd be off like a rocket making for the first fence. On the canter she first struck off on the wrong leg, then overshot the arena. By the time we got to the last two movements, she'd decided to concede and do what *I* wanted to do. Her final perfect corner was too late. It was an abysmal demonstration of how not to ride a horse. Still, that's why we were here, for both of us to gain experience, and while the marks weren't good, at least we weren't bottom!

We set off for the show-jumping arena slightly less nervous than we had been at the start, and ready for experience number two. The course wasn't big. There was nothing there over 2 ft 6 in (0.76 m).

As long as we took things at a fairly steady pace and didn't worry too much about flashy style, we should be able to get round. The first fence was fine – the second an inelegant disaster. The crossed poles weren't high, but when I asked Kate to take off she said 'No way', put in another short stride and then leapt like a cat straight up in the air. I almost went right over her head, and on landing spent an uncomfortable few minutes getting back in the saddle and finding my stirrups. The next two fences were less dramatic. Then came the wall. It wasn't big but the approach was uphill into the face of a Bodmin Moor gale. She ducked out of the first approach, leaving me firmly in the saddle, and determined that we'd get over at the second attempt. We didn't. Not on the third go either – so the bell rang, and we were eliminated.

It was an awful long walk back to the horse lorry, and it took ages to unsaddle her, and re-dress her ready for the journey back to the stables some twenty-five miles away.

When I got home, I was so angry and disappointed at having failed that I couldn't stay in the house. I took the dog out for a walk, sat under a tree in the middle of a huge, empty field and had a good cry. They were tears of frustration more than anything. All that running, all that work and training for nothing. We'd been eliminated on day one before we'd even got to within sniffing distance of the cross-country – the one phase I'd really wanted to ride. So I was out of the competition. Frustration turned to resignation and I made alternative plans for the following day, and got ready to go out for dinner with friends. I might be miserable but I was also hungry. We locked up the house, took the car out of the garage, and I walked to the top of the drive to close the gates. As I pulled them to, I heard the phone ringing. 'Leave it,' I thought. 'No, it might be important.' So I ran back down the drive, unlocked the house and answered the phone. 'Are you happy about the cross-country course tomorrow?' It was Sue Armstrong. 'Oh, no,' I thought. 'She doesn't know I've been eliminated.'

'I'm not riding it,' I said. 'I'm out of the competition – hadn't you heard? We had three refusals at the wall.' 'That doesn't matter,' she said. 'You can still ride tomorrow. You can go *hors concours*. That means you ride, but the score doesn't count. It's the only way you'll ever get experience of a cross-country course, and if the riding clubs don't let you do it, no one else will.'

'But I haven't walked the course.'

'That's all right,' she said. 'Get there early tomorrow and I'll walk it with you and help you work out your route.'

It was like being given an injection of pure sunlight. I dashed back up the drive, fell into the car and said, 'I'm still riding tomorrow.' If our friends and my husband thought I was the most capricious and changeable female they'd ever met, they had the manners, and the good nature, not to mention it.

Our first cross-country
Walking my first cross-country course was a formidable experience. Nothing was very big, but obviously my experience of fences had been limited to those at the riding school. There were some here I'd never seen before, and they frightened the life out of me. The coffin was the first frightener. The approach was downhill with a pole in; then one stride, over a ditch, one stride, and out over another pole. Right after that, frightener number two, a Cornish bank, and towards the end of the course a jump up on to a bank with a brush fence on the other side. The coffin I decided to dodge through by missing the first pole, and taking just the ditch and the second fence. The final bank I would miss out altogether. But the Cornish bank in the middle

of the route *had* to be jumped – there was no other way round the course. Sue explained how I should ride at each fence, helped me decide on my line and approach, and did a marvellous job of boosting my courage. I had two hours before I had to set off on the first stage of the roads and tracks, so I settled down in the car for a sleep to 'ride' the course in my mind from the start to finish.

Kate was in fine fettle. When we set off on the first stage she was keen to get moving with the anticipation of something more interesting ahead than yesterday's boring dressage. The steeplechase course was the first major test. She'd never seen these big sloping brush fences before and three strides out I felt her check at the first and have a good hard look. Oh no – I thought – not today. So I kicked, urged her on, and we flew over. There were five fences, each to be jumped twice, and as we started on the second circuit there was a strong, confident pull to her stride. We met each fence perfectly, at speed and without any resistance. As we cantered towards the end of the second phase, and slowed down to a trot, I felt relief that we'd managed the first test without mishap – and Kate showed every sign of wanting to tackle anything I cared to face her at.

Schooling over a difficult combination with one stride between two rustic elements. It was a fence Kate hadn't seen before, and she was slightly apprehensive on the approach, which is why she is screwed in mid-air (below)

By the second attempt, she had gained confidence and rode through without a fault (right)

As it was we had now started on the third phase of the day, the long section of roads and tracks. We took a steady trot along lanes, over open moorland, and through a forestry plantation, where I was able to let her have a good canter to keep her on her toes, and ensure that we finished within the time allowance.

We got back to the start of the cross-country with time to spare in addition to the compulsory ten-minute stop, and that's when I started to feel nervous. It was stage fright, and cowardice, but I'd come this far and wasn't going back. Besides, Kate was raring to go – if I'd chickened out then she'd never have forgiven me.

Two minutes before the off I remounted and just walked quietly getting my nerves under control. The girl who was setting off before me looked green. 'Why do we do it?' she said, echoing my own feelings. The starter called me up to the line, explained that I must start from a standstill, and set his watch ready to count me down. Ten seconds to go. Then three, two, one – off. Kate leapt off the line like a racehorse and made straight for the first fence – a nice low inviting brush line. Three strides out she actually started to dodge about as if she was going to refuse. I couldn't believe it. 'Go on', I shouted, urging her forward with voice and legs – and she did. It's funny, but on at least three occasions since she's dodged and weaved her way into the first fence on a cross-country course, and I'm sure it's one of her 'confidence' tricks. She's putting me to the test before we start out on a really big course. She wants to know whether or not I mean business – when I make it clear that I *do*, she just keeps on going and rarely shows any sign of stopping.

But at that first fence, in our first competition, it was unnerving to say the least. Fence number two was a log pile – we were over that safely, then going downhill to the coffin, I dodged in through the side, over the ditch, scrambled out over the second pole, and careered off uphill to the left and the Cornish bank. I took a straight line in and a firm hold as Kate leapt on to the bank. For a split second she teetered on the edge as she realized that there wasn't solid ground ahead of her but a drop down of about 2 ft 6 in. Her speed and impulsion kept her going, and we landed safely on the other side. All the horrors I'd had about dropping off that fence were left behind as we headed downhill to a tiger trap and then a trakehner.

This was a pole over a ditch with a steep slope on the far bank. Kate got to the edge of the ditch – saw a gaping black hole in front of her, and stopped dead. I turned her and tried again – same response. I'd been eliminated the day before so I could go on having as many tries to get over the fence as I liked, but in my mind I'd decided to ride the course for real, so I had only one more attempt left. As she got to the edge I just kept pushing and pushing. Eventually she summoned up her courage and leapt from a standstill over the ditch, clear of the pole and on to the far bank. At the top of the slope there was another small rustic fence, the Helsinki steps, and after that a pole with a long steep slope behind it. A number of very good horses in the earlier classes had stopped dead here.

The fence was partly shaded by overhanging trees and they obviously didn't like the thought of jumping into a black hole. I wasn't risking another stop with Kate, so I shortened the reins, gathered her up, and willed her over the pole. She took it suspiciously, landed badly, and I fell off. But we were over the fence, and I took it as a psychological victory. After that we had the most marvellous ride. It was if Kate had suddenly realized what was going on. This wasn't just another training session over the same four or five fences, this was much more interesting. There were long gallops, and big jumps. She stopped being wary and hesitant, and started to enjoy herself, and so did I.

The course dropped downhill, through two fields and back over the coffin, which I took in full this time and bounced through without a fault. Then it swept away from the main spectator area over land which sloped gently uphill, and needed to be ridden carefully so that the horse didn't wear itself out coping with the gradient. At the top of the hill we took the easy, long route through a V fence, then turned right-handed and started back downhill to home.

We went clear over the bullfinch, the elephant trap and the lap fence. The piano wires was a tricky combination of poles with one or two strides in between. We didn't have the accuracy to do it in style – but we got through and were just two fences from home. In front of me was the bank I'd decided to miss out. For a second I wondered if I shouldn't try it after all. She was riding with such strength and confidence I was tempted to have a go.

But I'm a coward at heart, and decided to stick to my original plan so we dodged through the gate at the side of the fence, and bounced through the poles and brush that made the last obstacle.

I was exhausted and elated – I couldn't believe that I would have enjoyed it so much. After being screwed up with fear and tension just five minutes before, the way I felt now I'd be happy to ride round again. Kate looked pretty pleased with herself too. She'd done everything I'd asked of her – and more. We were both green raw beginners, but I think that in those five minutes we'd learned more about riding together than we had in the five weeks before.

A hunter trial

Two weeks later the Lamerton Hunt staged a hunter trial. There were twenty-two fences spread out over a fairly flat course, and flushed with our success in Cornwall, we drove the fifteen miles to the location feeling, not confident, but certainly less terrified than before.

After walking the course I knew there'd be two major problem areas. The first was the river. Kate hated getting her feet wet. There's never any shortage of water on Dartmoor and when I ride her over the moor I take every opportunity to walk her into and through the moorland streams and rivers. But she's crafty, and if she thinks she can clear the water by jumping it – rather than putting her toes in it – she will. Asking Kate to get her feet wet or muddy creates the atmosphere of disgust you'd expect from asking a fashionable lady in snow-white, suede Gucci boots to paddle in a slurry heap. She *loathes* it, and I doubt that I will ever totally cure her of it . . . though I'm still trying.

At Lamerton the water was shallow – but wide. I'd have to be firm, and ready to counter any attempt to run out. The second problem was a whacking great ditch towards the end of the course. It had a brush fence in front, and the horse probably wouldn't have even seen the gaping great hole until it was already in mid-air. But *I* knew it was there – and that was enough. I couldn't face the thought of jumping it, and decided to take the coward's way out by crossing a small wooden footbridge instead.

The course rode well. Kate minced about on the bank above the water, but she eventually went in, and rode the next eight fences with style and vigour. The course followed a large figure-of-eight pattern. At the half-way stage was an interesting combination of fences in a wood with a big solid steeplechase fence on the way in. It was wider and thicker than any Kate had ridden before. She attacked it boldly, but thought she had to bank it – that is jump on top, and then push off, as she had on the Cornish bank. As her left foot went in she realized it wasn't solid, and screwed in mid-air to leap clear. The force in her hindquarters threw me off balance, and I rolled in a messy heap over the top of her neck. I bounced on my bottom, and was laid out. The base of my spine had taken the full weight of my fall, and knocked the stuffing right out of me. I lay on the ground for ages just to get my breath back.

When I got back on again, my spine was tingling, but not hurting too much. We finished the course – missing out the ditch – without any further mishap, and I immediately paid my entrance money to go round again in the next class.

Here was an opportunity to practise over new jumps, and I couldn't waste it. Second time around the water was no problem. Kate has an extremely good memory, and between us we managed to right all the mistakes we'd made at the first attempt. We even cleared the steeplechase fence – properly this time. I finished the day thinking that if Kate had come this far and done this well in just five months then the coming year would be a real challenge to us both. She obviously had more than potential – she was rather special.

The following day she had a rest – and I could hardly walk. The base of my spine was so painful that moving was an effort, getting in and out of the car almost impossible, and standing up straight completely impossible. As the week wore on, either the pain decreased or I just got used to it. Either way, by the following Sunday I was walking the course in preparation for my final hunter trial of the season. There was nothing 'trappy' or particularly frightening. Most of the fences were well built and solid with a good clean approach line. Only the ski-jump gave me the collywobbles. It was built into the side of a bank, three railway sleepers high. You took off on a downhill slope and landed on a slope which meant that for a brief second you were flying through the air with the ground falling away beneath you.

The class before me was for the juniors. I watched those little mites popping over this fence on their 14 hands 2 in ponies and felt ashamed of myself – a grown woman, on a big horse scared stiff – and *they* were making nothing of it.

By the time the starter counted me down into the off, I'd gone through my usual attack of nerves and was ready for Kate to play up at the first fence. She obliged with her, by now usual, zigzag approach, but we cleared the first hurdle and settled into a strong steady pace with the whole of the course before us. By the third fence my back was showing signs of wear. As long as I could stay with my weight on my feet, and my body balanced over my knees, I was fine, but as soon as I sat in the saddle to start pushing, the pain jabbed up my spine. Kate sensed that I wasn't riding her with any strength or firmness, and grabbed her opportunity to prove who was really the strong member of the partnership.

She dodged out of a jump over a pile of logs, and there was nothing I could do to stop her. I was concentrating too hard on fending off the pain as my bones were jarred to the left. I used my crop on her flanks, just one sharp clip, and told her this was no time to muck about. We cleared the next two, and the ski-jump loomed over the next bank. We trotted up to it – she stopped, had a good look, and when I made our second approach popped over the top without hesitating. Going downhill was agony, but the small fence at the bottom was just a pole at ground level over a narrow ditch. It was such a small, inconsequential jump, the sort you can take on a cantering stride and not even know it's there.

Kate skidded to a halt, and with no power in my legs to hold on – I fell off yet again – and landed on my back. The fence judge helped me into the saddle – and I had another go. This time she completely demolished the fence so I turned her quickly hoping to jump the ditch – all two feet of it – while the pole was down.

But she wasn't having it, made a right hash of the approach, and I landed in a heap on the ground for the second time. I got back in the saddle, aching too much to want to argue, and ploughed on. Kate was having a marvellous time. She galloped on, leaping wildly over the next four obstacles, while I tried to persuade myself that if only I could get my back in a comfortable position on the saddle I'd be able to control her and salvage something from the shambles.

We reached a trakehner, a pole 2 ft 6 in high set at a forty-five-degree angle over a ditch. As we met the take-off point, she dodged to the right, flew the ditch and I capitulated. My back felt as if it was about to snap in half, and Kate was making the most of it. I went home sore, and chastened. A week and two visits to the osteopath later, friends gave me a back protector for my birthday – but that solved only part of the problem. Kate had proved herself to be a willing and capable pupil. When she jumped she was bold and accurate, she absorbed the tension and atmosphere of a competition and thrived on it. But she was also intelligent, crafty and full of spirit. As soon as she sensed that I wasn't asking her to give one hundred per cent, she simply wouldn't give it, and played the prima donna instead.

As for me, I still had so much to learn. The physical and technical side I could be taught – but the psychological side I had to work out for myself. Quite simply, big fences scared me, and at that stage anything over 2 ft 6 in was big.

When youngsters are learning to ride, or doing anything for that matter, they don't see danger. So by the time they reach their teens or early twenties, they've seen and jumped every combination of fence that's going, and as the obstacles get bigger they simply take them in their stride. But here I was at the ripe old age of thirty-three trying to cram into just a few months a set of experiences that others had accepted after a lifetime of familiarity. I saw dangers and problems at every fence that must have sounded silly to seasoned onlookers. But to me they were real, and until I'd sorted out my own confidence, I wasn't going to be much help to Kate.

More training

Throughout the winter we got back to basics. We worked on dressage movements, and entered a few indoor jumping competitions, at which she started winning rosettes. Nothing spectacular, a couple of thirds and fourths, which I took home and tied to the spaghetti jar. I didn't dare pin them up in her stable in case she ate them! For whatever else Kate had proved she was good at, the thing she did best of all was eat. I've never seen a horse consume so much food. Anything that looks even slightly palatable is sucked up like dust into a vacuum cleaner. She even started eating the straw in her bed – which is one reason why she's stabled on a deep litter of wood shavings. Whenever I go into her stable she always snuffles and rummages around my pockets and hands to see what titbits I've brought her. Carrots and mints are fine, but for a real treat she likes digestive or cheese-flavoured salty biscuits. She always curls her lip back and makes a funny face when she chews them – but she keeps coming back for more, so presumably it's an expression of pleasure.

The winter of 1978 was diabolical. Snow and ice clogged the roads and the ground froze rock hard so we couldn't get the horses out to be exercised. The nearest indoor school is fifteen miles away from where she's stabled, which would have been ideal if we could have got to it. But the roads were so slippery you could hardly walk down them, let alone drive a horse-box, so in desperation we laid old bedding straw in one corner of a field and just rode them round and round like circus ponies. It was boring but at least it got them moving and was better than being stuck in a stable for twenty-four hours.

Spring came late to Devon in 1979. It seemed for months as though every time I took Kate out for a ride we had to cope with pouring rain, biting winds or rock-hard ground. It must have been difficult for her to work out exactly who I was. Sometimes I'd manage to ride for four days with a break of just two or three and then be back again for a few more days. Other times I'd disappear for anything up to two weeks at a time, make a flying visit of one day, and then be absent again for three or four days. The only continuity she has even now is with Shirley, the girl who runs the livery stable, and attends to her every need, from grooming and rugging-up in the morning, to bedding-down for the night. Shirley is also the person who feeds her, so I'm afraid that I come a very poor second to her in popularity.

Despite all these problems through the long winter of 78/79 Kate and I came to know and understand each other. What conclusions she's come to about me I have no way of knowing, but I discovered her tantrums and tactics, her personality and charm. She'll suddenly decide she's had enough of practising a halt, or correct strike-off at the canter, and when asked to do it will thrash and lunge about, nostrils flaring, eyes staring, out of pure temper. She'll get herself all worked up, then calm down

Going down

An essential part of our training: getting Kate used to water

Right: A good confident leap over a wide ditch

Coming up

and go on as if nothing had happened. In the stable she makes a fuss whenever you fit or tighten a girth or surcingle, and when I'm fitting bandages or boots to her front legs she always turns her head towards me, and 'snuggles' into my neck with her soft nose. I grew to love her more and more, and as a bonus her work improved by leaps and bounds.

I'd set my sights on competing again in the riding club two-day event in October – it seemed an obvious yardstick for gauging our progress over a year. So as the weather warmed up, and the days grew longer we started to enter another round of riding club competitions, for what was called combined training – dressage and show-jumping. The first was a fiasco. Kate went back to her old game of trying to jump everything in sight before and during the dressage test, and we had marks ranging from two – which rates as bad – to four – insufficient.

The second outing was better – and we actually managed two sevens which carry the description 'fairly good'.

Rosettes for the spaghetti jar
On our third outing we tried a slightly more difficult dressage test and went back to scores of two and three, but in June we finally got it together. A girlfriend of mine, Wendy Jackson, who was more interested in dressage than jumping, had spent hours working with her on the flat while I was in London – and it paid off. She did a good test, went clear in the show-jumping, and brought home a rosette for second place. At last, I thought, we were getting somewhere. But though Kate's riding was improving, her condition wasn't. Although we kept pumping food into her she started to look thin and ribby. We called in the vet who said she was as fit as a fiddle – just bored. She needed a holiday. So in mid-July she was turned out into a field full of lush rye grass, where she could eat her head off for four weeks and not do a stroke of work.

Every day that I was home I went to see her, to feed her with bran and oats as a 'hard' food supplement to the grass, and to cover her with fly repellant as she was being bitten to death by the midges. She came out in a few lumps and bumps, but her tail was the real casualty. One day it was long and glossy, the next it looked like a well worn loo brush. She'd rubbed her bottom with such relish to relieve the itching and irritation of the flies, that she'd worn away the hair on one side of the dock – it looked awful and took nearly four months to grow.

On Thursday, 9 August, her holiday was over – with a vengeance. I now had to get her fit, harden up her muscles and strengthen up her legs ready for the autumn programme of one-day events and hunter trials. I worked to a carefully planned fitness routine. For the first four days we just walked for an hour a day, then for two days, an hour and a quarter. On day seven we introduced a little trotting, and over the next four days increased the work to an hour and a half.

On 19 August she cantered for the first time. After that we went back to the old routine of schooling, jumping, and hacking.

The rest had done her a power of good, and when I entered her in the restricted novice class of a one-day event on 26 August, just as a gentle warm-up for the season, she was raring to go. Her dressage was passable, but I made an error and was penalized. The show-jumping was accurate and clear but her cross-country was a revelation. She chewed up the ground with a strong impatient gallop and flew over the fences as if they weren't there. We took second place, and another rosette for the spaghetti jar.

She won her second rosette of the season just two weeks later. Before we even started, the day had a good feel about it. I'd walked the course, and came away feeling less shattered by the obstacles than at any time before. Right at the end of the cross-country phase were a set of double banks that worried me slightly, but apart from that the big problem was going to be the water jump. It had a small log in front, with about 4 ft of water beyond – none of it deeper than 10 in. Kate still loathed water – but I knew that if I could keep her going strongly into the fence, she'd be in the wet before she even realized it.

Warming up for the dressage test she felt calm and supple and from the second we went into the arena I knew that for once we were really working together. She responded well to each request for a change in movement. Her head came down as she relaxed on to the bit, and I knew that this time she was really concentrating. As we cantered on the left rein – disaster – she struck off with the wrong leg, but when I brought her back to the trot and asked her to canter again, she did it perfectly, without getting into a paddy. We finished the test, I saluted to the judge, and left the ring knowing that we had just ridden what was probably the best dressage test of our partnership. We weren't perfect – far from it – but we'd scored a series of fives, sixes and two sevens which put us in third place in an entry of over twenty horses.

She took a brick out of the wall in the show-jumping ring, but so did the horse who was lying equal third. So as we gathered in the collecting ring before the start of the cross-country, I began to feel, for the first time ever, a real sense of competition – and the cement mixer in my stomach started working overtime. I know that once I go over the finishing line I shall be excited and elated with the sheer relief of having got round, and I always try to convince myself to feel before I start, the way I *know* I'll feel when I've finished – but I can't.

Kate produced her usual dodging and weaving technique for the first fence, but got over safely and went strongly down hill into a bullfinch, and on to the water. I took up a firm contact, and kept pushing. With just one stride to go she saw the water and stopped. Her hooves were right up against the log – and I was urging her forward with such determination that she couldn't

The rosettes that Kate and I have won, now displayed on my spaghetti jar

185

back off. If she had put so much as one foot back we'd have been given a refusal. But she didn't. Instead she daintily picked up her right foot, lifted it over the log and prodded about in the water to find how deep it was, and if the ground underneath was solid. Once she'd planted it firmly on the ground I assumed that we'd gather momentum and be off. But no. Instead she picked up the left foot, and repeated the rather elegant performance so that eventually she stood with front legs in the water, hind legs on dry ground, and her body suspended over the log, while I continued to push, kick and shout, 'Stop mucking about, Kate.' Obviously convinced that it was safe to proceed she powered off through the water in a great show of spray, and headed off uphill towards the next fence.

The rest of the course was a high-speed blur of trees, marker posts and the occasional strong flight through the air over a fence, without even a hint of hesitation. At the end of the day we finished fourth. Our 'rivals' in third place had covered the cross-country course in a time that was three seconds less than ours. But the spaghetti jar had another colourful addition, and I had an even greater determination to get Kate over her phobia about water.

The two-day event again
The riding club two-day event that was my goal for the end of the season had shrunk to one day, and changed location to another farm high on Bodmin Moor. It was a pity that we wouldn't be able to put our year's work to the test over the same ground, but it was nevertheless a good marker – a point at which we could assess our progress as a team over twelve months.

Sunday, 30 September 1979, was a cold, miserable, damp day. I had to ride my dressage test at 10.52 a.m. so if I was to have enough time to prepare the horse, load her into the box, drive the thirty or so miles to the competition site, and still have about an hour in hand to settle and work her in, we would have to leave home at 7.30 a.m. 'We' being not just me and the horse, but what had become known as the Katie Lou Fan Club and consists of my mother, father and mother-in-law, and a few loyal friends. My father adores Kate and thinks she's the best thing that ever lived on four legs. He's chief groom and takes charge of getting her dressed, rubbing her down, and walking her to cool her off or stop her getting bored between rounds. Mother is chief groom's assistant, and rolls bandages, folds blankets, and generally keeps things in order. Mother-in-law is in charge of catering, supplying hot coffee, soup and egg pie throughout what can often be long and cold days on exposed and out-of-the-way farms.

As anyone who rides as an amateur will tell you, family and friends are invaluable if you can persuade them to lend a hand with the horse or just turn up to give moral support – and mine are great.

We arrived with time to spare – and I needed it. The dressage arena was on the side of a sloping, exposed field. The slope I could cope with providing I had Kate's undivided attention. But the wind, which had been a fairly gentle, gusty thing down in the valley, sliced across the open moor with an icy, wintry ferocity that she didn't like one bit. After half an hour she was still on her toes, and when the judge called us into the arena I was ready for an eventful four and a half minutes.

I didn't dare let her go for a second – holding her together to keep her light on her toes and stop her from slopping forward going downhill and prevent her from lengthening her stride going up to ease the gradient. Riding across the centre of the ring she was pushing against a solid wall of wind and I could feel that if I moved just one wrong muscle we'd bounce around like an uncontrollable ping-pong ball. I was glad to finish – and stunned by the dressage judges sheet. We'd scored an eight for one of the movements which rated as 'good' and got a four for the walk with the comment, 'Horse rather sleepy at the walk'. If only you knew, I thought.

We had a clear round show-jumping, and almost two hours to wait before the final phase. I'd walked the course the night before the competition and looked at parts of it again soon after I'd arrived in the morning, but this gap gave me a chance to walk it again with my instructor, and talk through those fences I thought might pose a problem. Half an hour before I was due to ride, the light rain that had developed at lunch-time turned into a thick moorland mist, and by the time the starter sent me off we couldn't see the first fence – let alone the rest of the course.

Fence number three had been one of my bogies. It was V-shaped, with the first pole at forty-five degrees, and had one stride on to the second pole. Kate had jumped fences like this before without hesitation, but this one was sited on the crest of a small hill so the approach was uphill which made the fence look bigger, and the pole behind much closer, than they really were. She went into it strongly, then dodged to the left at the last second.

I couldn't believe it. It was such a small, ordinary fence. But she wouldn't take the second attempt either – nor the third. We were eliminated. But told we could ride the rest of the course just for the fun of it, which we did.

The mist was so thick it was impossible to see any of the fences until you were almost on top of them. Walking the course three times had paid off. I was able to head in the right direction with some certainty, and Kate bowled over the ground as if impatient to make up for lost time. She never once felt like stopping from then on and approached each fence with ears pricked on a strong, forward stride. As soon as she landed she was off impatiently as if to say, 'That was fun, where's the next one?'

If she hadn't stopped at just that one fence we'd undoubtedly have been placed, but the fact that she didn't take home another set of ribbons didn't bother me at all. Her stop had been my fault as much as hers. If I'd looked for an alternative route through the third fence she might have taken it at the second attempt – so it had taught *me* a good lesson in tactical riding. That apart, the faint promise of willingness and ability, which had been there the year before, had, without doubt, developed into a commitment. I wasn't looking for prizes – more for proof that we hadn't both wasted our time. And she'd given me that in full measure.

The Cornwood trial

Two weeks later we met another landmark. The hunter trial at Cornwood where the horse, the course, and my back had defeated me the year before. Walking the course on the morning of the ride, the fences looked smaller and less imposing than I remembered. Even the notorious ski-jump looked fairly straightforward and eminently jumpable.

It wasn't cockiness or big-headedness – just the result of a year's hard work. Two-thirds of the way round they'd built a V-fence, and I looked hard and long at every possible jumping angle. After Bodmin I wasn't going to get caught a second time! There were twenty fences on the course and after a wild and joyous gallop between the first two, which took us careering up a sharp incline into a coppice, she settled into a steady rhythmic stride that ate up the ground, and the fences, without a break.

The approach to fence fifteen, the V, was flat and open, the fence itself had been built between three trees so the horse was being asked to jump from sunlight into shade, at an angle. I took a confident hold and rode her at the first element. We reached the take-off point, started to rise, and she reared off to the left. I didn't stop to work out what I'd done wrong, just turned her quickly, took the fence from a different angle and she ploughed over. It meant riding the long way round to get over the second element which wasted precious seconds, but she jumped cleanly, and without resistance, and powered on and over the last five fences.

Looking forward

There was just one more hunter trial the following week-end, before the end of the season. The terrain was tricky, the fences imposing, but she sailed the course with a confidence and spirit that gave us a clear round and a fast time.

When we got back to the stables that night I packed away my crash-helmet and back-protector, as I wouldn't need them again until the spring, and decided that whatever our ups and downs, we'd had a good year together, Kate and I. She was fit and bold, and took a real joy in jumping that rarely let me down. To the seasoned rider or horseman our. major disasters and minor triumphs, my fears and sentiments may seem silly and naïve – but they're honest. We won't ever make Badminton or Wembley, and I won't ever have the temperament that enables me to sail over big fences with careless nonchalance. But we *do* have fun and she's contributed in full to her half of the partnership.

As I write this, Dartmoor has lost its brash summer green and turned leaf-gold and bracken-burgundy as a late, misty autumn creeps over Devon. Throughout the winter there's indoor show-jumping. She's already won a third over fences at 3 ft 6 in and in the new year we're planning a series of dressage courses, with the spring and summer beyond offering new challenges to us both.

Best of all, there will be hours and hours of riding over Dartmoor. Together we'll drink in the clear crisp air of a winter's morning, curse the wet and cold of a rain storm, and wonder at the pattern of frost on a bare hawthorn tree.

Kate isn't just a conveyance, an extension of some alter ego or even a plaything to while away my leisure hours. She's very much a part of my life, though I may at times have called her every name under the sun, and she certainly invokes every reaction from exasperation to elation.

She provides me with relaxation, a challenge, the exhilaration of speed, the feeling that I can be as free as air, and have harmony with another living creature. In return, I've given her a piece of my heart.

Addresses

British Horse Society
British Equestrian Centre
Kenilworth
Warwickshire
CU8 2LR
Coventry [0203] 52241

The Pony Club
British Equestrian Centre
National Agricultural Centre
Kenilworth
Warwickshire
CU8 2LR
Coventry [0203] 52241

Riding for The Disabled
Avenue 'R'
National Agricultural Centre
Kenilworth
Warwickshire
CU8 2LR
Coventry [0203] 56107

Association of British Riding Schools
Chesham House
56 Greenend Road
Sawtry
Huntingdon
Cambridgeshire
PE17 5UY
Ramsey [0487] 830 443

Master of Foxhounds Association
Secretary – Mr A. H. B. Hart
Parsloe Cottage
Bagendon
Cirencester
Gloucestershire
GL7 7DU
North Cerney [028 583] 470

British Field Sports Society
59 Kennington Road
London SE1 7P2
01-928 4742

League Against Cruel Sports Ltd
1 Reform Row
London N17 9TW
01-801 2177

The Jockey Club
42 Portman Square
London W1H 0EN
01-486 4921

Shire Horse Society
East of England Showground
Peterborough
Cambridgeshire
PE2 0XE
Peterborough [0733] 234451

Horse Rescue Fund
English Cottage
Great Common
Ilketshall St Andrew
Nr Beccles
Suffolk

**Horses and Ponies
Protection Association**
Greenbank Farm
Fence
Nr Burnley
Lancashire
BB12 9QJ
Nelson [0282] 65909

**International League for the
Protection of Horses**
67a Camden High Street
London NW1 7JL
01-388 1449

The Registrar
Farriers' Registration Council
4 Royal College Street
London NW1 0TU
01-387 9729

The Secretary
The Society of Master Saddlers
Leather Trade House
9 St Thomas Street
London SE 1 9SA
01-407 1582

Index

191

Photo Acknowledgements
The author and publishers would like to thank the following for the use of their photographs: Col. Mike Ansell, p. 98; A. C. Arthur, p. 114 (below); *Birmingham Post and Mail Ltd.*, pp. 168-9; Camera Press, pp. 10-11 (above and below); *Daily Mirror* (Manchester), pp. 164, 165; W. Everitt, p. 61; Leslie Lane, pp. 76-7, 97, 101, 111-2 (above and below), 120, 122, 144 (above and below), 153 (above and below); Bob Langrish, p. 154 (above and below); Lock Studio Five, Stow-in-the-Wold, pp. 156-7; Marston Photographics, pp. 18-19; Jim Meads, pp. 126-7, 129, 131, 135 (above and below); Judy Meakin, p. 114 (above); Provincial Press Agency, Southport, p. 167; Riding for the Disabled Association, pp. 140, 142, 143; the *Sun*, pp. 6-7; Syndication International, p. 10;

The remaining photographs were all specially taken for the book by Gordon Moore of Devon Commercial Photos.